TEACHING MODERNIZATION

Studies in Latin American and Spanish History

This series bridges the divide between studies of Latin America and peninsular Spain by employing transnational and comparative approaches that shed light on the complex societies, cultures, and economies of the modern age. Focusing on the cross-pollination that was the legacy of colonialism on both sides of the Atlantic, these monographs and collections explore a variety of issues such as race, class, gender, and politics in the Spanish-speaking world.

Volume 6
Teaching Modernization: Spanish and Latin American Educational Reform in the Cold War
Edited by Óscar J. Martín García and Lorenzo Delgado Gómez-Escalonilla

Volume 5
The Configuration of the Spanish Public Sphere: From the Enlightenment to the Indignados
Edited by David Jiménez Torres and Leticia Villamediana González

Volume 4
The Brazilian Truth Commission: Local, National and Global Perspectives
Edited by Nina Schneider

Volume 3
José Antonio Primo De Rivera: The Reality and Myth of a Spanish Fascist Leader
Joan Maria Thomàs

Volume 2
Conflict, Domination, and Violence: Episodes in Mexican Social History
Carlos Illades

Volume 1
Metaphors of Spain: Representations of Spanish National Identity in the Twentieth Century
Edited by Javier Moreno Luzón and Xosé M. Núñez Seixas

Teaching Modernization

Spanish and Latin American Educational Reform in the Cold War

Edited by

Óscar J. Martín García and
Lorenzo Delgado Gómez-Escalonilla

berghahn
NEW YORK • OXFORD
www.berghahnbooks.com

First published in 2020 by
Berghahn Books
www.berghahnbooks.com

Library of Congress Cataloging-in-Publication Data
Names: Martín García, Óscar José, editor. | Delgado Gómez-Escalonilla, Lorenzo, editor.
Title: Teaching modernization : Spanish and Latin American educational reform in the Cold War / edited by Óscar J. Martín García and Lorenzo Delgado Gómez-Escalonilla.
Description: New York : Berghahn Books, 2019. | Series: Studies in Latin American and Spanish history; volume 6 | Includes bibliographical references and index.
Identifiers: LCCN 2019040175 (print) | LCCN 2019040176 (ebook) | ISBN 9781789205459 (hardback) | ISBN 9781789205466 (ebook)
Subjects: LCSH: Educational change--Spain--History--20th century. | Educational change--Latin America--History--20th century. | Education and state--Spain--History--20th century. | Education and state--Latin America--History--20th century. | Cold war--Social aspects--Spain. | Cold war--Social aspects--Latin America.
Classification: LCC LA911.82 .T43 2019 (print) | LCC LA911.82 (ebook) | DDC 379.46--dc23
LC record available at https://lccn.loc.gov/2019040175
LC ebook record available at https://lccn.loc.gov/2019040176

British Library Cataloguing in Publication Data
A catalogue record for this book is available from the British Library.

ISBN 978-1-78920-545-9 hardback
ISBN 978-1-78920-546-6 ebook

Contents

Illustrations

Figures

Table

Acknowledgments

As the editors, we would like to point out that the research that has made this publication possible has been funded by the research project "International Relations and the Modernization of the Spanish Educational and Scientific System, 1953–1986" (Spanish Ministry of Economy, Industry, and Competitiveness, HAR2014-58685-R). We are sincerely grateful for this support, which was essential for the completion of this study.

Chapter 1

Educational Reform, Modernization, and Development

A Cold War Transnational Process

Óscar J. Martín García and Lorenzo Delgado Gómez-Escalonilla

International Aspects of Educational Reform

The objective of this book is to analyze the set of external factors that intervened in the processes of educational reforms that took place in Spain and several Latin American countries during the 1960s and 1970s. The book pays special attention to the role played in such processes by the United States, non-state actors, international organizations, and the theories of modernization and human capital. A collective approach is used that includes contributions by several international history scholars and historians of education who examine programs of educational modernization in various case studies resulting from the interaction between international and domestic elements in the context of the cultural Cold War.

The origin of this book was a research project on the international dimensions of educational and scientific modernization in Spain in the 1960s and 1970s. The initial focus of the research was therefore on Spain. However, in the course of the project, we found there were obvious analogies with other educational reforms in that period in South America. For this reason, we thought it would be relevant to incorporate into the present volume several studies on Latin America that complemented the Spanish case. Such an approach would allow the educational transformations that occurred in Spain to be contextualized in a more global framework. However, it is our purpose not to make a systematic comparison between Spain and other Latin American countries but rather to analyze each case included in the book in a concrete way and try to establish connections between both sides of the Atlantic. In this sense, this volume does not claim to be comprehensive. A good number of significant Latin American cases and educational experiences are not included here. Instead, the book is intended to open up new perspectives for debate and to deepen existing ones in order to encourage further research that gives priority to a comparative approach and integrates new case studies.

The methodological approach adopted in this volume is not intended to apply central concepts and approaches as unitary axes with which to endow the chapters with methodological homogeneity. It is not the book's goal to reflect a particular methodological approach as a whole. Indeed, one of its strengths is the rich variety of analytical tools used by the different authors. Thus, there are chapters that organize and analyze their content around concepts such as "private diplomacy," "public diplomacy," and "academic dependency"; others put the focus on the United States and the spread of its influence through a mix of demand factors and supply of educational assistance. There are also contributions that adopt a transnational perspective and focus on non-state actors, as well as those that inquire into the influence of educational discourses and practices sponsored by various international operators. In summary, regarding the selection of chapters, the book speaks with different voices and approaches on a coherent and common theme: the study of the external dimensions of educational modernization within the framework of the Cold War.

United States, a Leading Force in the Modernization of Developing Countries

The educational reforms described in this book represent an unprecedented advance in attempts to modernize the educational systems of countries such as Spain, El Salvador, Chile, and Brazil. In the case of Spain, Mariano González-Delgado and Tamar Groves (chapter 4) consider that the process that led to the General Education Law of 1970 was the "most important reform in the history of Spanish education in the twentieth century." Likewise, Héctor Lindo-Fuentes (chapter 7) argues the educational reforms in El Salvador initiated in 1968, which ended in July 1971 with the promulgation of the General Education Law, constituted "a deep and comprehensive overhaul of the nation's public school system," an ambitious educational plan aimed at transforming the Central American country "into a modern, urban, industrialized nation." For his part, Colin Snider (chapter 8) points out that the university reform of 1968 "marked a transformational moment that dramatically changed the development of higher education in Brazil in a myriad of ways."

The United States was a leading force behind these processes of educational reform. From the beginning of the 1960s, the US government began to show greater interest in the role of education in its relations with the countries of the periphery and global semi-periphery. In September 1961, a report entitled "International Educational and Cultural Policies and Programs for the 1960s" collected the proposals of several working groups assembled by the Kennedy administration in order to elaborate "a philosophy and objectives for educational, cultural and scientific activity for the decade of the sixties as they relate to both governmental and private sectors." According to this report, education was a basic ingredient of the early stages of economic development. The takeoff toward the modernization of backward countries would involve training through modern educational systems to create human capital with the necessary technical capacities to solve the problems of underdevelopment. Therefore, "an increased effort in international programs in education, culture and science is as important as any effort our country may undertake, and that without it, our efforts in the areas of politics, of military assistance and of economics can never be truly effective." [1] In that same year and in a similar vein, President John F. Kennedy highlighted the importance of education for United States foreign policy toward the Third World:

> As our own history demonstrates so well, education is in the long run the chief means by which a young nation can develop its economy, its political and social institutions and individual freedom and opportunity. There is no better way of helping the new nations of Latin America, Africa and Asia in their present pursuit of freedom and better living conditions than by assisting them to develop their human resources by education.[2]

The US government saw education as a development factor at a juncture where the socioeconomic growth of poor nations became a fundamental objective of the Kennedy administration's foreign policy. Washington's interest in promoting education and development in the Third World was also part of the US response to the international challenges arising from the interaction between decolonization, the Cold War, and the expansion of communism in many regions of the planet. With such an international panorama, facts like the launching of Sputnik (1957), the Cuban Revolution (1959), the support of Nikita Khrushchev for anticolonialist movements (1961), and the increasing economic, technical, and military aid of the Soviet Union to newly independent nations all elevated communism as an alternative model of modernization to US capitalism in the Third World. According to US Deputy National Security Adviser Walt Rostow, such events had high potential to project "an image of communism as the most efficient method of modernizing underdeveloped regions" (Simpson 2008: 8)—even more so considering the interest and admiration of postcolonial leaders for the rapid industrialization experienced by the USSR, which, in a few decades, had gone from being a backward and agrarian country to becoming one of the world's main economic powers (Engerman 2004: 51–52).

Given this challenge, the Kennedy government created the US Agency for International Development (USAID) in 1961 and promoted initiatives such as the Decade of Development in order to expand the US vision of modernization in the periphery and global semi-periphery. According to this vision, democracy, capitalism, and technocratic reform represented the pillars of an ideal of progress that ran counter to the class struggle and the Marxist utopia embodied by the USSR. Within this liberal conception of modernization, education could contribute to promoting development in a framework of order and stability. In other words, education could help foster the economic growth necessary to face revolutionary threats in places like Cuba, the Congo, Laos, or Vietnam, where ignorance, poverty, frustration and political instability were fertile breeding grounds for radical ideas and movements (Gilman 2003: 48–49; Latham 2003a: 3–4). As we will see, the governments of many developing countries enthusiastically adopted this notion of education. For example, Lindo-Fuentes (chapter 7) points out that in 1962, in the inaugural address of Colonel Julio Rivera, the new Salvadoran president, education was presented as a way for his country to both modernize its economy and defeat communism.

The US emphasis on educational issues was also closely related to a series of internal and external factors that gained intensity during these years. First, the educational expansion at the domestic level was one of the priorities of US leaders from the arrival of Kennedy in the White House. Interest in the stimulus of education continued and was accentuated with the Great Society of President Lyndon B. Johnson. Second, decolonization generated new dynamics of global social transformation whose repercussions were more accentuated in a growing youth sector desperate for change and education. Likewise, there were the effects on the Third World of the economic boom experienced by all the capitalist First World countries that also reached the communist

Second World, with the consequent emergence of an incipient society of mass consumption in some parts of the Southern Hemisphere. As a result, several countries in the periphery and semi-periphery global witnessed the growing role of an urban middle class with expectations of economic growth and increased purchasing power. These new intermediate social strata demanded the expansion of education and a rapid modernization of their countries, thus influencing domestic and international politics.[3] Immersed in this epoch of a "revolution of expectations," the foreign actions of the United States had to confront this "combination of hope and urgency."[4]

The confluence of all these processes caused an explosion of demand for education in Third World countries, as well as in others that were at an intermediate stage of development. As stated in another official report in 1961, the "passion for education" from the beginning of this decade became a "rising tide in the newly developing nations."[5] As a result of this sharp increase in popular aspirations for education—and encouraged by the theories of modernization and educational development, and by the progressive importance of technology and demographic growth—there was a dramatic global upsurge in demand for education between the 1950s and 1970s. Consequently, during these years there was a remarkable educational expansion, clearly observable in the increase in the number of students. A palpable example of this phenomenon was Latin America, where the student population (at all levels) went from 30.5 million to 78.7 million between 1960 and 1977.

The enormous expansion of educational demand in the postwar period threatened world stability and provoked what Philip H. Coombs (1968) called a "world educational crisis" (Arnove 1980: 48; Meyer et al. 1979: 37–56).[6] Consequently, educational reform went from being a primarily domestic issue to an international one. It became a central component of North-South relations and East-West competition. Thus, from the beginning of the 1960s, educational modernization became a battlefield in the struggle between the Americans and the Soviets for winning the hearts and minds of the inhabitants of postcolonial and developing societies. In fact, in 1965, LBJ announced—along the lines already initiated by the Kennedy administration—the call for a special task force on international education to recommend a broad and long-range plan of worldwide educational endeavor. Based on the recommendations of that task force, the International Education Act of 1966 would be prepared, in charge of coordinating its activities at the Interagency Council on International Educational and Cultural Affairs. This agency included all government agencies with significant programs in this field: the Department of State, USAID, Peace Corps, Department of Defense, Department of Health Education and Welfare, and US Information Agency (USIA).

An Antidote against the Cuban Revolution: United States and Latin America in the Development Decade

For the analysts and strategists of the US Department of State, the situation in Latin America clearly illustrated the capacity of the international communist movement to exploit political and social instability in the underdeveloped areas of the planet. The Latin American region became a hot zone in the ideological competition of the Cold War in the second half of the 1950s. From this time onward, the political situation south of the Rio Grande attracted increasing attention from US foreign policy makers. They viewed with concern the hostile reception and anti-Americanism that accompanied the official tour of Richard Nixon in several Latin American countries in 1958. The visit of the then US vice president to countries such as Uruguay, Peru, and Venezuela raised numerous student protests, which in some cases resulted in serious incidents (Black 2007: 356–363).

Nevertheless, the true turning point in this regard occurred with the Cuban Revolution in 1959 (McPherson 2003; Rabe 1988). As Thomas Wright points out, such an event "embodied the aspirations and captured the imagination of Latin America's masses as no other political movement had ever done" (2001: 1). The victory of the guerrilla forces over the regime of Fulgencio Batista served as an example of inspiration for many other revolutionary movements from the Andes to the Southern Cone (Gleijeses 2009). This was why Fidel Castro's assault on the established power base ignited all the alarms in Washington, especially when the approach of the new Cuban authorities to the USSR triggered the fears of the US leaders regarding a possible spread of the Castro virus to other poor societies of the hemisphere (Latham 2000: 75–77). This threat lasted throughout the following decade, as indicated by information prepared by the Department of State in 1968: "The Latin American countries remain a prime target of direct and indirect subversion by Cuba, the Soviet Union, and, to a lesser extent, Communist China."[7]

To contain this threat, the Kennedy administration launched the Alliance for Progress (AfP) in 1961. This initiative was aimed at ending poverty, illiteracy, instability, and authoritarianism in the Latin American subcontinent by carrying out reforms in the fields of education, health, housing, agriculture, and the distribution of wealth. It was a matter of carrying out, under the aid and tutelage of the United States, a peaceful revolution from above that fostered economic growth and constrained communism in the region (Darnton 2012; Rabe 1999). The start-up of the AfP was accompanied by a whole informative, propagandistic, and cultural offensive orchestrated by the USIA, aimed at presenting the United States before Latin American public opinion as an advanced and benevolent leader, committed to development aid in a region burdened by the legacy of Spanish imperialism and by the influence of communist and Castroist ideas (Field 2012; Latham 2000: 70–72; Taffet 2007). The emphasis on concepts such as democracy in action, self-help, and cooperative effort accompanied the deployment of an important package of economic aid, mostly in the form of loans. The final result would be very different from the initial purpose outlined by Kennedy to modernize Latin American societies, taking as a reference the United States model. In general terms, the AfP has been described as "a remarkable policy failure of the Cold War" (Rabe 2012: 90).

Support for education occupied an important place in this endeavor. The US government encouraged the establishment of bilateral and multilateral programs of educational assistance considering this field "a critical factor in the social and economic development of the region." Under this impulse, some of the educational programs analyzed in this book were launched and implemented, such as the educational reform in El Salvador, the Reforma Universitária in Brazil, and the agreement between the University of Chile and the University of California. Brazil and Chile also received, together with Colombia, "the bulk of US assistance to Latin America."[8]

Moreover, throughout the 1960s, the university students and youth media "were singled out for special treatment as key targets for USIA/USIS [US Information Service, now USIA] personal and media contacts."[9] As in the Spanish case discussed in this book, students constituted a strategic sector in Latin American countries. The limited educational opportunities in this subcontinent made them a "vulnerable" sector for communist infiltration and subversion. In addition, in the universities—the extraction quarry of future national leaders—there was a growing critical attitude toward the United States, which contributed to identifying student leaders as a "target group of critical importance."[10] As an official memo in the summer of 1968 said, "The danger is that the students, in their desperate search for a way out of the morass of underdevelopment, may swing toward a sweeping, destructive, ideological solution."[11] To avoid such a threat, US leaders stimulated cooperation with national governments and international organizations in order to modernize education systems, promote development, and end the structural causes of student discontent

Programs like the AfP and organizations like the USAID rested on a vision of the United States as a bulwark of modernity and as the benevolent leader of the "Free World." As such, the US superpower had a moral obligation to share the concepts and methods that would encourage the economic and political development of backward countries and inoculate them against communism. According to this narrative, the American experience could provide a "historical guide" for nations like Brazil, Chile, and El Salvador that faced the challenge of modernization, in such a way that contact with the North American experience would help pull these countries' "malleable" societies out of their state of political immaturity and economic backwardness.

Starting from the international context described here, this book includes several chapters that analyze the role of the United States in educational reforms that were carried out in some Latin American countries with the support of the USAID and AfP. The book also contains chapters on the US influence on the educational modernization of Spain. As pointed out by Lorenzo Delgado Gómez-Escalonilla and Patricia de la Hoz Pascua (chapter 2), the US superpower was the main source of both direct and indirect economic aid and technical advice for the educational reforms that took place in Spain at the end of the 1960s. All these contributions pay attention to the work of the US government and state agencies that operated in the field of education at the international level. However, as we will see, US assistance in this field was not limited to the efforts made by official institutions and agencies.

Other International Agents and Non-State Actors

The transnational shift experienced by historiographical research has increased the interest in nongovernmental organizations as actors in international relations. In recent decades, a body of research has gone beyond the state-centered approaches in the study of international politics and has expanded the spectrum of agents involved in cultural and educational practices abroad, including nongovernment actors such as private foundations, think tanks, universities, research institutes, informal networks, and particular individuals (see, e.g., Kramer 2009; Laville and Wilford 2006; Lucas 2003; Parmar 2012; Weisbrode 2013).

Much of this literature has followed an approach similar to that of Sarah Snyder, for whom transnationalism is not a "separate field of historical inquiry" but rather an "approach or methodology that enables international historians to study new actors" (2003: 100–102). From this perspective, although without forgetting the influence of the US state, this book includes two chapters, those of Francisco Rodríguez-Jiménez (chapter 3) and Fernando Quesada (chapter 9), on the educational work of the Ford Foundation in Spain and Chile, respectively. Other contributions, such as that of Snider (chapter 8), also examine the educational work of non-state actors, for example, the University of Houston, which developed an intense transnational work within the framework of the reform of higher education in Brazil in the 1960s. Lindo-Fuentes (chapter 7) also pays attention to the role of Harvard University in the introduction of educational television in El Salvador.

Moreover, it is worth noting the United States was not the only official actor that participated in educational programs in Latin America and Spain. In the field of development, the AfP, the USAID, and other US government agencies did not act alone. The work done in this regard by the governments of countries such as Japan, the Federal Republic of Germany, Great Britain, and France should not be forgotten, and this book focuses on activism in the educational sphere of international institutions such as the United Nations Educational, Scientific and Cultural Organization (UNESCO), the Organization for Economic Cooperation and Development (OECD), and the World Bank (WB).

These entities constituted the backbone of the "international development community" as denominated by Héctor Lindo-Fuentes and Erik Ching (2012: 10–12). This community was formed between the 1950s and 1960s in the context of the Cold War and was composed of national governments, official agencies, multilateral institutions, and non-state actors. The objective of this conglomerate of international operators was to promote economic growth and political stability in backward countries. Throughout the 1960s, this community also devoted important efforts to the dissemination of Western visions of development in areas such as education, in which international communism projected an increasing influence (Dorn and Ghodsee 2012). Organizations such as UNESCO, the OECD, and the WB functioned as forums for the circulation of educational discourses that echoed the theories of modernization and human capital elaborated in Western universities, mainly in the United States.

The Regional Conference on Free and Obligatory Education in Latin America, organized by UNESCO in May 1956 in Lima, marked the beginning of the enthusiastic commitment of various international bodies toward modernization and educational reform. Another important subsequent step was the Conference on Education and Economic and Social Development in Latin America, promoted in 1962 by UNESCO and other international entities. Also at that time, the OECD (1965) launched the Mediterranean Regional Project, aimed at analyzing the needs of human resources to promote economic development in several Southern European countries, including Spain. Through these types of conferences and projects, transnational circuits of aid and knowledge dissemination in the education field were created. Such networks materialized throughout the 1960s with the aim of (1) promoting and institutionalizing, at a global level, a concept of education associated with economic growth and social progress, and (2) using education and development as antidotes to the expansion of communism in developing nations (Frey et al. 2014; Jolly et al. 2004; Sharma 2017; Stokke 2009).

Therefore, during the 1960s and 1970s, the external influence on the educational reforms carried out in Spain and Latin America was the result of cooperation between the US superpower and other international actors and institutions. In the educational field, Washington established fluid collaborative relationships with international entities over which it exercised a certain ancestry, as can be seen in David Corrales Morales's contribution on the World Bank (chapter 5). A similar approach is glimpsed in the contribution of Lindo-Fuentes (chapter 7), who highlights the similarity of interests, visions, and practices in the field of development between the United States and UNESCO led by René Maheu from 1962 to 1972. Not in vain, during that period the UNESCO Executive Board openly endorsed the AfP sponsored by the US government.

On this issue, it is worth remembering, as did a report by the US delegation to UNESCO at the height of 1967, that the United States had been one of the founding members and main contributors to this organization since its creation after World War II. As such, the US superpower had "played a major role in shaping UNESCO's policies and programs." This document suggested retaining such a position of influence, as UNESCO offered "a multilateral base of support for the pursuit of US policies on behalf of international education and development aid." Thus, if, on the one hand, the entrance in this institution of a good number of new independent nations had generated certain distortions for the United States, on the other, it had caused UNESCO's main concerns to become aligned with priority issues for the US foreign agenda, such as the development and the training of human capital. In addition, the international organizations working in the educational field offered a multinational umbrella that allowed US modernizers to apply their educational notions in countries where direct US intervention could meet with rejection from students, teachers, and other social and political groups. International institutions such as UNESCO allowed the US government to have some capacity for maneuver, where political circumstances made educational intervention "counterproductive or, at best, ineffective." [12] On this question, US officials recognized that the aforementioned bodies "can proceed with a freedom of action frequently impossible for a single nation, and they can often count upon a warmer reception than a single nation, with its capacity to stir up fears, would enjoy."[13] Likewise, the educational programs endorsed by such institutions enjoyed a modernizing prestige that facilitated their acceptance by the technocratic elites of developing countries "as a mobilizing mechanism to 'catch up' in the modern world, as well as a way to obtain legitimacy in the international community" (McNeely 1995: 502).

In the analyzed cases, educational cooperation between governments, nonofficial actors, and international organizations was also often mediated by a series of individuals such as Ricardo Díez-Hochleitner, Joaquín Tena Artigas, Robert J. Alexander, Rudolph Atcon, Kalman Silvert, Frank Tiller, Joseph Lauwerys, Wilbur Schramm, Philip H. Coombs, and Peter Fraenkel, among others. These individuals were affiliated with Western universities, private foundations, professional bodies, government agencies, and multilateral institutions. They were part of a community of knowledge professionals, or an "epistemic community" (Adler 1992; Haas 1992), composed of international experts, social scientists, and intellectuals. Its members played a key role in the processes of production and transnational circulation of the "semantics of modernization" (Schriewer 1997: 28), which led to the educational reforms implemented in the countries of the Southern Hemisphere during the 1960s and 1970s.

Among these experts, the figure of Rudolph Atcon, whose advisory work on the modernization of university systems in Brazil and Chile, is analyzed by Snider (chapter 8) and Anabella Abarzúa Cutroni (chapter 10), respectively. At the beginning of the 1950s, this Harvard University doctor supervised, as an international expert, various educational projects in Brazil. At the end of the decade, he carried out consultancy functions at the service of international entities such as the Organization of American States and UNESCO in several Latin American countries (Venezuela, Chile, Colombia, the Dominican Republic, Honduras, Mexico, and Argentina). In the realization of this effort, he collaborated and established contacts with various US actors, both with official agencies for development and with foundations and universities in that country. During the second half of the 1960s, Atcon played an important role in the university reform approved in Brazil in 1968. As a result of work in different areas of the region, he published influential studies, such as "The Latin American University" in 1961. However, his advisory work was not without controversy, as shown by the criticisms made by students, professors, academic authorities, and even UNESCO colleagues due to the political nature of some of his recommendations.

Despite the rejections aroused on some occasions, the studies and publications of these experts became reference works for international missions and local technocrats who participated in the design of educational programs in developing countries. In this respect, the work of Wilbur Schramm analyzed by Lindo-Fuentes (chapter 7), "Mass Media and National Development" (commissioned by UNESCO), is a good example of the important role played by these experts in the intersection between Western social sciences, the agenda of international development organizations, and the Cold War. Sometimes, the members of this transnational expert and discourse community took on important roles as "informal" or "private" diplomats. That is, these individuals acted as part of a "parallel diplomacy" that complemented the official diplomatic channels, even reaching into areas where the latter did not. The study of the figure of Ricardo Díez-Hochleitner as mediator between the Spanish dictatorship and the US authorities or the WB is illustrative in the sense of the maneuverability of these actors integrated into epistemic communities and with strong international contacts. This position allowed them to develop a work of interlocution sometimes more decisive than that of the state mechanisms themselves.

Corrales Morales (chapter 5) and Delgado Gómez-Escalonilla and Hoz Pascua (chapter 2) describe different aspects of this mediating activity, which turned these experts into "informal governance actors." This concept was coined by Dino Knudsen (2012: 8–9) with the purpose of overcoming the dichotomy between state and civil society that until recently predominated in historical studies of international relations. The approach of these and other historians reflects the influence of the cultural and transnational turns in the new diplomatic history, which has led to a line of inquiry that seeks "to introduce new layers of investigation by focusing on what can be termed the informal or unofficial realm of diplomacy" (Scott-Smith 2014: 1–7). It also highlights the importance of tracking the itinerary of these communities of experts, formal and informal, and their training and interaction circuits.

Finally, these international experts established close links of cooperation and advice with social scientists and local academic authorities. This was the case, for example, of the New York University political science professor Kalman Silvert. As can be seen from Quesada (chapter 9), this specialist in Latin America and a consultant for the Ford Foundation established contacts with a good number of prestigious Latin American academics and joined the main intellectual networks of the region. In fact, Silvert was the first president of the Latin American Studies Association, created in 1966 with the support of the aforementioned philanthropic foundation. Also worthy of note is the harmony between these international experts, US foundations, and the members of the technocratic elites of developing countries. Among these modernizing elites were the education ministers of countries such as Colombia (Gabriel Betancourt), Ecuador (Walter Béneke), Brazil (Flávio Suplicy de Lacerda), Spain (José Luis Villar Palasí), and Chile (Juan Gómez Millas). The latter was, according to Quesada, held in very high esteem by officials of the Ford Foundation, who considered him a figure committed to the modernization of Chilean universities. Indeed, all these ministers showed a favorable attitude to the technocratic reform of the educational structures of their countries, under the guidance of US consultants and international organizations. From their positions of influence in the governments of developing nations, these technocratic leaders supported the primacy of technical-scientific knowledge above ideologies and politics, which put them in harmony with the principles that international experts and US social scientists had been articulating ever since the 1950s. Like these, the technocrats were also fervent defenders of order and reforms from above as an antidote to the Marxist revolution.

During the 1960s, the US ideas of modernization often fitted right in with the institutional and political priorities of the technocratic leaders of the developing countries, who constituted an audience eager to listen to the international consultants and US modernization theorists and apply their recipes. Although they sometimes rejected the recommendations of certain international experts when the local political circumstances so advised, the technocratic elites of countries such as Spain, Brazil, Chile, and El Salvador used to share the views on the education of their counterparts in international organizations and in US development agencies. Such technocratic sectors, often trained in the West, acted as the primary interpreters of US foreign policy makers and other international actors in their plans for the countries of the global periphery. Their leadership represented an assurance of order and development in the face of the possible destabilizing effects of modernization. From Washington and other Western capitals, they were seen as rational, modern, pragmatic, active, and efficient forces, whose countries, like those studied here, needed to get on board the development train (Simpson 2008: 6). These technocratic elites would come to identify themselves with those whom Federico Romero (2014: 694–695) calls the "political entrepreneurs" of developing countries, who used Cold War discourses such as modernization to shore up their internal power based on a new language of developmental legitimization.

US Involvement in the Global Semi-Periphery: From Political Development to Authoritarian Modernization

In the past two decades, an influential body of research has presented the Cold War as an ideological struggle between two visions on the nature of global social change and the definition of modernity (Cullather 2004b; Engerman 2004; Latham 2000). From this perspective, the East-West conflict is seen as a competition to "engineer the developing world's transition to modernity—and in the process, attempting to win the 'hearts and minds,' or the ideological loyalties of its population" (Van Vleck 2009: 4). On the American side, modernization theory occupied a central place in the competition between two opposing models of development, each aspiring to transform the Third World into its image and likeness (Westad 2000: 554–57). This theory provided the conceptual framework that articulated a series of precepts about the American capacity to end underdevelopment, instability, and the revolutionary threat in the Global South (Latham 2000: 4–5). It worked as an ideological device, whose main principles were used by US officials as a political instrument, analytical model, rhetorical tool, explanatory framework, and value system in the exercise and legitimization of US global power (Simpson 2008: 7).

Although its historical roots can be found in the Enlightenment, imperialist ideologies, and the Keynesian reforms of the interwar New Deal period (Ekbladh 2009; Shibusawa 2012), modernization theory represents a specific phenomenon of the Cold War in the middle decades of the twentieth century. It was the US response to the political and intellectual challenges imposed by decolonization, global social change, and international communism in the Third World. As such, modernization was used, on the one hand, as a tool for scientific analysis and political control of the profound transformations being produced by the decolonization processes. On the other, it fulfilled a normative function, which prescribed how "traditional" societies should evolve toward a modernity epitomized by the American model.[14]

However, modernization theory was not an exclusively US phenomenon. It was global and transnational in scope. In fact, it provided the general cognitive framework used by the "international development community" when interpreting and addressing the problems of the nations of the Global South. Both as an intellectual theory and as a political instrument, modernization described and prescribed for these countries a linear and liberal path toward the ideal of progress, as opposed to the promises of social justice and material equality promoted by the dialectical and revolutionary model proposed by communist forces (Latham 2003b: 721–22).

The paradigm of modernization was based on a series of principles and assumptions that served as a reference point for the intervention of the United States and other international actors in the newly emerging nations during the 1960s (Del Pero 2009: 21). Throughout that decade, US scholars and intellectuals such as Lucian Pye, Daniel Lerner, Max Millikan, and Walt Rostow, among others, connected such principles with each other, reinforcing them and forming a coherent and attractive body of doctrine that permeated the formulation of the US foreign policy toward developing countries. In synthesized form, such a mold involved the following assumptions:

(1) the difference and the hierarchy between modern and traditional societies;
(2) a vision of the latter as societies lacking cultural maturity and political sophistication, weighed down by an archaic mentality and therefore tending toward radical political behavior;
(3) the conviction that contact with the West would speed up the development of traditional societies toward modernity;
(4) the view of the political, economic, and social system of the United States as the ultimate expression of modernization; and
(5) the belief that economic and sociocultural development would serve as the foundation for political epiphenomena such as democratization.

In reference to the last of these five points, US social scientists and modernizers believed developing nations would enter political modernity when they reached certain levels of industrialization, urbanization, education, and expansion of communications. In their opinion, the economic development of traditional societies would be followed by a transition to more sophisticated, modern political forms similar to those of the Western democracies.[15] This vision, which closely linked economic and political development, was routinely incorporated into US diplomacy's analyses of the socioeconomic and political evolution of backward countries. For instance, US officials thought a "viable democracy in Spain" would appear only "through gradual evolution, accompanied by improved living standards and considerable growth of the middle class."[16]

Consequently, modernization was presented at the end of the 1950s and in the early 1960s as an altruistic, pluralist, and reformist solution to the risks posed by decolonization and underdevelopment. In 1961, the USIA included modernization as one of its five long-term priority themes based on the "US conviction that the modernization of newly developing nations could best be achieved through democratic, pragmatics, means."[17] However, as the 1960s progressed, that same theory soon became a framework through which to legitimate US alliances with the authoritarian regimes of the Third World, or with countries, like Spain, that were at an "intermediate" stage of development.

In the course of the 1960s, instability and sociopolitical chaos spread in the postcolonial regions. This situation, coupled with the growing communist threat over these parts of the globe, led US officials to give greater weight to the counterinsurgency aspects of their foreign policy toward newly independent nations. The initial reformist liberal approach to the decolonization and modernization of the Third World was giving way to support for authoritarian and military options. The strategic need to combine anti-communism and modernization led US foreign policy makers to help strong anti-liberal regimes to the detriment of weak representative governments, which were considered susceptible to falling into the hands of radical forces. Consequently, the maintenance of order and stability, rather than the promotion of democracy, became the main objective of US policy toward the countries of Asia, Africa, and Latin America throughout the 1960s (Field 2014; Simpson 2008).

At the same time, as the 1960s progressed, more prominent US academics watched with concern as the fragile postcolonial nations faced turbulent modernization processes, some of whose ramifications (erosion of authority, rising popular expectations, social conflict, political instability) could be exploited by the communists. Walt Rostow (1960) saw the communists as the "scavengers of the modernization process" who sought to take advantage of the conflicts and social pressures unleashed by rapid development. For this renowned theoretician of modernization, the new states that were going through accelerated and convulsive processes of social change were "highly vulnerable" to subversion fomented by revolutionary forces.

Based on this type of approach, various US academics and intellectuals believed it was therefore necessary that the "takeoff" toward the modernity of these nations be led by strong authorities, capable of promoting the development of their countries under conditions of stability and order that would close the doors to communist opportunism. The aim, in other words, was to ensure the necessary social discipline to carry out modernization from above so as to block the way of revolution from below. Over the course of the 1960s, modernization theorists and US social scientists increasingly began to see in military and dictatorial governments the best guarantee to impose the authority needed to preserve the anti-communist status quo during the chaotic modernization of traditional societies. According to this approach, by promoting economic development within a framework of social order, these autocracies would help put their nations on the road to democracy. The American social science establishment thus came to see right-wing authoritarian regimes as an effective vehicle for boosting economic growth, containing communism, and, as a result, facilitating the establishment of pluralistic systems in their countries in the long term (Latham 2012: 153).

As a consequence, in a context in which social science, geostrategy, and US national interests were closely linked, the normative priority of modernization theory went from "democracy" to "stability" as the political and moral ideal for developing countries (O'Brien 1972: 351–353). This orientation was expressed by numerous academic works that appeared during the first half of the 1960s (Bienen 1971: 9–21). In general terms, these contributions presented the military dictatorships allied with the United States as the ideal agents to promote a stable modernization that would lead to the future democratization of traditional societies that at that time tended toward turmoil and could be easily manipulated by the "delusions of communism" (Herman 1995: 136).[18] As a memorandum sent to the Department of State from a conference held in 1961 at the Brookings Institution explained, from the late 1950s, American political theorists and academics had begun to see the reactionary and militaristic forces "as a sort of panacea for the ills of underdeveloped countries," on account of their ability to steer development "under non-Communist auspices."[19] Thus, an emerging academic consensus was built around an authoritarian version of modernization that conceived of anti-communist dictatorships as a temporary necessary evil in defense of long-term freedom (Schmitz 2006: 2–3).

Such ideas were used by US diplomats to justify their superpower's support for authoritarian governments in developing countries, such as some of those included in this book. In this regard, General Francisco Franco's dictatorship in Spain and the military regimes of El Salvador, Brazil, and, subsequently, Chile as of 1973 were seen from Washington as agents of development and important bastions in the struggle against international communism. The US government channeled substantial amounts of economic, technical, and military aid to these autocratic regimes in order to promote the "healthy" and "stable" development that would close the way to communist subversion in two areas that held great geostrategic value in the Cold War: Southern Europe and Latin America.

In the discourse of the US leaders, democracy used to be conceived as a final goal of the modernizing process, always situated in the medium-long term. The immediate geostrategic needs ended up turning that discourse into a litany with dubious effects on reality, as evidenced in the Spanish case (Delgado Gómez-Escalonilla 2015a). However, the support of the US Department of State for anti-communist dictatorships was not always shared by its partners in the "international development community." This was the case of the Ford Foundation in Chile. As Quesada (chapter 9) says, the foundation did not share the policy of the Nixon administration toward the government of Salvador Allende and the subsequent dictatorship of Augusto Pinochet.

Human Capital and Education

In addition to its structural aspects, modernization theory, as an expression of liberal-internationalist ambitions for social engineering, had a social-psychological and cultural dimension that has been little explored. In the 1960s, prominent social scientists such as Walt Rostow, Daniel Lerner, David McClelland, and Alex Inkeles thought modernization was not only an economic, social, and institutional process but also a cultural and mental one. These authors considered countries like the ones studied in this book to have one key feature in common, despite their different historical trajectories and their diverse geographical, economic, and political circumstances: the level of psychological and cultural evolution in their societies was not comparable to that of the Western First World, which was made up of the rich, modern nations that shared a cultural heritage and similar political institutions compatible with those of the United States.

From this perspective, the democracies of the Free World were characterized by the sociocultural hegemony of values related to empiricism, rationality, science, efficiency, and political moderation. On the contrary, traditional societies were seen as "people afflicted with a sense of fatalism, debility of mind as much as material condition" (Latham 2003a: 7). In other words, the aforementioned authors substituted the biological racism of social Darwinism for cultural and anthropological approaches. Such a vision associated the ideal of modernity with the cultural patterns of the Western world while contrasting it with the irrational customs and habits characteristic of underdeveloped societies.

Unlike the developed nations, traditional societies suffered—according to the view of the US social scientific establishment—from a cultural backwardness that, on the one hand, hindered economic growth and, on the other, made them vulnerable to radical and communist ideologies. From this perspective, the irrationality and the superstition inherent in underdeveloped societies were the origin of such problems as inequality, poverty, corruption, radicalism, and underdevelopment. In the same vein, some of the most renowned proponents of modernization cited in this book, such as Wilbur Schramm and Max Millikan, thought change in mentalities, beliefs, and cultural habits was one of the basic requirements for the promotion of progress in the countries of the Global South.

According to this ethnocentric and paternalistic notion of modernization, developing nations were not genetically inferior but culturally backward. The stagnation of these societies was because of not biological reasons but the perpetuation of traditional ways of life. These were the causes of a state of prostration that could be overcome only by adopting the methods and ideas that had fostered prosperity in Western democracies. This approach was also shared by sectors of the technocratic elites of the countries of the world's semi-periphery. For example, Laureano López Rodó, a technocrat leader influenced by the ideas of Walt Rostow, well connected with the United States, and responsible for the Development Plans that were made in Spain between 1962 and 1973, thought the decisive element for modernization of this country was the acquisition of a "development mentality." In statements to the press in October 1965, he said, "Structures cannot be transformed if mental attitudes are not modified before and the old atavisms are banished" (quoted in González-Fernández 2016: 314).

According to this thinking, the progress of backward nations depended not only on Western development aid programs but also on contact with the values and rational attitudes of the "modern man."

That is to say, the "minor" nations must emulate the most advanced nations, which in turn had a moral obligation to guide the underdeveloped peoples toward maturity. This view led the United States and its allies in the global mission of modernization to place great importance on the dissemination in developing societies of modern concepts, values, and practices on which the advances of the Western world had been based. Thus, modernization was not only a "normative vocabulary" in the hands of the US cold warriors but also a cultural good that could be transmitted through different channels such as technology, technical assistance, mass communications, and education (Cullather 2004a: 227; Isaac 2007: 741).

Philanthropic officials, technocrats, social scientists, and modernizers linked to Western governments and institutions viewed education as one of the main instruments to instill in these societies a "new sense of rationality, efficiency, and respect for empiricism in contrast to native passivity" (Latham 2003a: 3). For them, education was considered an instrument of sociocultural transformation that would shape Third World societies in the image and likeness of Western powers and end traditional habits that hindered their development. As mentioned, an OECD report in 1966 on the Spanish case said the construction of modern and efficient education systems in developing nations was a necessary condition for "breaking the stereotyped schemes of a mentality excessively attached to the traditional" (quoted in De Miguel 1976: 20–21).

From this perspective, education—and the incorporation in it of advances in fields such as mass communication—represented an essential instrument to disseminate to "backward" societies the attitudes, methods, and modern ideas—efficiency, productivity, pragmatism, moderation—necessary to (1) promote economic growth compatible with the transatlantic security agenda, (2) prevent the spread of revolutionary ideas among sectors such as students and the future elites, and (3) neutralize the revolutionary potential in these societies and get them closely linked to the Western world. From this conception of education as an instrument for development and as a weapon in the Cold War, projects emerged, such as educational television analyzed by Lindo-Fuentes (chapter 7). Educational television was an initiative encouraged for the whole of the American subcontinent as part of the promotion of technological education.[20]

This approach to education was in line with the Chicago School human capital theory propounded since the late 1950s by several economists: Theodore Schultz, W. Arthur Lewis, Frederick H. Harbison, and Gary Becker, among others. In 1960, Schultz popularized "human capital theory" during a conference of the American Economic Association over which he presided. This theory held that training the workforce was crucial to "the productive superiority of technically advanced countries" (1968: 135–136). In 1964, the standard reference work in this field appeared as "Human Capital: A Theoretical and Empirical Analysis, with Special Reference to Education," written by Becker. This scholar, who would later receive the Nobel Prize in Economics, highlighted the central role of education and human resources in the promotion of economic growth (Dorn and Ghodsee 2012: 383–85).

Generally speaking, all these authors regarded education as representing a valuable productive investment to train a qualified workforce that could respond to the needs of global capitalism (Jones and Coleman 2005: 31). Such a modernizing and technocratic conception of education as an engine of national development formed the basis of a "developmental educational ideology," which attained a high degree of academic and institutional prestige in the 1960s. Its principles shaped the paradigm that dominated the educational debate and permeated the policies in this field of governments and international organizations such as UNESCO, the WB, and the OECD (Fiala and Gordon Lanford 1987: 318–319).

These organizations saw in the training of human capital the main resource with which countries like Brazil, Spain, Chile, and El Salvador could reach the First World (Ossenbach and Martínez Boom 2011). An economicist approach to education that had a decisive influence on the education policies implemented by developing countries in the 1960s. For instance, the three Development Plans promoted by the technocratic sectors of the Spanish dictatorship from 1962 to 1973 conceived of education as a fundamental part of economic growth (Milito Barone and Groves 2013: 137). In a similar vein, the aforementioned OECD (1965) report attached great importance to education and the training of human capital to respond to the "needs of skilled labor that economic development implies." Likewise, in 1965 the Director of the Analysis Division of the Department of Social Sciences of UNESCO pointed out that investment in the "training of manpower and human resources in an economic and professional sense" was vital for developing countries to "break the vicious circle of poverty and social systems that impede development." (UNESCO 1965: 22)

The US propaganda and public diplomacy agencies also invested considerable effort in disseminating the human capital approach to education among academic authorities, teachers, and students of semi-peripheral nations.[21] A good example of this was the presentation given by US Ambassador to Spain Angier Biddle Duke before a young audience at the Institute of North American Studies of Barcelona in November 1965. On this occasion, he said, "In advancing industrial societies, where productive requirements relate directly to education, a growing faction of unskilled citizens has little to offer to community."[22]

Similar opinions could be found in articles collected in journals—such as *Noticias de Actualidad*, *Atlántico*, and *Facetas*—distributed by the USIA among the cultural, intellectual, and educational elites of Spain. For example, the last issue of *Noticias de Actualidad* in 1961 included an article entitled "Education and Economics." The text emphasized that the progress of any "modern economic society" needed the training of technical, scientific, economic, and administrative personnel. The progress of the United States, itself, and other advanced nations had been based, according to the article, on educational opportunities and investment in human resources.[23] Through this type of articles and other channels—such as exhibitions and documentary screenings—US public diplomacy disseminated in Spain the technocratic, depoliticizing, and developmental vision of education apropos to the human capital theory.

However, it must be emphasized that although this educational ideology provided a general outline that guided the conceptions and methods of action of international experts and institutions, there was still room within this framework for varied and heterogeneous educational discourses, such as those expressed by US specialists in the Brazilian university reform, as studied by Snider (chapter 8). This case highlights the different US approaches that, based on a technocratic and modernizing conception of education, participated in guiding educational reform in that South American country. As such, Snider's contribution questions the vision of the US superpower as a homogeneous imperial power, which spoke with a single voice on issues related to development.

The Spanish Case: Development and Dictatorship

This book pays special attention to Spain. The literature on Cold War modernization has selectively focused its interest on the impact of the narratives and practices of modernization in societies that were decolonized after World War II. There are also several works on nations that, despite having achieved independence much earlier—most notably Latin American countries—faced the challenge of postwar development in a context of instability and potential communist threats. The emphasis on US discourses and programs of modernization in postcolonial and Third World societies has seemed to obviate the investigation of other cases such as Spain, which does not fit into an interpretive framework mainly built around the Third World–postcolonial axis limited to Asian, African, and Latin American experiences. Although modernization was a global and transnational project in character and scope, research is scarce on those countries, like Spain, that occupied an intermediate position between the First World and the Third World based on their level of economic development and their social structure.

In September 1953, the Eisenhower administration and the Franco dictatorship concluded a military pact that began a long period of collaboration between the United States and Spain. This agreement allowed the superpower to establish, under very advantageous conditions, military bases of high strategic value on Spanish soil while giving Spain economic, technical, and military aid (Álvaro Moya 2011; Calvo González 2001; León-Aguinaga and Delgado Gómez-Escalonilla 2018; Liedtke 1998; Puig Raposo and Álvaro Moya 2004; Viñas 2003). From then, and until Franco's death in 1975, matters of security occupied a high priority in US foreign policy toward Spain. As an official report put it in 1960, "Spain plays a strong role in our worldwide defensive strategy and our policies toward that country are, in a sense, dictated by our security interests."[24] The strategic relationship established with the United States contributed to breaking the international rejection that the Franco regime suffered because of its affinity with the Axis powers in World War II. Even so, at the end of the 1950s, US diplomacy still regarded Spain as an isolated and underdeveloped country, at a great distance from its Western European neighbors. As an official report pointed out in 1959, throughout its recent history, Spain had "lagged behind as neighboring countries modernized themselves," their standard of living being the lowest of any Western European country except Portugal.[25]

However, after the Stabilization Plan of the Spanish economy that was launched that same year, this country went through an unprecedented phase of economic expansion from 1960 to 1973. During this period, the Spanish economy grew at an annual rate of more than 7 percent, surpassed within the OECD only by Japan. The accelerated industrialization and tertiarization of the economy provoked deep demographic and social changes that led to a rapid urbanization of the country. At the same time, an incipient mass consumer society emerged, and new habits and more open and plural forms of lifestyle appeared. Factors such as tourism, television, the decline of the rural population, the increase in per capita income, and the emergence of new middle classes helped foster secularization and modernization of Spanish attitudes and behaviors (Townson 2007).

Because of the important economic advances achieved by Spain in these years, the country ceased to be a recipient of aid from the USAID in 1962. Around the same time, US diplomacy began to describe Spain "as the most developed of the underdeveloped nations."[26] For US analysts, Spain was a country midway between the Global North and the Global South. This characterization referred not only to its geographical position at the southern border of Europe but also to its intermediate socioeconomic and cultural status with the Atlantic Community, comprising the affluent nations that shared political institutions similar to those of the United States, and Third World societies. Such a position, a "bridge" between the center and the periphery of the world economy, along with its important strategic location, makes Spain an interesting focus of study for evaluating the incidence of Cold War modernization.

US diplomats favorably received the new socioeconomic dynamics set in motion in Spain, since they converged with their defensive objectives in the Iberian Peninsula. For this reason, they hailed the fast and robust economic development of Spain as "a necessary concomitant to the US joint-use of Spanish [military] bases and facilities."[27] Likewise, in the summer of 1963, a report of the US Policy Planning Staff enthusiastically stressed, "Spain, economically, has now very nearly reached the take-off stage," which would definitively put the country on the path toward modernization.[28] Similar optimism could be detected two years later in another memorandum, which highlighted that Spain was "undergoing a rapid economic and social transition which is breaking down the decades of isolation."[29]

However, the profound social and economic transformations witnessed by Spain during the 1960s also gave rise to strong protest movements, especially in sectors such as universities, which weakened the Franco dictatorship and jeopardized the defensive priorities of the United States in this country. In 1960s Spain, there was no threat as powerful and imminent as that projected in Latin America by the Cuban Revolution and the spread of insurgent movements in various parts of the hemisphere. However, US diplomats still viewed with some concern the increase in discontent and conflict in a context of sweeping and chaotic social change. In addition, Franco's aging and the weakening of his regime were occurring in parallel. All these factors could complicate a future succession of the dictator that was favorable to the geostrategic interests of the US superpower (Martín

García 2013). In the face of such danger, the US government promoted and assisted various modernization programs in different fields such as the economy, agriculture, education, science, the Armed Forces, and public administration. In general, the US involvement in these programs had a double purpose. First, it was about promoting an orderly capitalist development that, in turn, underpinned the political stability required for the maintenance of US military bases in Spanish territory. Second, it was intended to create the economic, social, and cultural conditions necessary to prepare a future post-Franco transition that would be peaceful, moderate, and compatible with the military objectives of the United States (Delgado Gómez-Escalonilla 2010).

Thus, the assistance of the superpower with the educational reforms that took place in Spain at the end of the 1960s and the beginning of the 1970s must be understood within this context. That is, it was part of the US modernization effort that sought to create the human capital necessary for the promotion of economic development that, in turn, would pave the way for an evolutionary and favorable regime change to Western defense interests in the Iberian Peninsula. In this sense, in addition to reducing conflict on university campuses, US assistance to educational reform tried to encourage economic growth, which would contribute to "expand and strengthen the social basis for the evolution of a popularly based political system and to provide an element of stability during the crucial transitional period following Franco's demise."[30] But in the educational reform, the Americans collaborated and assisted the Spanish authoritarian technocrats, who intend not to democratize the country but to safeguard the survival of the Franco regime.

In any case, though the United States encouraged and intervened in Spanish educational reform as part of its international political agenda in the framework of the Cold War, it did not take the simple form of external imposition by a hegemonic power. In fact, Spanish government officials and academic authorities showed great interest in US assistance in the modernization of the obsolete and archaic educational system of their country. As Delgado Gómez-Escalonilla and Hoz Pascua (chapter 2) show, in the context of the negotiation that led to the renewal of military agreements between the two countries in 1969 and 1970, the Spanish dictatorship actively sought American aid to launch an educational reform that would consolidate the path of economic growth and contribute to prop up its political survival.

Therefore, although, as we have seen, educational modernization fitted in with US priorities and interests, it was largely the negotiating pressure of the Spanish authorities that led to the United States' commitment to its educational plans (Delgado Gómez-Escalonilla 2010). Thus, if the Cold War imposed on the authorities of countries such as Spain a subordinated geopolitical status, then these countries also played their tricks to take advantage of the opportunities for agency opened by the bipolar competition itself (Van Vleck 2009). In this way, the educational reform became an important space for interaction, negotiation, and collaboration between Madrid and Washington.

Indeed, the Spanish government sought US aid in the field of educational reform as part of their authoritarian modernization project, which aimed to expand the dwindling social bases of Franco's regime by promoting economic growth, mass consumption, and social and political demobilization (González-Fernández 2016). Franco's regime aspired to obtain greater consent and popular support at a juncture in which victory in the Spanish Civil War in the late 1930s had lost the capacity for cohesion and social control, as highlighted by the student protests. The Spanish authorities saw in the US aid for the modernization of the educational structures of the country an element of legitimization that allowed them to connect with the expectations of improvement in living conditions that were spreading in Spanish society. Likewise, the Salvadoran leaders thought an elaborate educational reform program that enjoyed the approval and assistance of Washington and international organizations would promote economic growth, neutralize the expansion of communism, and legitimize a military regime that felt threatened by the revolution in Cuba.

The main architects of the development of this relegitimization operation sponsored by Franco's dictatorship were the technocratic leaders. In the second half of the 1950s, Spanish technocrats climbed to positions of power in the apparatus of the authoritarian state. Their goal was to undertake the economic transformations that, under the cloak of Western capitalism, would ensure the continuity of Franco's rule. The technocrats sought to achieve a "reactionary utopia" based on the promotion of economic development and social depoliticization. Both were considered necessary conditions for the perpetuation of Franco's regime as an anti-liberal but modern state. For this, they chose to seek advice and external support, serving as intermediaries between the international currents of the time and their adaptation to Spanish reality (Delgado Gómez-Escalonilla 2015b).

The links of the Spanish authoritarian technocrats with organizations such as the International Monetary Fund, the OECD, the WB, and UNESCO were extremely useful, as it enabled them to serve as mediators with those who had the resources and methods that, coming in from outside, could help pull the country out of its backwardness.

Spanish technocrats aspired to become the agents of a project of controlled change "from above," from the state apparatus. In the context of the 1960s, the Spanish technocratic elites—as was the case with some of their Latin American counterparts—embraced the formulas devised by US social scientists, which would branch out and become strong in international organizations (Delgado Gómez-Escalonilla 2015b).

Education Reform, Technocrats, and Discontents

Throughout this book, it can be seen that the discourse of educational modernization was not forcibly imposed on the political, economic, and intellectual elites and societies of Southern Hemisphere countries. As González-Delgado and Groves (chapter 4) explain, educational transfers do not occur exclusively as a hierarchical imposition on the part of international organizations and governments. For these authors, the introduction and development of certain educational policies under Franco's dictatorship in Spain occurred in response not only to a transnational process but also to one in which local actors were able to wield considerable influence. For his part, Snider (chapter 8) points out that in the case of the *reforma universitária* in Brazil, the recommendations of US experts and agencies were accepted or rejected by the military dictatorship in accordance with its own interests. As happened in the Spanish case, the Brazilian rulers adopted those US notions that fitted their own views on education, development, and social order while rejecting those that worked against their political priorities.

Thus, it is convenient to take into consideration the interests and the agency capacity of developing countries. Although these nations were subject to US hegemony, their educational reforms responded to a two-way dynamic in which, together with the influence of US models, there were processes of collaboration and negotiation between the parties involved. That is to say, these educational reforms were more the result of coproduction than of the domination of imperial power. For John Krige (2006: 4–6), the concept of coproduction, "draw[s] attention to the creativity of both partners." It "implies that empire building is a fluid process" in which the developing nations "selectively appropriated and adapted features of the US agenda and . . . made them their own."

Therefore, the reforms discussed in this book were not just a Western educational archetype imported and implanted artificially in developing nations and without any connection to the socioeconomic and educational situation of these countries. Rather, these reforms responded to several educational needs and problems of underdevelopment that had long been recognized in both the domestic sphere and international forums. For example, in Brazil, the situation of education and its contribution to national progress was a crosscutting concern shared by different political regimes. As Snider (chapter 8) shows, both the governments that emerged from the military coup of 1964 and their predecessors elected at the polls emphasized the urgency of modernizing education as a vehicle to resolve the social and economic backwardness of that country.

However, it should be emphasized that in the mid-twentieth century, educational reform in developing nations was not a matter of exclusive interest of the political elites.[31] In the 1960s, countries such as Spain, Chile, Brazil, and El Salvador witnessed an intense social, academic, and intellectual debate on the modernization of the educational system and its implementation at the service of the needs of development. For example, as noted in a chapter on the Brazilian case, the important educational reform of 1968 "did not emerge out of the bureaucratic ether" but rather "marked the culmination of a public debate between the Brazilian state and society that dated back to the late 1950s" (Snider 2013: 101). It can be said, therefore, that the educational reforms of the late 1960s and early 1970s were preceded by a climate of public discussion about education and modernization. These reforms were the result of a wealth of social demands and expectations, public debates, and educational experiences and innovations that had been ongoing since the 1950s. For example, the approval of the General Education Law of 1970 in Spain was preceded by a series of student protests, the publication of books and newspaper articles, and various pedagogical and educational modernization proposals that had been introduced since the 1950s, as González-Delgado and Groves explain (chapter 4).

To know in depth the sociopolitical and cultural environment that preceded and surrounded the implementation of educational reforms, it is necessary to pay attention to the demands, mobilizations, and educational and pedagogical proposals arising from the base of civil society, especially among the movements of students and teachers. In this regard, it should be noted that Cold War modernization studies have generally placed their focus on the core from which the modernization ideas emanated, concentrating on the official programs and narratives used by US experts, social scientists, and diplomats. But there is also a body of historical and anthropological research that has assessed the local effects of US-led modernization programs in developing nations. This literature has paid attention to the encounters on the ground between modernization and its target groups, as well as to the processes of reinterpretation and local adaptation of the approaches disseminated by US modernizers and diplomats (Adas 2006; Escobar 1995; Mitchell 2002; Scott 1999).

In this line, in recent decades, works have appeared that analyze how modernization was received, answered, or reappropriated in developing societies, as its application in different cultural and political contexts provoked widely varying reactions and results. Some of these works include theoretical proposals that combine top-down with bottom-up perspectives in the study of diverse Latin American cases. Such studies have introduced new local actors—such as youth activists, union leaders, women, and peasants—in the study of modernization, thus contributing to expanding the framework of who "counts" in the international history of the Cold War (Field 2012; Joseph and Spenser 2008; Lindo-Fuentes and Ching 2012).

Building on this literature, the works included in this book by Óscar Martín García (chapter 6) and Héctor Lindo-Fuentes (chapter 7) are interested in conflicts and social struggles led by students and teachers in connection with educational modernization. As said earlier, at the end of the 1960s, Philip H. Coombs pointed to the emergence of a global educational crisis. In his opinion, this crisis resided in the inability of obsolete educational systems of developing countries to adapt to the demands arising from rapid social change. One of the principal manifestations of this incongruity between the old educational structures and the new economic, social, and cultural realities was the growing frustration, discontent, and disaffection of young people and students, as can be seen in the chapter by Martín García. In the 1960s, these groups demanded educational reforms to solve pressing problems for the university community, such as overcrowding in the classrooms, lack of resources, and insufficient student participation in university management or limited teacher training. As Samantha Christiansen and Zachary Scarlett (2013: 6) point out, "one important catalyst that sparked social movements in Europe and the United States, as well as in the Third World, was an active concern over education and educational reform."

Faced with this situation, Western government officials and international bureaucrats considered it necessary to implement educational reforms that modernized educational systems, fostered economic growth, and neutralized student discontent. According to Martín García (chapter 6), US officials perceived such student unrest as the result of the pressures and imbalances caused by the impetuous social change over archaic educational structures. This amounted to identifying the deficiencies of the educational systems such as problems related to development and technical and administrative issues, which could be solved through the application of scientific knowledge of international experts. In some cases, such a position implied a certain disdain for the demands of students and professors, whose opinions were hardly considered in reforms generally conceived and implemented from above.

There were also exceptions to this rule. Abarzúa Cutroni (chapter 10) refers to the capacity of student organizations to influence educational reforms at the Universidad de Concepción in Chile. Along this line, various chapters emphasize the agency capacity of students. Quesada (chapter 9) argues the Ford Foundation was receptive and tried to incorporate student approaches into the modernization programs of the University of Chile. According to Snider (chapter 8), student pressure caused Brazilian academic authorities to distance themselves from an expert as prestigious and renowned as Rudolph Atcon. In any case, the implementation of educational reforms was very often accompanied—as can be seen in the cases of Spain, Brazil, and Chile—with important signs of student unrest and protest. The Salvadoran case deserves special mention, where the opposition of teachers to the General Law of Education approved in 1971 fueled a strong social polarization that led to civil war.

Therefore, it can be said the educational plans promoted by local technocrats, international experts, and US modernizers met on more than one occasion with rejection from below, especially from students. At times, international experts considered the most politicized and active student groups a force contrary to the modernization of higher education. So, it was not entirely strange, as can be seen from Abarzúa Cutroni (chapter 10), that in some cases, these advisers recommended the national university authorities to constrain student groups. There were also proposals, such as the one developed by the UNESCO expert Joseph Lauwerys for the Universidad de Concepción in Chile, that suggested the participation of students in the reform process through the consultation of their representative organizations.

To conclude, in the study of the educational reforms of the 1960s and 1970s, it is essential to go beyond the sanitized reports of local technocrats and international institutions and to pay attention to the tumultuous national and international picture of these decades. It is necessary to bear in mind that these reforms often took place in a local and international environment of social and political ferment, in which the attitudes of actors such as students and teachers acquired great importance. Sometimes, these local and grassroots actors rejected reforms they considered technocratic, hierarchical, and designed by neocolonial experts (such as Atcon) to satisfy the interests of US capitalism.

Such resistance, in cases of dictatorial systems like the Spanish one, was accompanied by a simultaneous phenomenon among sectors of the most conservative political and social elites. Although the projects of educational modernization in these countries were pushed from above to prop up the authoritarian order, the immobilist establishment sectors were wary of the potentially liberalizing effects of the reforms. In the end, the transnational process that articulated educational reform, modernization, and development failed to fill the "revolution of expectations" unleashed in the 1960s and 1970s. The reactions it provoked were disparate, but its influence on a number of Global South societies was indisputable.

Óscar J. Martín García is a tenure-track researcher in the Ramón y Cajal Program in the Department of Political History, Theories, and Geography of the Universidad Complutense de Madrid. His professional career as a social and diplomatic historian began in 2003. Since then, his investigation has focused on two different lines of inquiry: social movement studies and international history. Within this second field, he has specialized on the United States and United Kingdom's soft power, public diplomacy, and foreign policy toward the Iberian dictatorships during the Cold War. On these topics, he has authored various articles in refereed journals such as *Contemporary European History*, *Cold War History*, and *Contemporary British History*. He has recently coedited—with Rósa Magnúsdóttir—the volume *Machineries of Persuasion: European Soft Power and Public Diplomacy during the Cold War* (2019).

Lorenzo Delgado Gómez-Escalonilla is Senior Researcher at the National Research Council of Spain, Doctorate in Contemporary History at the Universidad Complutense de Madrid, Research Fellow at the Centre d'Histoire des Relations Internationales Contemporaines (Paris 1), and Researcher Participant at the International Visitor Leadership Program. A specialist in the history of international affairs, he has extensively published on several dimensions of Spanish foreign relations, including propaganda and public diplomacy; cultural, educational, and scientific transfers; and military assistance. Recent publications include *Westerly Wind: The Fulbright Program in Spain* (2009); "La diplomacia pública de Estados Unidos: Una perspectiva histórica"

(2014); *US Public Diplomacy and Democratization in Spain: Selling Democracy?* (2015); "Modernizadores y tecnócratas: Estados Unidos ante la política educativa y científica de la España del desarrollo" (2015); *La apertura internacional de España: Entre el franquismo y la democracia (1953–1986)* (2016); "El factor exterior en la consolidación y desarrollo de la dictadura" (2018).

Notes

1. Simultaneously, an Assistant Secretary of State for Educational and Cultural Affairs (Philip H. Coombs) was appointed for the first time to take charge of this initiative.
2. "International Educational and Cultural Policies and Programs for the 1960s," September 1961, Papers of Arthur M. Schlesinger, Series 10.2, Subject File 1961–64, Box WH-16, John Fitzgerald Kennedy Library (JFKL).
3. For Cyrus Schayegh (2012: 617), it is necessary to pay more attention to the demands and attitudes of these local middle classes born in the heat of developmentalism in peripheral countries. According to him, the sociopolitical and cultural rise of such urban groups helps "to understand interactions between the Cold War and Third World development, and the interplay in the latter process, between societal and state actors."
4. "The United States Information Agency during the Administration of President Lyndon B. Johnson," November 1963–January 1969: 2–5, Administrative History, United States Information Agency (USIA), Box 1, Lyndon B. Johnson Presidential Library (LBJL).
5. "The Role of the Department of State in Educational and Cultural Affairs," 18 October 1961, Thomas Bowman Personal Papers, Research Files, 1956–1982, Box 1, JFKL.
6. Coombs had direct knowledge of such questions from his responsibility as US Assistant Secretary of State for Education and Culture and later as Director of UNESCO's International Institute for Educational Planning. He was also a member of the international committee appointed by UNESCO to advise on the elaboration and implementation of the General Education Law in Spain in 1970.
7. "Latin America: Area Program Memorandum," 18 July 1968, Leonard Marks Personal Papers, Box 2, LBJL.
8. "The Department of State during the Administration of President Lyndon B. Johnson," November 1963–January 1969, vol. 1, part II, Administrative History, Department of State, Box 1–4, LBJL.
9. "The United States Information Agency during the Administration of President Lyndon B. Johnson," 5–79.
10. "Latin America: Regional Program Memorandum," 31 August 1967, Leonard Marks Personal Papers, Box 1, LBJL.

11. "Latin America: Area Program Memorandum."
12. "National Policy Paper UNESCO, 1967," August 1968, Record Group 353, Inter-Agency Youth Committee, General Records, 1959–1973, Box 10, National Archives at College Park (NACP).
13. "Basic Philosophy, Objectives and Proposed Role of the Concerning US Policies and Programs in the Educational and Cultural Fields during the 1960s," 26 March 1961, Papers of Arthur M. Schlesinger, Series 10.2, Subject File 1961–64, Box WH-16, JFKL.
14. The scholarly literature on modernization theory and US foreign policy is quite broad (see, e.g., Cullather 2004b; Ekbladh 2009; Engerman et al. 2003; Gilman 2003a; Latham 2012).
15. A main proponent of this type of explanation was Seymour Martin Lipset (1959), who in one of his most cited works established a direct relationship between political development and other socioeconomic variables. Like modernization theorists, Lipset was also adviser to the US government.
16. "The Outlook for Spain and Portugal," 26 September 1961. Papers of President 1963–1969, National Security File-National Intelligence Estimates, Box 5, LBJL.
17. "The United States Information Agency during the Administration of President Lyndon B. Johnson," 5–16.
18. Among those works were Gutteridge (1964); Huntington (1962); Janowitz (1964).
19. "Brookings Paper on Political Development," 2 May 1961, National Security Files, Departments and Agencies, Box 283A, JFKL.
20. "The Department of State during the Administration of President Lyndon B. Johnson."
21. According to the US official discourse, American history emphasized that human capital was an essential factor in the modernization and material advancement of societies. "International Educational and Cultural Policies and Programs for the 1960s."
22. "Visit of Ambassador and Mrs. Duke to Barcelona," 15 November 1965, RG59, Department of State (DS), Central Foreign Policy Files, Education and Cultural Exchange, 1964–1966, Box 402, NACP.
23. *Noticias de Actualidad* 13, no. 20 (15 December 1961): 20.
24. "Comments on 'Authoritarian Regimes' Receiving US Assistance (Military or Economic)," 2 May 1960, RG59, DS, Lot Files, Bureau of European Affairs, 1956–66, Spain, Box 5, NACP.
25. "Spain: A Preoccupation Profile," 11 November 1959, RG 306, USIA, Office of Research (OR), Classified Research Reports, Box 3, NACP.
26. "USIS Country Plan for Spain, FY 1962," 7 March 1962, RG 306, USIA, OR, Foreign Service Dispatches, 1954–1965, Box 4, NACP.
27. "Statement of US Policy toward Spain," National Security Council Report, 10 October 1960 (quoted in Landa et al. 1993: 787).
28. "The Succession Problem in Spain," 17 July 1963, RG59, DS, Policy Planning Council, Planning and Coordination Staff, Subject Files, 1963–73, Box 16, NACP.

29. "Memorandum for the President: Visit by the Spanish Foreign Minister," 4 March 1965, RG59, DS, Central Foreign Policy, 1964–1966, Political and Defence, Box 2663, NACP.
30. "Addendum to the CU Contribution for a Country Guidelines Paper on Spain," 1963, RG59, CU, Policy Review and Coordination Staff, Country Files, 1955–66, Box 31, NACP.
31. As Schayegh (2012: 618) points out, although the development programs in Third World countries were led from above by the elites of the state, it is necessary to consider the pressure exerted on these states by rising expectations and social demands, especially of the new urban middle classes with growing political and cultural power.

References

Adas, Michael. 2006. *Dominance by Design: Technological Imperatives and America's Civilizing Mission*. Cambridge, MA: Belknap Press.
Adler, Emanuel. 1992. "Conclusion: Epistemic Communities, World Order, and the Creation of a Reflective Research Program." *International Organization* 46 (1): 367–390.
Álvaro Moya, Adoración. 2011. "Guerra Fría y formación de capital humano durante el franquismo: Un balance sobre el programa estadounidense de ayuda técnica (1953–1963)." *Historia del Presente* 17: 13–25.
Arnove, Robert F. 1980. "Comparative Education and World-Systems Analysis." *Comparative Education Review* 24 (1): 48–62.
Atcon, Rudolph P. 1961. *The Latin American University: A Key for an Integrated Ap[p]roach to the Coordinated Social, Economic and Educational Developmen[t] of Latin America*. Tegucigalpa, D.C.
Becker, Gary. 1964. *Human Capital: A Theoretical and Empirical Analysis, with Special Reference to Education*. New York: National Bureau of Economic Research.
Bienen, Henry. 1971. *The Military and Modernization*. Chicago: Atherton.
Black, Conrad. 2007. *The Invincible Quest: The Life of Richard Milhous Nixon*. London: Quercus.
Calvo González, Óscar. 2001. "¡Bienvenido, Míster Marshall! La ayuda económica americana y la economía española en la década de 1950." *Revista de Historia Económica* 19 (S1): 253–275.
Christiansen, Samantha, and Zachary A. Scarlett, eds. 2013. *The Third World in the Global 1960s*. New York: Berghahn Books.
Coombs, Philip H. 1968. *The World Educational Crisis: A Systems Analysis*. New York: Oxford University Press.
Cullather, Nick. 2004a. "Miracles of Modernization: The Green Revolution and the Apotheosis of Technology." *Diplomatic History* 28 (2): 227–254.
——. 2004b. "Modernization Theory." In *Explaining the History of American Foreign Relations*, ed. Michael Hogan and Thomas Paterson, 212–221. Cambridge: Cambridge University Press.

Darnton, Christopher. 2012. "Asymmetry and Agenda-Setting in US-Latin American Relations: Rethinking the Origins of the Alliance for Progress." *Journal of Cold War Studies* 14 (4): 55–92.
De Miguel, Amando. 1976. *Reformar la universidad*. Barcelona: Euros.
Del Pero, Mario. 2009. *Eccentric Realist: Henry Kissinger and the Shaping of American Foreign Policy*. Ithaca, NY: Cornell University Press.
Delgado Gómez-Escalonilla, Lorenzo. 2010. "After Franco, What?' La diplomacia pública de Estados Unidos y la preparación del post-franquismo." In *Claves internacionales en la Transición española*, ed. Óscar J. Martín García and Manuel Ortiz Heras, 99–127. Madrid: Los Libros de la Catarata.
——. 2015a. "Consistency and Credibility: Why You Cannot Collaborate with Dictatorships and Sell Democracy." In *US Public Diplomacy and Democratization in Spain: Selling Democracy?*, ed. Francisco J. Rodríguez Jiménez, Lorenzo Delgado Gómez-Escalonilla, and Nicholas J. Cull, 201–228. New York: Palgrave Macmillan
——. 2015b. "Modernizadores y tecnócratas: Estados Unidos ante la política educativa y científica de la España del desarrollo." *Historia y Política* 34: 113–146.
Dorn, Charles, and Kristen Ghodsee. 2012. "The Cold War Politicization of Literacy: Communism, UNESCO, and the World Bank." *Diplomatic History* 36 (2): 373–398.
Ekbladh, David. 2009. *The Great American Mission: Modernization and the Construction of an American World Order*. Princeton, NJ: Princeton University Press.
Engerman, David C. 2004. "The Romance of Economic Development and New Histories of the Cold War." *Diplomatic History* 28 (2): 23–55.
Engerman, David, Nils Gilman, Mark Haefele, and Michael Latham, eds. 2003. *Staging Growth: Modernization, Development and the Global Cold War*. Boston: University of Massachusetts Press.
Escobar, Arturo. 1995. *Encountering Development: The Making and Unmaking of the Third World*. Princeton, NJ: Princeton University Press.
Fiala, Robert, and Audri Gordon Lanford. 1987. "Educational Ideology and the World Education Revolution, 1950–1970." *Comparative Education Review* 31 (3): 315–333.
Field, Thomas. 2012. "Ideology as Strategy: Military-Led Modernization and the Origins of the Alliance for Progress in Bolivia." *Diplomatic History* 36 (1): 147–183.
——. 2014. *From Development to Dictatorship: Bolivia and the Alliance for Progress in the Kennedy Era*. London: Cornell University Press.
Frey, Marc, Sönke Kunkel, and Corinna Unger, eds. 2014. *International Organizations and Development*. London: Palgrave Macmillan.
Gleijeses, Pero. 2009. *The Cuban Drumbeat*. Chicago: University of Chicago Press.
González-Fernández, Ángeles. 2016. "La otra modernización: Tecnocracia y 'mentalidad de desarrollo' en la peninsula ibérica (1959–1974)." *Historia y Política* 35: 313–339.

Gutteridge, William, 1964. *Military Institutions and Power in the New States*. London: Pall Mall.
Haas, Peter M. 1992. "Introduction: Epistemic Communities and International Policy Coordination." *International Organization* 46 (1): 1–35.
Herman, Ellen. 1995. *The Romance of American Psychology: Political Culture in the Age of Experts*. Berkeley: University of California Press.
Huntington, Samuel, ed. 1962. *Changing Patterns of Military Politics*. New York: Free Press of Glencoe.
Isaac, Joel. 2007. "The Human Sciences in Cold War America." *The Historical Journal* 50 (3): 725–746.
Janowitz, Morris. 1964. *The Military in the Political Development of New Nations*. Chicago: University of Chicago Press.
Jolly, Richard, Louis Emmerij, Dharam Ghai, and Frédéric Lapeyre. 2004. *UN Contributions to Development Thinking and Practice*. Bloomington: Indiana University Press.
Jones, Phillip W., and David Coleman. 2005. *The United Nations and Education: Multilateralism, Development and Globalisation*. New York: Routledge.
Joseph, Gilbert M., and Daniela Spenser, eds. 2008. *In from the Cold: Latin America's New Encounter with the Cold War*. Durham, NC: Duke University Press.
Kramer, Paul A. 2009. "Is the World Our Campus? International Students and U.S. Global Power in the Long Twentieth Century." *Diplomatic History* 33 (5): 775–806.
Krige, John. 2006. *Hegemony and the Postwar Reconstruction of Science in Europe*. Cambridge, MA: MIT Press.
Knudsen, Dino. 2016. *The Trilateral Commission and Global Governance: Informal Elite Diplomacy, 1972–82*. New York: Routledge.
Landa, Ronald, James Miller, David Patterson, and Charles Sampson, eds. 1993. *Foreign Relations of the United States, 1958–1960: Western Europe, Volume VII, Part 2*. Washington, DC: United States Government Printing Office.
Latham, Michael E. 2000. *Modernization as Ideology: American Social Science and Nation Building in the Kennedy Era*. Chapel Hill: University of North Carolina Press.
——. 2003a. "Introduction: Modernization, International History, and the Cold War World." In *Staging Growth: Modernization, Development and the Global Cold* War, ed. David Engerman, Nils Gilman, Mark Haefele, and Michael Latham, 1–24. Boston: University of Massachusetts Press. "
——. 2003b. Modernization." In *The Modern Social Sciences*, ed. Theodore Porter and Dorothy Ross, 722–731. Cambridge: Cambridge University Press.
——. 2012. *Right Kind of Revolution: Modernization and US Foreign Policy from the Cold War to the Present*. Ithaca, NY: Cornell University Press.
Laville, Helen, and Hugh Wilford. 2006. *The US Government, Citizen Groups and the Cold War: The State-Private Network*. London: Routledge.

León-Aguinaga, Pablo, and Lorenzo Delgado Gómez-Escalonilla. 2018. "The Deployment of US Military Assistance to Franco's Spain: Limited Modernization and Strategic Dependence." *Cold War History*, published online 26 July. https://doi.org/10.1080/14682745.2018.1492554.

Liedtke, Boris. 1998. *Embracing a Dictatorship: US Relations with Spain, 1945–53*. London: Palgrave Macmillan.

Lindo-Fuentes, Héctor, and Erik Ching. 2012. *Modernizing Minds in El Salvador: Education Reform and the Cold War, 1960–1980*. Albuquerque: University of New Mexico.

Lipset, Seymour Martin. 1959. "Some Social Requisites of Democracy: Economic Development and Political Legitimacy." *American Political Science Review* 53 (1): 69–105.

Lucas, Scott. 2003. "Beyond Freedom, Beyond Control: Approaches to Culture and the State-Private Network in the Cold War." In *The Cultural Cold War in Western Europe*, ed. Giles Scott-Smith and Hans Krabbendam, 40–57. London: Frank Cass.

Martín García, Óscar J. 2013. "A Complicated Mission: The United States and Spanish Students during the Johnson Administration." *Cold War History* 12 (4): 311–329.

McNeely, Connie L. 1995. "Prescribing National Education Policies: The Role of International Organizations." Comparative Education Review 39 (4): 483–507.

McPherson, Alan. 2003. *Yankee No! Anti-Americanism in U.S.-Latin American Relations*. Cambridge, MA: Harvard University Press.

Meyer, John W., Francisco Ramírez, Richard Robinson, and John Boli-Bennet. 1979. "The World Educational Revolution, 1950–1970." In *National Development and the World System: Educational, Economic, and Political Change, 1950–1970*, ed. John W. Meyer and Michael T. Hannan, 37–56. Chicago: University of Chicago Press.

Milito Barone, Cecilia C., and Tamar R. Groves. 2013, "¿Modernización o democratización? La construcción de un nuevo sistema educativo entre el tardofranquismo y la democracia." *Bordón* 65 (4): 135–148.

Mitchell, Timothy. 2002. *Rule of Experts: Egypt, Techno-Politics, Modernity*. Berkeley: University of California Press.

O'Brien, Donal C. 1972. "Modernization, Order, and the Erosion of a Democratic Ideal: American Political Science 1960–70." *Journal of Development Studies* 8 (4): 351–378.

OECD. 1965. *The Mediterranean Regional Project: Spain*. Paris: OECD.

Ossenbach, Gabriela, and Alberto Martínez Boom. 2011. "Itineraries of the Discourses on Development and Education in Spain and Latin America (circa 1950–1970)." *Paedagogica Historica* 47 (5): 679–700.

Parmar, Inderjeet. 2002. "American Foundations and the Development of International Knowledge Networks." *Global Networks* 2 (1): 13–30.

Puig Raposo, Núria, and Adoración Álvaro Moya. 2004. "La guerra fría y los empresarios españoles: la articulación de los intereses económicos de

Estados Unidos en España, 1950–1975." *Revista de Historia Económica* 22 (2): 387–424.
Rabe, Stephen G. 1988. *Eisenhower and Latin America: The Foreign Policy of Anticommunism*. Chapel Hill: University of North Carolina Press.
——. 1999. *The Most Dangerous Area in the World: John F. Kennedy Confronts Communist Revolution in Latin America*. Chapel Hill: University of North Carolina Press.
——. 2012. *The Killing Zone: The United States Wages Cold War in Latin America*. New York: Oxford University Press.
Romero, Federico. 2014. "Cold War Historiography at the Crossroads." *Cold War History* 14 (4): 685–703.
Rostow, Walter W. 1960. *The Stages of Economic Growth: A Non-Communist Manifesto*. Cambridge: Cambridge University Press.
Schayegh, Cyrus. 2012. "Iran's Karaj Dam Affair: Emerging Mass Consumerism, the Politics of Promise, and the Cold War in the Third World." *Comparative Studies in Society and History* 54 (3): 612–643.
Schmitz, David F. 2006. *The United States and Right-Wing Dictatorships, 1965–1989*. New York: Cambridge University Press.
Schriewer, Jürgen. 1997. "Sistema mundial y redes de interrelación: la internacionalización de la educación y el papel de la investigación comparada." *Educación y Ciencia* 1 (15): 21–58.
Schultz, Theodore. 1968. *Valor económico de la educación*. México: UTEHA.
Scott, James C. 1999. *Seeing Like a State: How Certain Schemes to Improve the Human Condition Have Failed*. New Haven, CT: Yale University Press.
Scott-Smith, Giles. 2014. "Introduction: Private Diplomacy—Making the Citizen Visible." *New Global Studies* 8 (1): 1–7.
Sharma, Patrick Allan. 2017. *Robert McNamara's Other War: The World Bank and International Development*. Philadelphia: University of Pennsylvania Press.
Shibusawa, Naoko. 2012. "Ideology, Culture and the Cold War." In *The Oxford Handbook of the Cold War*, ed. Richard H. Immerman and Petra Goedde, 32–49. Oxford: Oxford University Press.
Simpson, Bradley R. 2008. *Economists with Guns: Authoritarian Development and US-Indonesian Relations*. Stanford, CA: Stanford University Press.
Snider, Colin. 2013 "A More Systemic Fight for Reform: University Reform, Student Movements, Society, and the State in Brazil, 1957–1968." In Christiansen and Scarlett 2013: 101–115.
Snyder, Sarah. 2013. "Bringing the Trasnational In: Writing Human Rights into the International History of the Cold War." Diplomacy and Statecraft 23: 100–116.
Stokke, Olav. 2009. *The UN and Development: From Aid to Cooperation*. Bloomington: Indiana University Press.
Taffet, Jeffrey F. 2007. *Foreign Aid as Foreign Policy: The Alliance for Progress in Latin America*. New York: Routledge.
Townson, Nigel. 2007. *Spain Transformed: The Late Franco Dictatorship, 1959–1975*. Basingstoke: Palgrave Macmillan.

UNESCO. 1965. *Los problemas y la estrategia del planeamiento de la educación: La experiencia de América Latina*. Paris: UNESCO.

Van Vleck, Jenifer. 2009. "An Airline at the Crossroads of the World: Ariana Afghan Airlines, Modernization, and the Global Cold War." *History and Technology* 25 (19): 3–24.

Viñas, Ángel. 2003. *En las garras del águila: Los pactos con Estados Unidos, de Francisco Franco a Felipe González (1945–1995)*. Barcelona: Crítica.

Weisbrode, Kenneth. 2013. *Old Diplomacy Revisited*. London: Palgrave Macmillan.

Westad, Odd Arne. 2000. "The New International History of the Cold War: Three (Possible) Paradigms." *Diplomatic History* 24 (4): 551–565.

Wright, Thomas. 2001. *Latin America in the Era of the Cuban Revolution*. London: Praeger.

Chapter 2

US Assistance to Educational Reform in Spain

Soft Power in Exchange for Military Bases

Lorenzo Delgado Gómez-Escalonilla and Patricia de la Hoz Pascua

From the start of the 1950s, the United States began an approach to the Franco regime guided by a strategic consideration: the desire to have military bases in the Iberian country. Bilateral pacts very favorable to American interests were signed in 1953, governing that security relationship and allowing for the progressive international rehabilitation of Spain. In the course of the 1950s, the country, with US support, joined organizations such as the International Monetary Fund (IMF), the World Bank (WB), and the Organization for Economic Cooperation and Development (OECD), contributing to the Spanish economy's change of course embodied in the Stabilization Plan of 1959. From then on, Spain furthered its integration into Western commercial and financial networks, giving rise to an economic growth that lasted throughout the following decade.

The connection to the United States also facilitated Spain's incorporation into the networks of training and exchange promoted by the American nation with Western Europe since the end of World War II: the Foreign Leaders Program, the Educational Exchange Program, the Technical Exchange Program, the Military Assistance Training Program and, already by the end of that decade, the Fulbright Program. These programs in the United States allowed for raising the level of some thousands of Spanish professionals: military men, technicians, businessmen, university professors, scientists, and so forth (Álvaro Moya 2011; Delgado Gómez-Escalonilla 2009, 2012; León-Aguinaga and Delgado Gómez-Escalonilla 2018). The training experience on North American soil favored the creation, still in the nascent stage, of nuclei of professionals in diverse sectors (companies, armed forces, mass media, research centers) who met the advances made on the western side of the Atlantic. The transfer of methods and knowledge to Spain was a consequence of such exchanges, although their pace and intensity would be disparate: faster in the business world and slower in the academic world, to cite just a couple examples at the risk of excessive generalization.

The United States became a fundamental point of reference for the modernization of the country, especially when there were still no equivalent lines of interaction with other European countries. Throughout the 1960s, relations with partners such as France and the Federal Republic of Germany began to intensify, but the United States remained the main foreign influence, at least until the following decades, when Spanish ties with the European community increased. When the Franco regime was preparing to undertake a profound reform of its education system, it logically turned to the United States in search of advice, financing, and training. As explained in the opening chapter of this book, this reform was part of a global framework of transformation connected with the expectations of economic growth and with the emergence of sectors of the population who saw in education a way to facilitate their social advancement. The role of education was highlighted by the theory of modernization and human capital, very much in vogue at that time, to provide the training foundations and changes of mind-set that were necessary to bring about the leap to development. The United States and the leading international organizations echoed these principles and provided knowledge and teaching strategies that favored curricular and methodological changes in the training of Spanish teachers (González Delgado and Groves 2016).

At the end of the 1960s, an educational reform program was forged that aimed to consolidate the economic and social changes of that decade that had made Spain "the Most Developed of the Underdeveloped Nations" (Martín García 2018). The political leaders who promoted that measure had already turned in the recent past to the United States and international organizations for support, seeking not only technical assistance but also ways to overcome internal resistance to their reform projects. That process coincided with the renegotiation of the bilateral pacts, making for a propitious juncture to favor US assistance to educational reform in Spain. In this chapter, we will analyze how those processes were combined and what their main results were.

Economic Development, Technocratic Cadres, and Incentives for Educational Reform

The 1960s were characterized in Spain by a strong industrial expansion driven by increased trade abroad, the influx of investment, and the opening up of new foreign firms in the country, to which were added the foreign currency generated by tourism and the remittances received from emigrants in Europe (Carreras and Tafunell 2007: 331–364). The tertiary sector registered a strong growth as a result of the migratory displacements from the countryside to the cities and from the center toward the periphery. The physiognomy of Spain as a rural country gave way to increased urbanization, accompanied by the enlargement of the middle class and the industrial workforce. More disposable income led to greater access to the consumer society and the acquisition of goods hitherto available to only a minority of the population (household appliances, automobiles, etc.). At the same time, lifestyles and customs were changing, stimulated by greater purchasing power and increased contact with the outside world. Rigid religious and conservative mentalities were giving way to new social molds that brought the Spaniards closer to other Western citizens.

Economic development was reflected in an increased demand for education, especially by the rising urban middle classes. At that time, there was an elitist system, in which only a minority acceded to higher education. University and technical education suffered from "unjust socioeconomic discrimination" (Campo 1968: 209–266). In this context, the reform of teaching, of universities, and of academic research was conceived as an essential factor to respond to the economic and social challenges that were posed to the country. Modernizing the education system would ensure the skilled workforce necessary to economic development and could reduce the student protests that were on the rise. The offspring of the emerging middle class demanded greater equality of training opportunities while they expressed their growing disaffection with the Franco regime. The Spanish dictatorship was losing the battle of ideas in the universities. Police surveillance and crackdowns alone could not stop the rebellion of students called to play an important role in the immediate political future (Carrillo Linares 2006; Hernández Sandoica et al. 2007; Valdevira 2006).

By that time, those with the greatest predicament in the ambit of Francoism power were termed "technocrats." Their political influence grew after the success of the Stabilization Plan, which corrected the dire course that the country's economic policy had been on and put it on the path of growth that other Western countries had undertaken a few years earlier. They were also the promoters of an administrative reform aimed at rationalizing the state bureaucratic structure. Their approach sought to give the Spanish dictatorship a new legitimacy, not just based on victory in the civil war but complemented by the expansion of social welfare and a rise in the population's living standards. The technocrats aspired to be the managers of a regime that was politically authoritarian but economically liberal. Their objective was to give Francoism the new underpinnings of industrial development, business training, and the nurturing of human capital as engines of economic growth that would meet the expectations of the urban middle classes and industrial workers. The reforms to be undertaken would be designed and executed from the machinery of the dictatorship, excluding any attempt at democratization.

This project of authoritarian modernization (Martín García 2015: 42–45) showed a clear interest in what was happening outside Spanish borders. Since the late 1950s, various ideas from the United States, integrated into the theoretical frameworks of modernization and human capital, had gained currency among those new leaders. Influences from German ordoliberalism and French indicative planning were also evident in these circles. Their commitment to the transformation of the country's structures was closely associated with the gradual integration of Spain into the Euro-North American orbit. Their vision was to make the country equal, in economic and organizational terms, to the Western democracies while maintaining its authoritarian political distinctness. To achieve this, they sometimes had to overcome the tenacious resistance they ran up against in the heart of the Francoist elite. Faced with such obstacles, they looked to outside assistance and support to impose their points of view in the interior. This connection made them the liaisons with the "international development community," as represented by organizations like the OECD, the IMF, the WB, and UNESCO (Frey et al. 2014). The institutional and personal links established in these forums provided action models and useful resources to undertake the controlled change advocated for Spain.

The sense of a close connection between economic development and educational reform took on increasing intensity throughout the 1960s. The Spanish elites conceived of investment in "human capital" as a strategic means to consolidate the economic modernization process (Miguel 1976: 15–21). Throughout that decade, the recommendations of the OECD and UNESCO, as well as previous experiences in educational planning developed for Latin America since the 1950s, were fundamental to reconceptualizing the education system. The country suffered from a lack of qualified personnel, investments in training, and educational planning. It was a matter not merely of insufficient budgetary means but also of an inefficient use of them. The proposals of the international organizations were converted into a blueprint, based on the conviction that economic progress should be accompanied by the promotion of educational achievement and scientific research (Delgado Gómez-Escalonilla 2015; Groves and González Delgado 2017: 139–142; OECD 1966; Ossenbach and Martínez Boom 2011; Santesmases 2008: 321–322).

The arrival of a technocrat, Manuel Lora Tamayo, at the Ministry of Education—renamed the Ministry of Education and Science (MEC) in 1966—in 1962 strengthened the collaboration with international organizations. Joint actions with the OECD and UNESCO led to successive reports adopted as guides, as happened with other Southern European countries through the Mediterranean Regional Project (OECD 1965). The neglect of teaching and scientific research was especially serious, given the growing need for training human capital, business education, and above all technology to sustain economic growth. In addition, these deficiencies directly affected one of the sectors most discontented with the dictatorship, young people, as evidenced by the student political protests; these added to the general demands for improvements in secondary and higher education, envisioned as a means of social uplift by the new middle and working classes.

Some of the recommendations of the international organizations were reflected in a series of legislative acts adopted to boost Spain's technical studies in 1957 and 1964: reform of the higher and intermediate levels of technical education, alongside the creation of new engineering schools and technical studies (Baldó 2010). Other measures were conceived to improve teaching and research structures—such as the creation of new divisions in the universities dedicated to the training of mathematicians, physicists, chemists, biologists, and geologists—in response to the shortage of such specialists that had been detected.[1] In 1965, the Law of University Education was passed to ensure stronger preparation for teaching faculty, to encourage full-time professors dedication and to make university departments the basic units of organization. In 1968, the first Research Personnel Training Scholarships for graduates were set up, which promoted the extension of studies abroad (Sánchez Ferrer 1996: 187). The improvement in the formation of human capital permeated Spain's developmental planning in the 1960s—the *Planes de Desarrollo*—but they were not ultimately supported by the allocation of sufficient resources. Despite the efforts undertaken to modernize the educational structures, Minister Lora Tamayo was unable to stop the student revolts, and in 1968, he submitted his resignation in the face of the repeated use of repression in response to them.[2]

He was succeeded as head of the MEC by another minister with a technocratic orientation, José Luis Villar Palasí. Shortly after taking office, the new minister sent General Francisco Franco a memorandum on the university situation. In his opinion, the resolution of the tensions in the universities should center on three premises: unified governmental response, political action, and university reforms.[3] For the first two, he encouraged increased coordination of action by the police and courts and greater severity of penalties. But for the government to limit itself to actions of public order would be a mistake, because repression by itself would escalate the spiral of subversion. For this reason, he proposed to the head of state the need for profound reforms at all levels of education and the creation of more primary and secondary education centers: above all, of three autonomous universities—at Madrid, Barcelona, and Bilbao—and of two higher polytechnic institutes, at Barcelona and Valencia. Acutely aware of the student revolts being unleashed in several countries in that hectic year of 1968, which were making the university a kind of "seismograph of the future," the minister warned about the risk of combating political dissidence in universities solely by means of force. In order not to jeopardize the survival of the regime, it was advisable to accompany force with the meeting of expectations, through educational reforms that fostered upward mobility. In this context, a strategy of comprehensive change was forged, initially spelled out in the White Paper on Education (MEC 1969), which embodied the principles of educational planning advocated by UNESCO and the OECD. Among its objectives were improvement in the training of university professors and an end to the marginalization of the university in the field of research.

On the road toward this reform, several Spanish experts had a special role, maintaining close contacts with the aforementioned international organizations and integrating themselves in the transnational educational advisory networks. Joaquín Tena Artigas and Ricardo Díez Hochleitner may have played the most salient part as "informal diplomats." Tena Artigas was involved from 1950 on in the general conferences of UNESCO and of the International Office of Education in Geneva, where in 1967 he was elected president. He also directed the Mediterranean Regional Project (1960–1964) and assumed a prominent role in the education group of the Spanish National Commission of UNESCO.[4] Díez Hochleitner was the main architect of educational reform in Spain at the end of the 1960s. His work on the international scene began as educational planning adviser of the Organization of

American States in the 1950s. During the following decade, he assumed the functions of executive secretary of the Education Task Force of the Alliance for Progress, collaborating simultaneously with UNESCO, where he came to occupy the position of director of the Department of Planning and Financing of Education. His international journey of those years included direction of the WB's Department of Investment in Education. In 1968, he became the technical general secretary, and then the undersecretary, of the MEC, positions from which he undertook the preparation of the White Paper and the General Education Bill of 1970 (Romero 1971: 218–220).[5]

The reform was conceived from the connection between education and employment as the formula for a more productive population to stimulate economic growth, consistent with the demands of an industrialized society and with the theories of human capital.[6] It also entailed a call for equality of opportunities, which meant correcting serious deficiencies such as the high rates of school failure, the poor state of many of the country's educational and scientific infrastructures, the limited opportunities for social mobility, and the rigid class structure reinforced by the coexistence of two educational networks, public and private. Likewise, the reformers wanted university teaching and scientific research to be more in line with the economic and social needs of the country. Implementation of the reform program also required improvements in the training of teaching staff. In July 1969, the network of the Centro Nacional de Investigaciones para el Desarrollo de la Educación (National Research Center for the Development of Education—CENIDE) and the Institutos de Ciencias de la Educación (Institutes of Education Sciences—ICEs) was created. Finally, even without making it explicit, they tried to "respond to the phenomenon of student discontent and protest" and "legitimize the social order on a new cultural basis." The reform project aspired to transform society "from the top down," from the sources of power of the Franco dictatorship, but its technocratic cadres were sensitive to the need to revamp an outdated system, and they trusted in the potential of education to build a society more open to the future (O'Malley 1995a; Ortega Gutiérrez 1992; Puelles Benítez 1992; Romero 1971; Viñao 2004).[7]

At the end of the 1960s, educational reform was proposed as a way to solidify a more productive society open to change—and to help stave off the university revolt. At the same time, the Spanish-American talks for renewing the bilateral agreements signed in 1953 were about to take an unexpected turn, given the difficulties in reconciling the initial positions of both countries. The convergence of both processes made for a direct involvement of the United States in the educational reform that was to be implemented in Spain, with the idea of discreetly laying some groundwork for a post-Franco era. The nonmilitary agreements (NMAs) were the result of this confluence of interests.

Education Reform and the Renewal of the US-Spain Accords

In the talks that got underway in the summer of 1968 for the renewal of the military pacts with the United States, the Spanish leaders proposed a much more stringent revision of the agreements than that of 1963, in an attempt to reduce their country's heavy dependence on US power. The objective was to decrease the concessions made to the US Armed Forces and to configure a more balanced strategic relationship, either through a mutual security treaty or with the admission of Spain into NATO. Franco pointed to the "need to present a united front" in the negotiations, while a campaign by the government-controlled media questioned the point of continuing the agreements if certain requirements were not met.[8] However, the stance of the Johnson and Nixon administrations showed little flexibility, pressured by a public opinion that was increasingly critical of the foreign aid associated with the Vietnam War and the exorbitant military spending it entailed. The difficulties in reconciling the claims of the two governments proved to be a deadlock in the first months of 1969. To unclog the process, it was decided to raise the tone of the agreements "in some way." In the absence of consensus on security-related guarantees, other factors came into play (Sánchez Gijón 1971: 262). Thus did players from nonmilitary fields become part of this negotiating process.

In early March, Villar Palasí wrote to Minister of Foreign Affairs Fernando M. Castiella, informing him that his department had designed an ambitious teacher training plan whose cost was estimated at $79,625,000. Recruitment for new university faculty was forecasted at one thousand teachers per year, so an urgent training program was needed. The national capacity to undertake this enterprise was limited, given the lack of sufficient and well-equipped scientific facilities and the gaps in some areas of study. Therefore, the MEC considered the possibility of including in the agreements negotiated with the United States a training program in that country for two hundred professors annually, assistance in Spain for another seven hundred, and the professional retraining in the United States of 150 full and associate professors. The estimated annual budget was $8,400,000, which in the five years of the agreement would be $42 million.[9] Villar Palasí also informed Castiella of the steps that had already been taken in terms of international assistance for educational reform. UNESCO had formed an International Advisory Committee, which included eminent North American specialists such as Philip H. Coombs (Assistant Secretary of State for Education and Culture under President John F. Kennedy and later director of UNESCO's International Institute for Educational Planning) and Cornell University President Dexter Perkins. In addition, it had set up an exploratory mission to advise CENIDE and prepare a request for assistance to the United Nations Special Development Fund. The WB had sent several missions to Spain to study the prospect of granting a loan dedicated to the construction and equipping of schools of basic, secondary, and technical education, as well as several ICEs. Together with these organizations, the collaboration of the Ford Foundation was managed to cover scholarships and advisers for CENIDE.[10]

Initially, Castiella's response to his colleague was not very encouraging. The bilateral agreements were confined primarily to the field of joint defense, so any marginal requests to the military were subject to the goodwill of the US government. But a few days later, he announced he had passed orders to feel out the Department of State on the matter.[11] The Spanish ambassador in Washington proposed to the US Asisstant Secretary of State that a new factor be introduced into the ongoing talks: a cultural educational program linked to the project of reform of the Spanish education system. That initiative had a strong social emphasis and clear popular appeal, and thus would mollify the critics of military assistance in both countries. Even so, the request was not made part of the formal negotiations.[12]

A few days later, the Directorate-General for North America of the Spanish Ministry of Foreign Affairs (MAE) conveyed to the US negotiators in Madrid the desire to include in the consultations the establishment of a joint committee on scientific and educational matters to explore further cooperation in three areas: "(1) ties between NASA [National Air and Space Administration] and its Spanish counterpart, INTA; (2) ties between the AEC [Atomic Energy Commission] and the Spanish Atomic Energy Junta; and (3) Educational Exchange." That committee would also draw up guidelines for a training program for Spanish teachers in American universities, which would be a splendid complement to the educational and scientific reform that was taking place in Spain, and for which financial assistance would be needed. [13] From the point of view of the US negotiators, there was no necessity for including the cooperation of the AEC and NASA with Spain in this initiative, which they thought was already developing successfully since its inception in the 1950s and early 1960s. On the other hand, they did see possibilities in inserting educational exchange into the negotiations to expand the bilateral defensive agreement. The inclusion of the educational component in the bilateral agreement caused doubts on the Spanish side. Their priority was not to reduce military aid, and they did not want cooperation in other areas to mean a diversion of resources from the main part. The MAE, however, began to actively collaborate with the MEC, and included Díez Hochleitner in the negotiations over these issues.[14]

The obstacles posed by the distance between the negotiating positions of Spain and the United States afforded an opportunity to bargain for more American help for the educational reform. In May, the US side accepted the Spanish proposal to sign a two-year extension (made official the following month) to allow time to negotiate a broader "framework agreement" for bilateral cooperation, which would include all fields: military, spatial, commercial and financial, cultural, and nuclear, as well as technical assistance for educational reform. In early July 1969, Díez Hochleitner traveled to Washington to meet with representatives of the US diplomatic corps, the US Information Agency, the WB, and the Ford and Rockefeller foundations. The purpose of this journey was to drum up support for the reform and for programs of educational and scientific cooperation.[15] In the middle of the same month, Castiella discussed with Secretary of State William Rogers some possible formulas for cooperation in nonmilitary matters, getting past the previous disagreements. In his opinion, the training of professors in the United States would assuage the criticisms of those who wished for greater liberalization, since it could "'carry the word' back to Spain."[16]

The attitude of the US governement was receptive. Its leaders thought their contribution "would certainly have a liberalizing effect on the Spanish cultural establishment" and, consequently, was "an opportunity we should not let pass." The planned reform was "largely based on US models." From Madrid, US Ambassador Robert C. Hill embraced the opportunity to integrate this type of nonmilitary aid to facilitate the acceptance of the renewal of agreements by both Spanish and American public opinion. In addition, he was in favor of involving the foundations and the US private sector. Above all, he regarded the modernization of the education system as essential to bringing Spain closer to the European family.[17] Along these same lines, it was also felt that "the assistance to the educational reform program may be related to base negotiations as a possible *quid pro quo* for our future military presence in Spain."[18]

The replacement of Castiella by Gregorio López Bravo as the head of the MAE in October of that year did not change the objective of exploring the nonmilitary dimensions of the bilateral relationship within the framework of an agreement with more of a global emphasis. In February 1970, the National Security Council accepted this option, with support from Henry Kissinger and the Department of State. The bilateral negotiations continued until the summer of 1970. The MEC sent the MAE a list of its priority projects, justifying the objectives, means, and assistance requested.[19] The efforts to get other ministries to define their preferences moved more slowly. The MAE noted that, for the time being, the point was to establish contacts and a permanent institutional collaboration to make use of the experience of US government agencies with a view toward the future needs of Spain. The MAE drafted a preliminary proposal of sectors that would appear in the agreement and then sent a brief consultation to the other ministries to help them complete or correct their requests.

Meanwhile, the American officials had expressed to their Spanish counterparts an interest "in exploring ways in which we might cooperate in the Spanish educational reform plan."[20] Senior officials of the MAE and the MEC (among them Díez Hochleitner) held new meetings with the US representatives to better define the framework for collaboration.[21] Simultaneously, the MEC, now with the support of the US government, intensified international support for educational reform. By an agreement signed in June, the WB granted a loan to cover half the cost of a program—whose total budget was to be $24 million—dedicated to the construction and start-up of educational centers and ICEs, together with the acquisition of equipment for CENIDE. The Ford Foundation donated $400,000 to fund scholarships for Spanish educators and the visits of foreign consultants who would assist CENIDE and the ICEs in the propagation of innovative pedagogical methods.[22] In addition, the UN Special Development Fund provided outside guidance to CENIDE, and international education experts from UNESCO and the OECD participated in the preparation of recommendations on the contents of the reform. Both directly and indirectly, the United States acted as the main source of foreign support, providing financing, training, experts, and material for development of the educational reform.

The Treaty of Friendship and Cooperation between the two countries was signed in August 1970. It was packaged as a way to move past the strictly military character of the 1953 pacts, though this glossed over the concessions that were once again made by Spain to the United States. The Spanish leaders recovered some semblance of sovereignty, but they did not achieve either a true bilateral defense treaty or the degree of strategic assurance that would have come from entry into NATO. The US administration was favorable to offering a more cooperative and less militaristic version of American relations with Spain. The text included almost all the areas of interest articulated by the Spanish side, although there were no specific references to how the NMAs were to be implemented.[23]

The agreement included various cooperation programs: Educational and Cultural; Scientific and Technical; Environment and Problems of Urban Development; Agricultural; Economic; Public Information. There was, of course, the collaboration for defense, on which everything else rested. Cultural and educational cooperation, as laid out in chapter 2 of the accord, would encourage the expansion of exchanges of professors, researchers, scientists, intellectuals, and students in all branches of knowledge, giving preference to the natural and applied sciences, economics, and the language and culture of each country.[24] Cultural and educational cooperation, together with scientific-technical cooperation, were the core of the NMAs. Although the nonmilitary components of the agreement took up thirty of the forty articles relating to other areas of cooperation, there was a firm commitment of only $3 million per year to cover them: $2 million for scientific and technical cooperation, and $1 million for cultural and educational cooperation. This was a substantial contribution, though considerably lower than the demands presented by the Spaniards and even the amounts suggested by the US advisers.

The Role of Education in Non-Military Cooperation

After signing the agreement, it was necessary to set up the application channels of the NMAs, present the concrete projects to be financed, and, most importantly, obtain the funds for this. In mid-September, the head of International Technical Cooperation of the MAE contacted all Spanish ministries and organizations interested in US aid, informing them it was necessary to maintain coordination and present "specific programs of real interest for Spain." This would depend on the effectiveness of the bilateral agreement that was conceived as a "propulsion element" for other more ambitious programs in the medium term. The response of the MEC was to accept the coordination of the MAE, but to request that the responsibility in the "technical aspects" be held "unequivocally by the MEC." His position regarding the distribution of the assigned credit was clear: "Perhaps the number one priority for a long time will be to channel all the help we can get to the Institutes of Education Sciences that we have created in each university, in order to contribute to the necessary teacher training at all levels to properly carry out the reform."[25]

The leaders of the MEC had been the driving force behind the process that led to the inclusion of the NMAs in the bilateral agreement with the United States, as a way of obtaining international funding for educational reform. Therefore, they called for the funds initially allocated to be used primarily—almost exclusively—in that direction. In addition, they had already prepared the projects to which they wanted that funding to be directed. Such an attitude provoked misgivings among their MAE colleagues, who found the reaction of the MEC officials "very elusive, seeming to imply with their actions that they are prepared to carry out the work of implementing the Agreement by themselves."[26] A subsequent meeting between representatives of both ministries served to smooth out the situation, at least temporarily. The MEC stressed its leading role in the whole process and the great interest that educational reform aroused, for both Spaniards and Americans. The issue of education should therefore be a priority. The MEC had projects for chapters 2 and 3 of the agreement (the only ones that had allocated resources) involving the training of university staff and faculty, the establishment of a scientific information system, and the creation of research centers. The MAE representatives affirmed the priority of education but indicated they would give full attention to the projects of other ministries as well.[27] From the Spanish side, it was thought that the $3 million obtained was an expandable amount, holding out the hope of obtaining at least $10 million if "political pressure" was exerted and projects of mutual interest were selected.

Meanwhile, the wheels began to turn. The MAE assumed the coordinating responsibility, and diplomatic officials held meetings with other official representatives to consider projects that could obtain financing. American managers were appointed to oversee these programs. The coordination would be carried out from the Department of State, while the MAE would serve as its counterpart on the Spanish side.[28] At the same time, US authorities were asked to let the resources of the Fulbright Program be used to support the educational reform and to allow priority to be given to the allocation of scholarships for "applied science, economics and the language and culture of both countries."[29] In mid-November, the Spanish Minister and Commissioner of the Development Plan, Laureano López Rodó, took advantage of his visit to the United States to meet with Herman Pollack and John Richardson, the Department of State officials principally responsible for the NMAs. To both of them, he insisted that cooperation in education, science, and technology was considered "a vital part" of the Third Development Plan (1972–1975). He also told them the proposals being prepared were pilot projects estimated at $3 million and that he and his colleagues in Spain hoped these would lead to a second, larger phase of the program.[30] Finally, he was firm in asserting "education comes first," that the reason for his visit was to show "the great interest of my government regarding education," and that he therefore recommended they focus their assistance on the same.[31]

Throughout that fall, the MAE was gathering requests from various ministries that included projects on pollution, urbanization and land issues, agricultural research, oceanographic research, nuclear energy for peaceful uses, industrial technology, information technology, and assistance to university teams and special schools. In parallel, from the Secretariat of the Development Plan, action guidelines were given to the different ministries to guide the projects to be presented in sectors prioritized in the Third Development Plan. Before the end of the year, an interministerial commission was established, chaired by one of the Deputy Commissioners of the Development Plan, which would be responsible for selecting the projects to be presented and the order of priority. The MAE would centralize the negotiations with the United States but would not be responsible for the selection. This procedure favored the criteria used by the MEC, at the expense of the MAE. Although they recognized the importance of the expansion of education, "as a truly capital point for the future of the country," MAE officials continually said this preference should not prevent the "other aspects of national development" from benefiting from the agreement with the United States.[32]

At the beginning of December, an American mission reviewed with its Spanish negotiators the list of projects prepared. The decision was that two blocks would be submitted, one with the projects for the amount of $3 million available and another for which alternative financing possibilities would be explored, depending on their viability. Shortly afterward, the final selection was made at a meeting of the Technical General Secretaries of the various ministries in the Commissariat of the Development Plan and sent to López Rodó for his approval. After that, the heads of the MAE communicated it to the US representatives in a series of meetings held in Washington at the end of January 1971. In the agreed distribution, $2.4 million would go to the MEC projects: (a) training of school administrators and university executives, $609,000; (b) National Service of Scientific and Technical Information, $300,000; (c) training of English teachers and help for

CENIDE, $307,000; (d) Institute of Molecular Biology, $986,000; and (e) Institute of Automátics (Robotics), School of Industrial Engineers of Barcelona, $98,000. A surplus of $600,000 remained for projects of other agencies, very far from their requests, which totaled $10,253,000.[33] The MAE informed the MEC that it had charged of "all the projects whose financing is firmly assured."[34] Two US missions moved in the following months to examine how to proceed with the projects that were already approved and explore the viability of some other projects (urban development, air pollution, oceanography) that could be financed with the remaining amount.[35]

Some of the MEC projects were slated to begin in the fiscal year 1971–1972, with the contracts for their implementation signed in July. Such was the case with the training of university administrators (twenty-five in the first year), which was commissioned by the Educational Technology Center of the Sterling Institute. The first phase consisted of pilot courses on advanced educational management, lasting several weeks in Madrid at the School of Public Administration; the second phase took place in US universities (especially the University of Wisconsin). The instruction of English teachers, run by Georgetown University, was also launched. Spanish teachers would receive training in advanced linguistics and techniques of teaching English as a second language for nine months, during which time American instructors occupied their posts in Spain (twenty-seven Spanish and twenty-five American professors participated that year). The founding of the Institute of Molecular Biology was also on track. The National Science Foundation was in charge of preparing the agreement with Professor Severo Ochoa, approving its constitution in March 1971. The other two MEC projects were still in the planning stage. The creation of a National Service of Scientific and Technical Training was entrusted to the General Director of Archives and Libraries, Luis Sánchez Belda, in collaboration with the Institute Service Information. Although an exchange of information missions was planned, it did not materialize until sometime later. The opening of the Institute of Automatics, linked to the new Autonomous University of Barcelona and the University of Southern California, was also delayed, because its construction was linked to the second loan requested from the WB, which was expected to come at the beginning of 1972.

At the end of September, it was decided to approve the projects already mentioned, which were considered "first priority," so that they could begin after completing the administrative processes in Washington.[36] According to the American negotiators, it was evident that "GOS attaches importance to non-military agreement far beyond modest financial outlay this far involved," conceiving it as a "significant gesture" of the relations of the United States with Spain.[37] The MEC had played an essential role in the creation of the NMAs and was their principal beneficiary in the initial stages of its execution, with the aim of bankrolling the reforms contained in the General Education Law that was passed at almost the same time as the renewal of agreements with the United States. But its strong role did not leave other sectors of the Spanish administration sitting passively by, as they got shunted aside in the distribution of American aid funds. The MAE reflected this situation at the end of 1971, which said the MEC had absorbed almost exclusively the funds anticipated in the NMAs. The imbalance that prevailed led them to speak of the "voracity" of the MEC, which had provoked the resentment of other ministries.[38]

Throughout this process, Díez Hochleitner was especially noted for his broad capacity for initiative, his involvement in educational reform, and his contacts with the US leaders. The Spanish diplomats watched with disgust as decisions in this area escaped their control. Díez Hochleitner's resignation as Undersecretary of the MEC in May 1972 led to a reorientation of how NMA funds were allocated. His resignation was linked to the counter-reformist turn that education policy was then taking after the passage of the General Education Law, which slowed down its implementation and deprived it of sufficient means to meet its goals (Aguilar Cestero 2007: 20). As can be deduced from the documents consulted, it is not clear that all the projects agreed upon within the framework of the NMAs were ever initiated, so at least some of the funds provided were lost. From the point of view of the MAE, the MEC was responsible for this situation.[39]

At the end of 1972, the MAE again gathered project lists from other ministries to prepare the solicitations for the fiscal year 1973–1974. By then, some things had seriously changed. The MEC ceased to have a determining influence on the NMA assignments, which resulted in a loss of the percentage allocated to its projects. These projects were no longer linked so closely with educational reform, although they affected it in a more indirect way. Their main objective was to promote the training of university faculty and researchers in US centers through a scholarship program. Along with this, a series of specific projects integrated in a program called "Frontiers of Science" were financed. On the other hand, the participation of other ministries as beneficiaries of the NMA initiatives was increased.

In the first of the indicated lines of action, the Director General of Cultural Relations (DGRC) of MAE proposed to the Department of State in November 1972 that the funds of the NMAs for cultural and educational cooperation be used mostly in a new scholarship program. To organize it, Dr. Frank Freidel, a member of the Committee on International Exchange of Persons (CIEP) and professor of US history at Harvard University, held talks with Spanish officials to determine the distribution by area. In January 1973, Freidel resumed these talks, accompanied by Dr. A. D. Van Nostrand, professor of American literature at Brown University and former CIEP adviser for American studies.[40] That same month, the DGRC took charge of Spanish direction of the program of cultural and educational cooperation. As a coordinating body, a Supervisory Committee was formed,[41] and a National Advisory Committee composed of "relevant personalities of the Arts and Sciences" was established. [42] It was further agreed to delegate the management of this program to the Fulbright Commission. In the fiscal years 1973–1974 and 1974–1975, an annual $800,000 was received for cultural and educational cooperation. In 1975, that amount was raised to $1 million in response to the "repeated wishes of the American representatives who have always believed that there is an imbalance in favor of scientific issues in the use of NMA funds."[43] The same amount was put in the budget for the following year, although only $961,000 was used. The agreement was in force until the fiscal year 1976–1977, reaching a total of $3,561,000 for this program.

Most of these funds (about $2,685,000, three-quarters of the total) was used to finance the stays of scholarship recipients. The objective was to have more qualified teachers to keep up with the rapidly growing demand for education. The recipients were "full and associate professors from Spanish universities interested in refreshing their knowledge or in updating themselves in new techniques of their specialty ; young tenured and untenured educators who will need to expand their studies ; and researchers belonging to the CSIC [Consejo Superior de Investigaciones Científicas] needing to gain stronger preparation in their specialties, techniques, or methods." During the four years of the cultural and educational cooperation program, 264 scholarships were awarded. By specialty, the most awarded were chemistry (44), biological sciences (40), medicine (34), biochemistry (26), physics (18), and mathematics (15).[44] The proportion of the scholarships allocated to the sciences comfortably exceeded those assigned to the humanities and social sciences, which indicates the US claims in that latter regard were not fulfilled. [45]

At the same time, the Fulbright Program continued granting scholarships, also with majority funding from the United States and a small contribution from the Spanish government. The orientation of educational reform modulated this program in the coming years, creating an Executive Committee in charge of specifying the guidelines.[46] In Program Year 1971, one of the priority lines was Educational Development, in a double sense:

> A. Education: preparation of specialists in education qualified to prepare teachers of the primary, secondary and university levels; this implies support of the new Institutes of Educational Science as well as the developing fields of pedagogy and psychology.
> B. Support for specific developing fields considered of vital importance: Mathematics, Physics, Economics, Sociology.[47]

The distribution by area of Fulbright scholars sent to the United States during the first half of the 1970s was as follows: Language and Literature (172—including those dedicated to American Studies); Economy and Sociology (92—socioeconomic planning); Applied Sciences (78—construction technology, agriculture, and forestry); Pure Sciences (52—mathematics and physics); Educational Sciences (50—pedagogy and psychology), and Humanities (33).[48] The priority of the scholarships allocated to Language and Literature was connected with the growing demand for qualified teachers of English, which, as part of the educational reform, became the primary foreign language for Spain's schools.[49] At the same time, US advisers were appointed to collaborate on several fronts: the training of professors in the fields where deficiencies had been detected (mathematics, physics, chemistry, economics, and sociology); application of modern techniques and methodologies in the ICEs of Madrid, Barcelona, and Santiago de Compostela; and coordination of curriculum at the Faculty of Economics of the Autonomous University of Madrid, the Faculty of Political Science and Sociology of the Complutense University of Madrid, the Technical School of Telecommunications of Madrid, and the polytechnic institutes of Madrid and Barcelona.

With the remainder of the NMA funds for cultural and educational cooperation, several smaller-scale projects were financed. Some of them were also connected with various aspects of educational reform: a seminar on North American studies in the University of Salamanca; an exchange of professors between the Maxwell School of Citizenship and Public Affairs of Syracuse University and the Faculty of Political Science and Sociology of the Complutense University of Madrid; courses of educational innovation and teacher training at the ICE in Santiago de Compostela; a study of the skills involved in the learning process; support for a business management and technology program at the Polytechnic University of Barcelona; and scholarships to the

International Marketing Institute.[50] The final report of that program indicated its activities had been "always focused on strengthening the academic, cultural, and administrative structures of higher education, especially within Spain." The main beneficiaries were Spanish professors and researchers whose visits to the United States allowed them to expand their training in new techniques and methodologies. A survey carried out to evaluate the effectiveness of the program yielded highly satisfactory results. A high percentage of the fellows rated their experience as very positive from the academic point of view (95 percent) and said they had improved their prospects in the professional field (78 percent).[51]

Other programs approved in the years that followed under the NMAs' chapter on scientific and technical cooperation were also linked to the MEC. Several of them were a continuation of the previous ones (molecular biology, automatics, and scientific information). The novelty was in the so-called Frontiers of Science, which had been gestated after the arrival of the CSIC of Federico Mayor Zaragoza. On his initiative, a commission was created to investigate the trends of science and define the priorities of the aid that could be requested from the United States. In March 1973, the first draft was submitted, and a modest sum was obtained for its inception in the fiscal year 1973–1974. Starting the next year, its amount increased substantially, becoming the one that obtained the most funding in successive budgets ($898,000 in the fiscal year 1974–1975, and more in the following years). The program encompassed projects in seven areas: use of agricultural byproducts, direct energy conversion with special emphasis on solar, physical-chemical study of molecules and processes of biological interest, basic research on the environment, special materials, protein metabolism and nutrition, and neuropsychobiology. These funds would allow for the acquisition of American material and equipment, as well as facilitate relations with scientists from the United States.[52]

Two Areas of Priority in the Scholarship Program: Biological Sciences and Medicine

Candidates from the biological sciences and medicine reached a notable proportion in the distribution by area of the scholarships awarded with NMA funds for cultural and educational cooperation, to which were added the resources granted in the research projects related to these two fields. In both cases, the preferences were associated with specific processes: the international boom during the 1960s and 1970s of research in biochemistry and molecular biology, with its correlate in Spain stimulated by the Nobel Prize granted in 1959 to Severo Ochoa, and the impetus derived from the expansion of the Spanish health system.

The degree of interest granted to biochemistry and molecular biology was part of a process of consolidation of a research community in Spain, which had not only a reference point in the United States but also a preferred place in training priorities. The formative current intensified especially after the 1960s because of the convergence of several factors. One was the Vietnam War, whose prolongation meant many young American scientists were incorporated into the Army, leaving vacant their positions in research centers and laboratories (as well as hospitals), which consequently received their European colleagues who came to replace them with open arms (Ávila de Grado et al. 2003). The other was related to the fight against cancer, which had become the second-leading cause of death in the 1970s, prompting President Richard Nixon to declare a "War on Cancer" (Marshall 2011). An extensive research program was undertaken through the National Cancer Institute.

In the Spanish case, the scientific recognition achieved by Ochoa came, together with the desire of the government of his native country to take advantage of these circumstances, to encourage the outward extension of national research and to advance the progress of a group of scientists, who knew how to use the possibilities of the "Ochoa effect" to consolidate and internationalize advances in biochemistry and molecular biology in Spain (Santesmases 2000). Since the death of Santiago Ramón y Cajal in 1936, the creation in 1953 of the Center for Biological Research (CIB) into the CSIC probably represented the most important milestone in this field (Segovia de Arana 2006: 31–42). The difficulties in developing their work were not minor, in an environment in which avant-garde knowledge was neither produced nor disseminated in the universities, nor was it reflected in research activity (Santesmases 2001: 14–35). Ochoa's availability and collaboration in support of the initiatives undertaken by his Spain-based colleagues represented the best drawing card before the political authorities, giving rise to increasing public support. At the same time, the CIB and the scientific activities of its researchers, with Alberto Sols at the helm, benefited from Ochoa's international influence, which facilitated the center's contacts with the most advanced training centers and professional circuits (Salas 2003; Santesmases 2001).

Both Ochoa and Sols had crossed the Atlantic to work in the laboratory of Carl and Gerty Cori, winners of the Nobel Prize in Medicine in 1947. Ochoa remained in the United States while Sols returned to Spain. In 1956, he joined the CIB, which was becoming a nurturing ground for biochemists and biologists in general—including, among others, Julio Rodríguez Villanueva, Margarita Salas, Eladio Viñuelas, Antonio García-Bellido, and David Vázquez. After passing through either the CIB or the University of Salamanca, many of these young researchers made a postdoctoral stay in the United States, where they completed their training and returned to Spain to develop their research projects further, despite the precarious nature of resources there. They also returned with updated knowledge in their areas and with experience in using new devices and techniques for their experiments. Upon returning to Spain, these researchers proceeded to train new disciples while at the same time reinforcing their scientific expertise and international prestige. Later, José Manuel Sierra Pérez, Joan Guinovart, Mariano Barbacid, César de Haro, and César Nombela participated in this training chain (see Figure 2.1). If they had previously left the United States with scholarships from US centers, the CSIC, or the Fulbright Program (García-Bellido, Nombela, and Sierra), then the NMA program reinforced the training trajectory (Haro, Guinovart,

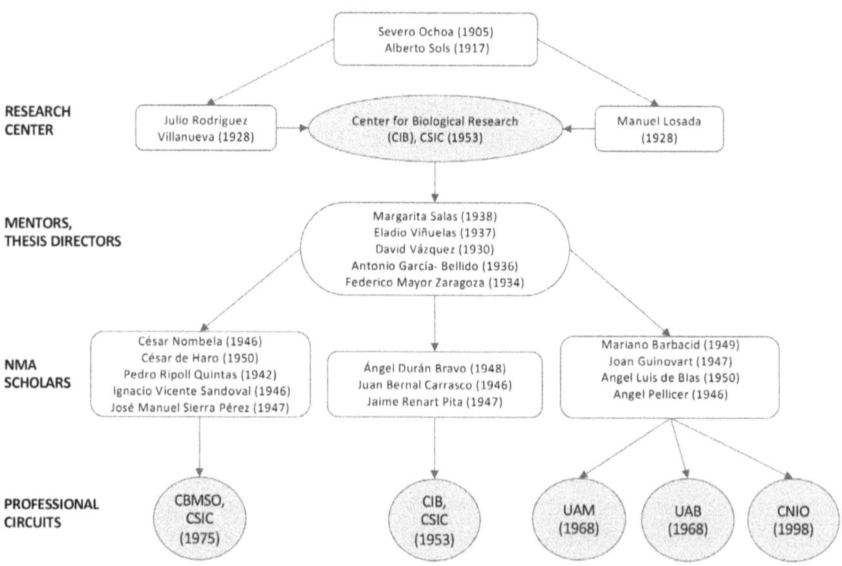

Figure 2.1 Molecular Biology, Biochemistry Centers and researchers trained in the United States. Figure created by the author.

Barbacid, Ángel Pellicer, and others). Likewise, the reform promoted by Villar Palasí and Díez Hochleitner gave them the opportunity to extend the scope of their institutional activities.

One of the objectives of the educational reform in Spain was to step up the research dimension of the universities and to recover some of the Spanish scientists who had successfully developed their professional careers abroad (the "brain drain"). Ochoa epitomized that category. To try to lure him back, Díez-Hochleitner visited him in New York and asked for his advice and collaboration. Ochoa also received offers of academic positions at the new Autonomous University of Madrid. He responded with a request to create a research center, which obtained support from the NMAs. In fact, the initiative started with a group of scientists from several centers of the CSIC and received the support of both university and political authorities. Ochoa encouraged the project to set up an Institute of Molecular Biology and became its main adviser. The objective was to create a research center and a school of biologists. NMA money obtained in 1972 and 1973 was used for the acquisition of scientific instruments and, to a lesser degree, books and journals. In the following two years, these funds were used to complete the provision of instrumental techniques and the training of researchers at the Medical Center of New York University, where Ochoa worked.[53]

The launching of the project took longer than expected and would count on fewer resources than anticipated. The removal from office of Villar Palasí in the MEC paralyzed operations in the middle of 1973; they got back on track after the ascension of Cruz Martínez Esteruelas to the ministry at the beginning of 1974 (with Mayor Zaragoza as Undersecretary). The Severo Ochoa Molecular Biology Center (CBMSO) was an important milestone in the consolidation of the efforts already underway. Earlier and with more modest pretensions, the Institute of Fundamental Biology had been established in Barcelona in 1970 under the inspiration of Juan Oró, from the University of Houston, and Jaume Palau, whose training had been developed in Great Britain (Santesmases 2000: 721–722, 726–728). The contingents of biochemists and molecular biologists who followed would find fertile ground for developing their biomedical research. The new researchers who were trained, after passing through prestigious international institutions, found more opportunities to continue their work in Spain: the CIB and the CBMSO, the autonomous universities of Madrid and Barcelona, and later the Center for Oncological Research in 1998 and the National Center for Cardiovascular Research in 1999 (Muñoz 2004).[54]

Medicine was another field of research emphasized in the awarding of NMA scholarships. In the United States, a hospital management model had been developing since the beginning of the twentieth century that would have an international reach, influencing, among others, Spanish health care. Spain had the Seguro Obligatorio de Enfermedad (Mandatory Illness Insurance—SOE), since 1949, extended to the entire population. However, the SOE and the welfare policies of the Franco regime were a mere palliative designed to make up for the social decline the dictatorship had ushered in. The state scarcely invested in this venture, which was funded primarily with the contributions of workers and employers. In mid-twentieth century, 43 percent of the Spanish population was still served by charity; Franco's regime "had opted for an individual, discriminatory insurance model with a residual presence of the State, while the West designed models of universal social assistance" (González Madrid and Ortiz Heras 2018: 370; see also Campos 2010; Perdiguero-Gil 2015).

In the 1960s, the Instituto Nacional de Previsión scarcely ran any hospitals of its own. It had to arrange for outside assistance, there was a huge delay for hospital care, and there were no specialties for graduates in medicine. Medical care for nonsurgical patients took place mainly in private centers. Surgical patients who could pay for the service were treated in hotel-like institutions called "sanatorios." Those who belonged to the SOE and resorted to its services were operated on in "residences" built by the Ministry of Labor in imitation of the "sanatorios" but without even minimal hospital quality (Nadal 2016). The first experiments with transforming the health system were in response to individual initiatives that later spread, encouraged by Spain's economic growth. One of the pioneers was Carlos Jiménez Díaz, who had had the opportunity to learn about British, German, and, above all, American medicine. In 1955, he created the Clínica de la Concepción in Madrid, establishing a network of contacts with the best US hospitals and importing the modern hospital concept in its threefold aspects of care, teaching, and research. He also put into operation a system of scholarships to train specialists. Sometime later, in 1959, Carlos Soler Durall founded the General Hospital in Asturias. His time as a postgraduate at Yale University had given him enough knowledge to implement a program similar to that of the United States, with a demanding selection of personnel, and centralized common services.

During those same years, and especially in the following decade, a group of young doctors who had recently graduated felt the need to leave Spain to specialize. Many of them went to the United States for training (Ruiz Fornells 1967). Upon their return, they set about applying the US model to the Spanish reality, becoming the architects of the main advances in medical training and research in the country. Such was the case of Diego Figuera Aymerich and José María Segovia de Arana, who had begun their medical journey at the Clínica de la Concepción. Figuera Aymerich and Segovia de Arana both completed specialization in US hospitals, and in 1964, both doctors launched, with a novel and pioneering orientation, the Puerta de Hierro Clinic in Madrid. This clinic was key to the modernization of hospital care in Spain, because through it a series of behavioral patterns were introduced into the Spanish system: full-time commitment of the doctors, hierarchical and specialized structure of medical services, freedom of recruitment of personnel, strong research ambitions, and the presence of postgraduates classified as interns and residents. All the service chiefs at that center had acquired their specialized expertise in the United States; many returned to the clinic, and many others visited the new hospitals that were opened in the following years, to which the "Puerta de Hierro model" was applied.[55] Jiménez Díaz, Segovia de Arana, and Figuera Aymerich became pioneers of a training circuit that began in their centers in Spain and culminated in specialized studies in the United States. NMA scholarships helped make the travels possible. Among those partaking were Juan Martínez López de Letona and Eduardo Sanz, who after their stays in the United States took positions as service chiefs at the Puerta de Hierro Clinic. Others also applied what they had learned in the United States to the new emerging hospitals in Spain, including Franco Sánchez Franco at the University Hospital La Paz, and Emilio Bouza at Hospital Ramón y Cajal (see Figure 2.2).[56]

Henceforth, the newly created hospitals applied modern methods of hospital management, and the training of specialists was systematized by the residency system. In 1966, the first call for vacancies of internal and resident doctors to work exclusively for the national welfare system hospitals appeared. At the end of 1974, the predominance of the public health system over the private was marked. SOE members made up 80 percent of the population, and a similar percentage of doctors worked for the Seguridad Social (Social Security) (Nadal 2016) —all this with a network of hospitals and more modern technical equipment, and with better trained human teams (see Table 2.1). The problem lay in the fact that the contribution of the state continued to be excessively low. At late as 1975, the financing in Spain was limited to 4.7 percent of the general budget, so the system could not be maintained for long (González Madrid and Ortiz Heras 2018: 376). With the dawn of

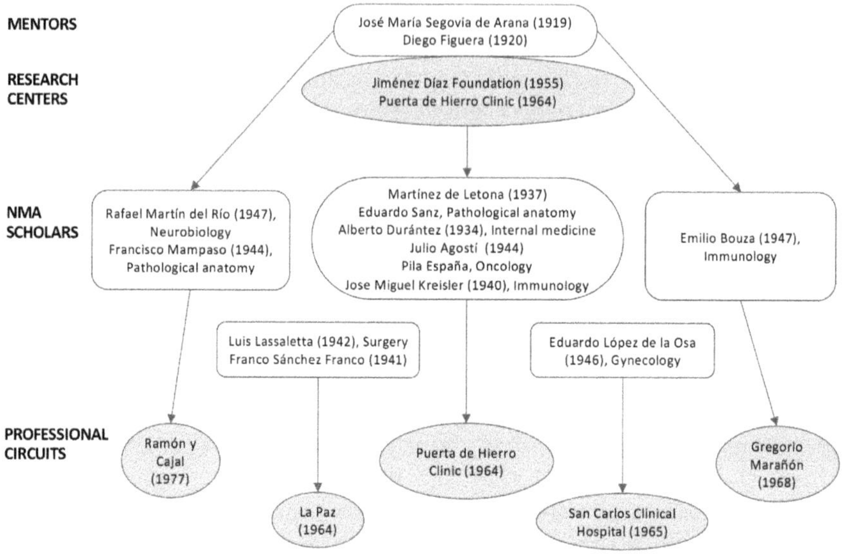

Figure 2.2 Hospitals and researchers trained in the United States. Figure created by the author.

Table 2.1 Creation dates of the new hospitals.

Clínica de la Concepción	1955
Hospital General de Asturias	1959
Clínica Puerta de Hierro	1964
Hospital Universitario La Paz	1964
Hospital Clínico San Carlos de Madrid	1965
Hospital Gregorio Marañón	1968
Hospital Doce de Octubre	1973
Hospital Universitario Ramón y Cajal	1977

democracy, the Ministry of Health and Social Security was created in 1977, establishing the MIR system (Médico Interno Residente/Hospital Resident) and family medicine the following year. Sometime later, in 1986, the General Law of Health arrived, presupposing the genesis of the current welfare system.

Conclusions

The reception that the educational reform received in Spain was at variance with what was desired by its promoters, who were aware of the suspicions it aroused even within the government. After its passage through the Cortes Españolas, the Franco government disposed of some of the most innovative proposals, as the more intractable elements in the dictatorship thought the program went too far and could set in motion changes of uncertain outcome. Also at that time, it was clear the new education law would not have enough financial backing to ensure its effective application, to which would be added the obstacles placed on its start up from various institutional structures. The reform clashed with strong corporate interests. It also faced the reservations of the Catholic Church that feared a loss of social and ideological influence by the extension of state intervention in education (Aguilar Cestero 2007: 30–33; Montoro Romero 1981: 61; O'Malley 1995a: 31; Viñao 2004: 85–86). The relatively democratizing mood that emerged from the ideas that inspired the reform contributed to the increase of these suspicions. The final report of the committee of international experts who analyzed it highlighting its potential to change "a traditional educational system, originally conceived to satisfy the needs of a privileged minority, in a modern and democratic system that should serve the great majority of the country."[57] The implementation of the reform was slow and incomplete, the latter being the case in some of its key aspects, like research in the National Institute of Education Sciences network (Escolano Benito 1982).[58]

This process also met with resistance from detractors of the Franco regime, who saw in the reform an initiative driven by an authoritarian regime and designed by technocratic cadres, without the participation of the educational community and whose ostensible inclinations toward democratization represented only a facade (Fernández de Castro 1973; Paris 1974). Many teachers, committed to antiauthoritarian and innovative pedagogical ideas, mobilized openly or clandestinely against the new reform law and promoted the creation of an alternative that embodied the germ of the public school model of the future democratic society (O'Malley 1995b): "'top-down' educational modernization that was launched with the reform of 1970 through the particular restructuring that Spanish technocrats carried out in conjunction with the open elements of the regime, carrying out the ideas, methods, and discourses of international organizations," were in contrast with "the 'bottom-up' proposals for democratization that started with teachers' movements" (Milito Barone and Groves 2013: 143).

It was also not lost on critics that behind the reform and the involvement of the United States in its promotion lurked shady American interests. Spain was no longer just a "satellite" of US military and economic designs: its action extended to cultural and scientific areas. Critics rejected the US contribution, arguing that both the WB's support for educational reform and the credits for research were aimed at advancing "imperial action" and "technological domination," within the "vaselinic effort [that] is applied to make evidence of Americanization seem tolerable for the future" (Vázquez Montalban 1974: 358–365). On this premise, measures aimed at overcoming inertia and deep-rooted hierarchies in the university came under fire, as inspired by foreign and technocratic influences (Romero 1971: 224–227). Likewise, the opposition to US "interference" extended to the student protests against the educational reform, showing the failure of the attempt to win support from leaders of that group (Martín García 2012; see also chapter 6).

In any case, the negotiation of the Hispano-American agreement of 1970 provided complementary resources in the educational and scientific fields, destined to support the reforms that were getting underway. The main institutional beneficiary of the contribution of the NMAs was the MEC, which had a training scholarship program in the United States (complementary to the Fulbright Program and with a larger allocation), with additional funding for some newly created centers and another program that allowed for subsidizing research in fields considered strategically significant. Some of the reform movement's leaders, such as Villar Palasí and Díez Hochleitner, had close relations with the United States.[59] From the American embassy in Madrid, this collaboration was conceived as a golden opportunity to influence "the future structure of Spanish society" by way of a "longer-range, lower-profile improvement of the educational system."[60] Such initiatives fit right in with the flexibility adopted by US policy in the face of the intense process of change that the country was going through. US policy aimed above all to defend its own interests and to avoid uncomfortable political commitments, which implied a dilemma between the immediate option of rapport with the dictatorship or support for the return of democracy to Spain. According to its promoters, this form of cooperation was an investment in the future, a sign of American solidarity with the progress and well-being of Spanish society. In this way, contacts were increased with individual and collective agents capable of supporting their positions outside the political arena.

Since the financing of these programs represented a quid pro quo for the use of military bases in Spanish territory, it could also be treated as an asset to be used in negotiations with Spanish leaders, be they Francoist or post-Franco. It is no coincidence that when the renewal of the bilateral agreements, scheduled for 1975, was being prepared, the instructions sent by Secretary of State Henry Kissinger to US Ambassador Robert J. McCloskey included considerable leeway in the area of nonmilitary cooperation. The idea was to "try to project an image of attaching importance to our non-military, as well as our defense, cooperation with Spain."[61] During the last years of the Franco regime and the beginning of Spain's political transition, the US contribution in these dimensions increased substantially, although still at more modest levels than Spanish negotiators desired. US foreign aid had been reduced by the cost of the Vietnam War and the budget deficit. The resources for the NMAs came mainly from the allocation for military spending in Spain, adding to what came from international organizations that had the United States as their leading partner and from philanthropic foundations in that country committed to its public diplomacy. This assistance had effects on the Spanish educational and scientific system. The resources that emanated from the United States boosted the renovation of some educational structures and improved the competence of a group of professors and researchers, especially in sensitive areas of the reform that was being attempted, although we still do not have a clear picture of its full scope. But it did not prevent the erosion of the image of the United States in Spain, which was identified in the public mind with the backing of the Franco regime to guarantee its military presence on the Iberian Peninsula.

Despite these censures, the Spanish authorities placed great interest in that flow of exchanges. The scholarships, integrated into the cooperation programs with the United States, were in those years the most important channel for the expansion of knowledge for scientists, university professors, and technicians. The target goals of the successive Development Plans were not fulfilled, which made the North American contribution all the more relevant in this area. From the Spanish perspective, help in the training of human capital for the reform of the educational and scientific-technical system became a counterweight for military collaboration with the United States, especially when the economic aid linked to the 1953 agreements was no longer received.

After the death of the dictator and the beginning of the political process that led to the establishment of a Western-style democracy, the Spanish government tried to count on the support of the United States. The 1976 treaty was conceived as an interim arrangement without any appreciable variations on the substantive issues, since it was thought the rebalancing of the strategic relationship would pass through the door of NATO (Powell 1996, 2011: 494–512). The problem was that this initiative aroused little enthusiasm in public opinion, especially among the opposition parties, so it was decided to put the matter on hold for the moment. However, the disagreements that affected things at the political level did not interfere with the continuity and deepening of the double facet of cultural-educational and scientific-technological cooperation. These dimensions were incorporated into the aforementioned bilateral treaty and would be integrated into the subsequent renewals of the Spanish-American agreements until the end of the 1980s. By then, the extent of such collaboration increased considerably: between 1977 and 1993, there were 2,630 scholarships and hundreds of projects, which received financing of more than $35 million.[62] The experience of the NMAs served as the basis for a much more intense collaboration in the immediate future, beyond their eventual contribution to the educational reform, which acted as their trigger.

Acknowledgments

This work was supported by the Ministry of Economy and Competitiveness of Spain and by the Junta of Castilla and León under the research projects "La modernización del sistema educativo y científico español en su dimensión internacional (1953–1986)" (HAR2014-58685-R) and "Asistencia exterior y modernización industrial y científico-técnica en Castilla-León: Análisis de potencialidades locales y opciones globales, c.1950-actualidad" (SA241P18).

Lorenzo Delgado Gómez-Escalonilla is Senior Researcher at the National Research Council of Spain, Doctorate in Contemporary History at the Universidad Complutense de Madrid, Research Fellow at the Centre d'Histoire des Relations Internationales Contemporaines (Paris 1), and Researcher Participant at the International Visitor Leadership Program. A specialist in the history of international affairs, he has extensively published on several dimensions of Spanish foreign relations, including propaganda and public diplomacy; cultural, educational, and scientific transfers; and military assistance. Recent publications include *Westerly Wind: The Fulbright Program in Spain* (2009); "La diplomacia pública de Estados Unidos: Una perspectiva histórica" (2014); *US Public Diplomacy and Democratization in Spain: Selling Democracy?* (2015); "Modernizadores y tecnócratas: Estados Unidos ante la política educativa y científica de la España del desarrollo" (2015); *La apertura internacional de España: Entre el franquismo y la democracia (1953–1986)* (2016); "El factor exterior en la consolidación y desarrollo de la dictadura" (2018).

Patricia de la Hoz Pascua is an archivist and historian. Since 2004, she has been working at the Fulbright Commission in Madrid, where she is in charge of organizing the historical archive with the aim of making the collection available to researchers. Moreover, she organized the private archive of Pedro Laín Entralgo for the Royal Academy of History and worked as a technical archivist in Manila for the project "Modernization of the National Archive of the Philippines": carried out by the CSIC Institute of History. Her duties included organizing the team of specialist materials, cataloging, managing databases, and preparing the microfilming of maps and plans. Recent publications include *Guía catálogo de la Sección de Documentos Españoles del Archivo Nacional de Filipinas* (2002), "La organización del archivo de la Comisión Fulbright y su interés para la investigación" (2012), and "El archivo de la comisión Fulbright y el estudio del intercambio educativo, científico y cultural entre España y Estados Unidos" (2017).

Notes

1. "Políticas científicas nacionales," 1964, Fondo Manuel Lora Tamayo, Box 4, Archivo General de la Universidad de Navarra (AGUN).
2. Lora Tamayo to Franco, 28 March 1968, in doc. 23440, Centro Documental de la Memoria Histórica, Archivo Fundación Nacional Francisco Franco (CDMH-AFNFF).
3. "La situación universitaria para octubre de 1968," 6 September 1968, Fondo Laureano López Rodó (FLLR), Box 5, AGUN.
4. He was also general director of primary education for the MEC (1956–1968), president of the Central Board of School Constructions (1956–1968), and president of the Interministerial Commission of Education and Employment (1970–1973). He was later director of UNESCO's Division of World Statistics on Education, Science, Culture, and Communications.
5. He also served as president of the CENIDE (1969–1973) and was an elected member of the UNESCO Executive Board (1970–1976) and, starting in 1973, patron of the International Council for the Development of Education. In this circle of Spanish experts, also noteworthy is the contribution of José Manuel Paredes Grosso, director of the Education Administration and Planning courses offered since 1966 at the National School of Public Administration, where many of the actors in the educational reform program got their training. Later he was named the secretary general of CENIDE. Also important to mention are José Blat Gimeno, a senior official of UNESCO who participated in the preparation of the White Paper as Deputy General Technical Secretary of the MEC with Díez Hochleitner, and Luis Cordero, who cooperated in several joint reports of the MEN-OECD and the Development Commission on Education (joined in the latter by Luis García de Diego and Luis Díaz Jarés).

6. In Spain, these theories were incorporated into the educational and social discourse (Romero and Miguel 1969).
7. The novelty was not so much in the foundations of that reform, taken from the previous experiences of other countries, as in its application in Spain (Gracia García and Ruiz Carnicer 2001: 325–329).
8. "Instrucciones de Franco para negociar con USA," October 1968, FLLR, Box 429/16, AGUN. Press campaign in docs. 4267, 19359, 19374–76, 19386, 19400, 19403, 20346, and 20349, CDMH-AFFF. On the negotiating process, see Pardo Sanz (2004: 169–183; 2005: 14–28); Powell (2011: 52–119); Viñas (2013: 382–408).
9. "A Request to the Unites States Government for Assistance in the Training of Spanish Higher Education Professors," R-9819/8, Archivo General de la Administración, Ministerio de Asuntos Exteriores y Cooperación (AGA-MAEC).
10. "Villar Palasí a Castiella," 4 March 1969, R-12190/6, AGA-MAEC.
11. "Castiella a Villar Palasí," 8 and 18 March 1969, R-12190/6, AGA-MAEC.
12. Department of State Telegram, 17 March 1969, RG 59, Subject Numeric File—Political and Defense (SNF) 1967–1969, Spain, Box 1623, National Archives at College Park (NACP).
13. "Spanish Base Negotiations, March 1969, Position Paper: Establishment of Joint Scientific and Educational Committee," and "Spanish Request for US Aid to Spanish University Reform Program," 24 March 1969, RG 59, SNF 1967–69, Spain, Box 1624, NACP.
14. Telegram, Ministry of Foreign Affairs, 25 March 1969, Europe 1961–1970, Spain, vol. 336, Archives du Ministère des Affaires Étrangères-France (AMAE-F).
15. "Negociations américano-espagnoles," 23 July 1969, Europe 1961–1970, Spain, vol. 335, AMAE-F.
16. "Broader Aspects of Future US-Spanish Relations (Part V of VII)," 15 July 1969, RG 59, SNF 1967–1969, Spain, Box 2493, NACP.
17. "US Policy Assessment," 8 October 1969, "Annual US Policy Assessment," 21 November 1970, RG 59, SNF 1967–1969, Spain, Box 2493, and SNF 1970–1973, Spain, Box 2599, NACP.
18. "The Educational and Cultural Exchange Program with Spain," 27 October 1969, Group IX, Box 240, Bureau of Educational and Cultural Affairs Historical Collection, University of Arkansas Libraries (BECA-UAL).
19. "Díez Hochleitner a López Bravo," 8 January 1970, R-12190/6, AGA-MAEC.
20. "Black Tie Dinner at the Spanish Embassy: Briefing Memorandum," 10 April 1970, RG 59, SNF 1970–73, Spain, Box 2598, NACP.
21. "Villar Palasí al Embajador en Washington," 3 March 1970, R-9564/7, AGA-MAEC.
22. "Ministerio de Educación y Ciencia: Resumen de actividades y realizaciones en 1970," February 1971, FLLR, Box 4/57, AGUN. For more information on these collaborations, see chaps. 2 and 4.

23. For example, the creation of a Spanish-American joint committee for mutual consultation and examination of scientific matters of common interest and the promotion of a research program were not achieved.
24. "Convenio de Amistad y Cooperación entre España y los Estados Unidos de América y Anejo," 6 August 1970, *Boletín Oficial del Estado*, 26 September 1970.
25. "Vallaure a Díez Hochleitner," "Díez Hochleitner a Vallaure," 17 and 22 September 1970, R-9564/7, AGA-MAEC.
26. "Nota informativa confidencial para el Sr. Subsecretario," 2 November 1970, R-9819/8, AGA-MAEC.
27. "Ejecución del Acuerdo con Estados Unidos: M°. Educación y Ciencia," 11 November 1970, R-9819/8, AGA-MAEC.
28. The responsibility in the Department of State fell to John Richardson (Assistant Secretary for Educational and Cultural Affairs) and Herman Pollack (Director of the Bureau of International Scientific and Technological Affairs). Both would be assisted by Allen V. Astin, former director of the National Bureau of Standards, and Duncan Clement, member of the Office of International Programs of the National Science Foundation. Councilor for Cultural Affairs and Information Albert Harkness Jr. was in charge of coordination at the Madrid embassy. In the MAE, the General Directorates of International Technical Cooperation, Cultural Relations, and International Economic Relations would be in charge of the coordination, headed by Francisco J. Vallaure, José Pérez del Arco, and José Luis Cerón, respectively.
29. "Annual Report: Program Year 1969," 5 October 1970, 54/10568, Archivo General de la Administración, Comisión Fulbright. "Nota para el Sr. Ministro," 14 October 1970, R-12486/14, AGA-MAEC. "Spanish Interest in the New US-Spanish Agreement of Friendship: Cultural and Educational Aspects," 14 October 1970, RG 59, SNF 1970–73, Spain, Box 2600, NACP.
30. Such expectations came from the promises made in August 1970, when the Nixon administration left open the possibility of increasing the figure of $3 million, provided it obtained additional budget approval from Congress.
31. The reports on both interviews are in R-12212/5, AGA-MAEC.
32. "Aplicación del Acuerdo con Estados Unidos: Relación con la Comisaría del Plan de Desarrollo," 27 November 1970, R-12212/5, AGA-MAEC.
33. "Reuniones en Washington sobre cooperación civil entre España y Estados Unidos en Acuerdo de 6 de agosto de 1970", 24 January 1971, R-9819/7, AGA-MAEC. The approved projects were those previously presented by the MEC. "US-Spanish Scientific and Technological Cooperation under the Agreement of Friendship and Cooperation," 16 November 1970, RG 59, SNF 1970–73, Spain, Box 2600, NACP. Villar Palasí to López Rodó, "Convenio de Amistad y Cooperación entre España y los EE.UU. de América: Proyectos españoles," 12 December 1970, FLLR, Box 74, AGUN.

34. "Vallaure a Díez Hochleitner," 9 March 1971, R-9819/8, AGA-MAEC.
35. "Misión norteamericana a España sobre cooperación civil," 14 April 1971, R-9819/7, AGA-MAEC.
36. "US-Spain Agreement of Friendship and Cooperation: Implementation of Non-Military Chapters," 16 October 1971, RG 59, SNF 1970–73, Spain, Box 2936, NACP.
37. "Non-military Aspects of US-Spain Agreement," September 1971, RG 59, SNF 1970–1973, Spain, Box 2936, NACP.
38. "Carta reservada de Vallaure al Subsecretario del MAE," 5 October 1971, R-9819/8, AGA-MAEC.
39. "Programa de Cooperación Cultural entre España y EE.UU. 1973/1976," 30 June 1976, Box 92/6, Archivo Comisión Fulbright España (ACFE). The information is contradictory in this regard. In any case, the projects on Molecular Biology, Automatics, and Scientific Information remained present in the successive fiscal year.
40. "Educational Exchanges with Spain under the Bases Agreement Program," April 1973, Council for International Exchange of Scholars, Box 431, BECA.
41. Also called the Tripartite Commission, it was composed of the Assistant Directors of Cultural Relations (Carlos M. Fernández-Shaw) and of International Cooperation of the MEC (Fernando Arias-Salgado Montalvo), and the Cultural Counselor of the US embassy (Millard L. Johnson).
42. Initial members of the Advisory Committee were Carlos Asensio, Juan Díez Nicolás, Alberto Dou, Manuel Gala, Federico García Moliner, Luis González Seara, Rafael Lapesa, Manuel Medina, Juan Pérez de Tudela, José Luis Pinillos, Julio Rodríguez Villanueva, and Andrés Pérez Masiá. "Acta de la reunión del Programa de Cooperación Cultural (PCC) entre España y los Estados Unidos," 24 January 1973, Box 3/1, ACFE. Joining subsequently were Javier Coy, José Ignacio Fernández Alonso, Diego Figuera, Peter Fraenkel, and Ubaldo Martínez. Minutes of PCC meeting, 9 October 1974, Box 3/1, ACFE.
43. "Programa de Cooperación Cultural . . ." Minutes of PCC meeting, 4 June 1974, Box 3/1, ACFE.
44. "Informe del Programa de Cooperación Cultural entre España y los Estados Unidos de América," 4 November 1976, and "Becas para españoles del Programa NMA," Box 92/7, ACFE.
45. The criteria for scholarships in are in the minutes of PCC meetings, 7 and 20 February, 8 and 21 March 1973, Box 3/1, ACFE.
46. Committee members included the Director General of Cultural Relations of the MAE (José Pérez del Arco), the Technical General Secretary of the MEC (Pedro Segú), the Counselor of Cultural Affairs and Information of the Embassy of the United States (Albert Harkness), and the Cultural Attaché (Millard L. Johnson).
47. Annual Program Proposal: Program Year 1971, 4 July 1971, Group III, Box 123, BECA.

48. Annual Program Proposal: Program Years 1971, 1972, 1973, 1974, and 1975, CU, Group III, Box 123. For more information, see Delgado Gómez-Escalonilla (2009).
49. These studies had already been established in the universities of Madrid, La Laguna, Valladolid, Barcelona, Zaragoza, Salamanca, Santiago de Compostela, Granada, Seville, Oviedo, and Deusto (see also Martín García and Rodríguez Jiménez 2013; Rodríguez Jiménez 2011).
50. "Brief Report on the Cultural Cooperation Program between Spain and the United States of America," 18 February 1976, Box 92/5, ACFE.
51. "Informe del Programa . . . ," "Informe sobre los ex-becarios del Programa de Cooperación Cultural entre España y los Estados Unidos (1973–1977)," June 1978, Box 74/1, ACFE.
52. "Fronteras de la Ciencia," March 1973, R-12212/2, AGA-MAEC.
53. "Proyecto creación Instituto Biología Molecular," s.f. R-9819/8, AGA-MAEC.
54. Some of the scientists trained in the United States returned to join this process, such as Barbacid, who returned in 1998 to direct the Center for Oncological Research.
55. Segovia de Arana was also dean of the Faculty of Medicine at the Autonomous University of Madrid, and outstanding driver of the MIR system. He held the position of Secretary of State for Health in 1979 and 1980 and participated in the drafting of the Health Reform, the remodeling of the National Institute of Health, and the creation of the Health Research Fund for the National Welfare State. Figuera Aymerich participated in several of these initiatives with his colleague, and he was a pioneer in heart transplant programs in Spain. In 1973, he joined the Advisory Committee of the NMA Program.
56. More complete information on all those NMA program grantees can be found in the Fulbright Commission database in Madrid. The paper files can be consulted in ACFE and AGA.
57. "Comité de Cooperación Internacional para la reforma educativa en España: Informe final," 1970, doc. 974, CDMH-AFFF.
58. The National Institute of Education Sciences was created in 1974 as successor to CENIDE. For an assessment of the educational reform made a few years later by some of its main protagonists, see Díez Hochleitner et al. (1977).
59 Villar Palasí as a former leader grantee, Díez Hochleitner as a former student of Columbia University. "Educational and Cultural Exchange: Annual Report for Spain for the Fiscal Year July 1, 1969–June 30 1970," 23 September 1970, Group XVI, Box 320, BECA.
60. "Annual Policy Assessment," 20 February 1971, RG 59, SNF 1970–73, Spain, Box 2599, NACP.
61. "Annual US Policy Assessment," 20 May 1972, RG 59, SNF 1970–73, Spain, Box 2599, NACP. "National Security Decision Memorandum 268: Renegotiation of Bases Agreement with Spain," 10 September 1974, in Viñas (2013: 417–418).

62. "The Cultural and Educational Exchange Program of the United States–Spanish Joint Committee for Cultural and Educational Cooperation, June 1977–June 1993," September 1995, Box 87/2, ACFE.

References

Aguilar Cestero, Raúl. 2007. "El despliegue de la Universidad Autónoma de Barcelona entre 1968 y 1973: De fundación franquista a motor del cambio democrático en Cataluña." *Cuadernos del Instituto Antonio de Nebrija* 10: 13–199.

Álvaro Moya, Adoración. 2011. "Guerra Fría y formación de capital humano durante el franquismo. Un balance sobre el programa estadounidense de ayuda técnica (1953–1963)." *Historia del Presente* 17: 13–25.

Ávila de Grado, Jesús, Manuel Perucho, and Carlos López Otín, eds. 2003. *El Fago phi 29 y los orígenes de la biología molecular en España*. Madrid: CSIC.

Baldó, Marc. 2010. "La investigación y la enseñanza técnica en el Ministerio de Lora-Tamayo (1962–1968)." In *Facultades y Grados: X Congreso Internacional de Historia de las universidades hispánicas*, vol. 1, 239–257. Valencia: Universitat de Valencia.

Boyd-Barrett, Oliver, and Pamela O'Malley, eds. 1995. *Education Reform in Democratic Spain: International Developments in School Reform*. New York: Routledge.

Campo, Salustiano del. 1968. *Cambios sociales y formas de vida*. Barcelona: Ariel.

Campos Marín, Ricardo. 2010. "El desarrollo de la salud pública en España durante el siglo XX." *Eidon: Revista de la Fundación Ciencias de la Salud* 32: 67–73.

Carreras, Albert, and Xavier Tafunell. 2007. *Historia económica de la España contemporánea*. 3rd ed. Barcelona: Crítica.

Carrillo Linares, Alberto. 2006. "Movimiento estudiantil antifranquista: Cultura política y transición política a la democracia." *Pasado y Memoria* 5: 149–170.

Delgado Gómez-Escalonilla, Lorenzo. 2009. *Westerly Wind: The Fulbright Program in Spain*. Madrid: Comisión Fulbright España-LID Editorial Empresarial-AECID.

——. 2012. "Objetivo: Atraer a las élites. Los líderes de la vida pública y la política exterior norteamericana en España." In *Guerra Fría y Propaganda: Estados Unidos y su cruzada cultural en Europa y América Latina*, ed. Antonio Niño and José Antonio Montero, 235–276. Madrid: Biblioteca Nueva.

——. 2015. "Modernizadores y tecnócratas: Estados Unidos ante la política educativa y científica de la España del desarrollo." *Historia y Política* 34: 113–146.

Díez Hochleitner, Ricardo, Joaquín Tena Artigas, and Marcelino García Cuerpo. 1977. *La reforma educativa española y la educación permanente*. Paris: UNESCO.

Escolano Benito, Agustín. 1982. "La investigación educativa en los Institutos de Ciencias de la Educación." *Studia Paedagogica* 9: 3–14.

Fernández de Castro, Ignacio. 1973. *Reforma educativa y desarrollo capitalista*. Madrid: Cuadernos para el Diálogo.

Frey, Marc, Sönke Kunkel, and Corinna Unger, eds. 2014. *International Organizations and Development*. London: Palgrave Macmillan.

González Delgado, Mariano, and Tamar R. Groves. 2016. "Influencias extranjeras en la formación continua del profesorado en el segundo franquismo." In *La formación del profesorado: Nuevos enfoques desde la teoría y la historia de la educación*, ed. Miguel Ángel Martín-Sánchez and Tamar Groves, 51–64. Salamanca: FahrenHouse.

González Madrid, Damián A., and Manuel Ortiz Heras. 2018. "El franquismo y la construcción del Estado de Bienestar en España: la protección social del Estado (1939–1986). *Pasado y Memoria* 17: 361–388.

Gracia García, Jordi, and Miguel A. Ruiz Carnicer. 2001. *La España de Franco (1939–1975): Cultura y vida cotidiana*. Madrid: Síntesis.

Groves, Tamar R., and Mariano González Delgado. 2017. "Chocando contra la cultura escolar: Las paradojas de la importación pedagógica en la España del desarrollismo." In *El factor internacional en la modernización educativa, científica y militar de España*, ed. Lorenzo Delgado Gómez-Escalonilla, Pablo León Aguinaga, Óscar J. Martín García, and Esther M. Sánchez, 129–151. Alicante: Biblioteca Virtual Cervantes.

Hernández Sandoica, Elena, Miguel A. Ruiz Carnicer, and Marc Baldó Lacomba. 2007. *Estudiantes contra Franco (1939–1975): Oposición política y movilización juvenil*. Madrid: La Esfera de los Libros.

León-Aguinaga, Pablo, and Lorenzo Delgado Gómez-Escalonilla. 2018. "The Deployment of US Military Assistance to Franco's Spain: Limited Modernization and Strategic Dependence." *Cold War History*, published online 26 July. https://doi.org/10.1080/14682745.2018.1492554.

Marshall, Elliot. 2011. "40 Years of the War on Cancer." *Science* 331 (6024): 1540–1544.

Martín García, Oscar J. 2012. "A Complicated Mission: The United States and Spanish Students during the Johnson Administration." *Cold War History* 13 (3): 311–329.

——. 2015. "Una utopía secular. La teoría de la modernización y la política exterior estadounidense en la Guerra Fría." *Historia y Política* 34: 27–52.

——. 2018. "'The Most Developed of the Underdeveloped Nations': US Foreign Policy and Student Unrest in1960s Spain." *International History Review*, published online 23 March. https://doi.org/10.1080/07075332.2018.1446999.

Martín García, Oscar J., and Francisco J. Rodríguez Jiménez. 2013. "¿Seducidos por el inglés? Diplomacia pública angloamericana y difusión de la lengua inglesa en España, 1959–1975." *Historia y Política* 29: 301–330.

MEC (Ministerio de Educación y Ciencia). 1969. *La educación en España: Bases para una política educativa*. Madrid: MEC.

Miguel, Amando de. 1976. *Reformar la universidad*. Barcelona: Euros.
Milito Barone, Cecilia C., and Tamar R. Groves. 2013. "¿Modernización o democratización? La construcción de un nuevo sistema educativo entre el tardofranquismo y la democracia." *Bordón* 65 (4): 135–148.
Montoro Romero, Ricardo. 1981. *La Universidad en la España de Franco (1939–1970): Un análisis sociológico*. Madrid: Centro de Investigaciones Sociológicas.
Muñoz, Emilio, dir. 2004. *Cuarenta años de la Sociedad Española de Bioquímica y Biología Molecular (1963–2003)*. Madrid: Sociedad Estatal de Conmemoraciones Culturales.
Nadal, Juli de. 2016. *La construcción de un éxito: Así se hizo nuestra sanidad pública*. Barcelona: Ediciones La Lluvia.
OECD. 1965. *The Mediterranean Regional Project*. Spain. Paris: OECD.
——. 1966. *La investigación científica y técnica y sus necesidades en relación con el desarrollo económico en España*. Madrid: Ministerio de Educación y Ciencia.
O'Malley, Pamela. 1995a. "Turning Point: The 1970 Education Act." In Boyd-Barrett and O'Malley 1995: 25–31.
——. 1995b. "Education as Resistance: The 'Alternativa.'" In Boyd-Barrett and O'Malley 1995: 32–40.
Ortega Gutiérrez, Félix. 1992. "Las ideologías de la reforma educativa de 1970." *Revista de Educación*, special issue: 31–46.
Ossenbach, Gabriela, and Alberto Martínez Boom. 2011. "Itineraries of the Discourses on Development and Education in Spain and Latin America (circa 1950–1970)." *Paedagogica Historica* 47 (5): 679–700.
Pardo Sanz, Rosa María. 2004. "Las relaciones hispano-norteamericanas durante la presidencia de L. B. Johnson: 1964–1968." *Studia Histórica: Historia Contemporánea* 22: 137–183.
——. 2005. "EE.UU. y el tardofranquismo: Las relaciones bilaterales durante la presidencia Nixon, 1969–1974." *Historia del Presente* 6: 11–41.
Paris, Carlos. 1974. *La universidad española actual: posibilidades y frustraciones*. Madrid: Cuadernos para el Diálogo.
Perdiguero-Gil, Enrique, dir. 2015. *Política, salud y enfermedad en España: Entre el desarrollismo y la transición democrática*. Elche: Universidad Miguel Hernández.
Powell, Charles. 1996. "Un 'hombre-puente' en la política exterior española: El caso de Marcelino Oreja." *Historia Contemporánea* 15: 257–288.
——. 2011. *El amigo americano: España y Estados Unidos de la dictadura a la democracia*. Madrid: Galaxia Gutenberg.
Puelles Benítez, Manuel de. 1992. "Tecnocracia y política en la reforma educativa de 1970." *Revista de Educación* S1: 13–29.
Rodríguez Jiménez, Francisco J. 2011. "¿'Misioneros de la Americanidad'? Promoción y difusión de los American Studies en España, 1969–1975." *Historia del Presente* 17: 55–69.
Romero, José L. 1971. "Del Libro Blanco a la Ley General de Educación." In *España: Perspectiva 1971*, 209–241. Madrid: Guadiana de Publicaciones.

Romero, José L., and Amando de Miguel. 1969. *El capital humano: Ideas para una planificación social de la enseñanza en España*. Madrid: Confederación Española de Cajas de Ahorro.

Ruiz Fornells, Enrique. 1967. "Presencia de la cultura española en los Estados Unidos a través del intercambio universitario." *Información Comercial Española* 409: 149–155.

Salas, Margarita. 2003. "La creación del Centro de Biología Molecular Severo Ochoa." *Arbor* 543: 81–86.

Sánchez Ferrer, Leonardo. 1996. *Políticas de reforma universitaria en España: 1983–1993*. Madrid: Instituto Juan March.

Sánchez Gijón, Antonio. 1971. "Acuerdos España-USA de 6 de agosto de 197." In *España: Perspectiva 1971*, 243–277. Madrid: Guadiana.

Santesmases, María Jesús. 2000. "Severo Ochoa and the Biomedical Sciences in Span under Franco." *Isis* 91 (4): 706–734.

——. 2001. *Entre Cajal y Ochoa: Ciencias biomédicas en la España de Franco (1939–1975)*. Madrid: CSIC.

——. 2008. "Orígenes internacionales de la política científica." In *Cien años de política científica en España*, ed. Ana Romero de Pablos and María Jesús Santesmases, 293–326. Bilbao: Fundación BBVA.

Segovia de Arana, José M., ed.2006. *La personalidad de D. Severo: recuerdos personales: Remembranza de Severo Ochoa en el centenario de su nacimiento*. Madrid: Farmaindustria.

Valdevira, Gregorio. 2006. *La oposición estudiantil al franquismo*. Madrid: Síntesis.

Vázquez Montalbán, Manuel. 1974. *La penetración americana en España*. Madrid: EDICUSA.

Viñao, Antonio. 2004. *Escuela para todos: Educación y modernidad en la España del siglo XX*. Madrid: Marcial Pons.

Viñas, Ángel. 2003. *En las garras del águila: Los pactos con Estados Unidos, de Francisco Franco a Felipe González (1945–1995)*. Barcelona: Crítica.

Chapter 3

Forerunners of Change?

The Ford Foundation's Activities in Francoist Spain

Francisco Rodríguez-Jiménez

> The Ford Foundation does not have the scale of resources capable of affecting changes in a whole sector of government, like the World Bank or the Inter American Bank can do, and even for them positive results of large investments are uncertain. In these conditions, the policy impact the Foundation could have depends on the quality and relevance of the research groups it supports, their ability to shape opinion and, ultimately, on the issues and actors involved in the policy making-process.
>
> —Simon Schwartzman, "Educating the Ford Foundation"

Introduction

The United States has been characterized as an "informal empire." For the configuration and management of that informal empire, it was crucial to "maintain alliances and nurture friends" (Scott-Smith 2008: 23). Following this logic, other authors have affirmed the United States "is prepared to exert imperial control over relatively small states that compose its 'frontiers,' but it depends on consensual acquiescence and common elite interests with its spheres of influence" (Maier 2006: 65–67). To that end, the North American nation exerted its influence abroad, not only through the traditional forms of hard power but also through the diffusion of its socioeconomic model, its institutional guidelines, and its cultural products—in short, its "soft power," the term coined by Joseph Nye in 1990.

The majority of pioneering studies on the American "informal empire" have centered on examining the economic sphere. It soon became clear that, rather than a simple imposition of the "American way of life," there was actually a gradual acceptance, sometimes an embrace, other times a rejection, of the models that issued forth from the United States. More recently, analyses have emerged of the different messages deployed by Washington in its ideological struggle against Moscow, the agencies that carried them out, the programs for the training and exchange of personnel, the cultural transfers, and so forth (see, among others, Barjot 2002; Berghahn 2001; Cull 2008; Delgado Gómez-Escalonilla 2009; Ekbladh 2009; Gienow-Hecht and Donfried 2010).

What role did US philanthropic foundations play in that story? Were they philanthropic transmitters of the American informal empire's creed or, on the contrary, active participants in its composition? What was the degree of autonomy of these foundations in the vicious atmosphere that the intense politicization of the Cold War created? Although the literature on the matter has not stopped growing, many questions remain open (Gemelli and Macleod 2003; Krige and Rausch 2012; Parmar 2012). Proof of this can be found in the persistence of two contrasting, almost antagonistic, narratives. On the one hand are those who emphasize the "voluntary benevolence and generosity"[1] of the philanthropic Americans, minimizing or ignoring the less-than-altruistic motivations for that generosity. On the other hand, partly as a consequence of the long shadow of the cultural-ideological Cold War, there is the point of view of those who see spies everywhere, alongside puppet foundations that were always at the service of the White House.[2]

That latter interpretation loses sight of the fact that the philanthropic concerns did not always have Washington's favor. Sometimes they shared goals; other times they utterly disagreed. There were even moments of judicial conflict. One of the moments of greatest tension was experienced in 1959 when the Ford Foundation (FF) sponsored, with more than a million dollars, a series of studies that questioned the attitude of the US government during the McCarthy era. Part of the Washington establishment was suspicious of some of the philanthropic foundations' projects.[3] Earlier in the decade, episodes of greater judicial pressure were experienced. In 1952, a House of Representatives committee held hearings to determine whether educational and philanthropic foundations were using their resources for un-American and subversive activities. Among those who had to testify were the presidents of the Ford Motor Company and the Ford Foundation, Henry Ford II and Paul Hoffman, respectively (Augier 2011: 105).

As it happens, the existing literature on philanthropic foundations is relatively recent and not very extensive. That leaves, therefore, much ground to be broken and many details to be clarified about the intervention of foundations abroad. Until just a few decades ago, work in diplomatic and international relations history gave most, in fact almost all, of its attention to the state. Situated halfway between the public and the private spheres,[4] the foundations were excluded, or at best kept in the periphery, from most of the historical narratives. This is similar, by the way, to what happened with unions (Rodríguez-Jiménez 2016; Waters and Goethem 2013), arms control communities, scientific groups like the Federation of American Scientists (Risse-Kappen 1994: 196), and all other NGOs and international actors and their ideas and international agendas. Ditto for supranational institutions such as the Office of the United Nations High Commissioner for Refugees as well as the World Health Organization (Chorev 2012; Loescher 2008).

Founded in 1936, the Ford Foundation would become one of the largest and most influential institutions of its kind in the 1940s and 1950s. The relationship with its parent, the Ford Motor Company, was not always harmonious; the interests of the presidents of one and the other did not always coincide. The FF would inject millions of dollars for medical research, among other areas. As David Engerman notes, "Enthusiasm and funding for behavioral sciences did increase in the Cold War, led by the FF's allocation of $43 million to the field in the mid-1950s" (2007: 604). The promotion abroad of American studies as an academic field, an ideological-cultural counterpoint of the Marshall Plan, was one of the first areas where government-philanthropy collaboration was forged. Not everything, however, was harmonious between the different actors involved. "These ventures were ideologically intertwined, but organisationally separate," Volker Berghahn (1999: 416) explains. Everyone did not always row in the same direction. Not even internally: within the official diplomatic structures, there was a debate (never entirely resolved) about what should be the extent of government intervention in these matters. Also noteworthy was the support of the FF and the Rockefeller Foundation to the Free University of Berlin.[5] In fact, West Germany became one of the areas where more American studies programs were launched—a cultural proselytism that fell within the strategies for the "ideological-cultural reeducation" of these countries.

Indeed, Western Europe was seen as the primary battlefront of the Cold War, "perhaps not the least because the Ford Motor Company had major investments there" (Berghahn 2012: 262) The main activities of the FF were concentrated in Western Europe starting in the 1940s. Then, the focus shifted to Eastern Europe, especially after the Soviet intervention in Hungary in 1956. Only in the 1960s and 1970s did Latin America, Africa, and Asia become the center of attention and budget reallocation. That was the general scenario. But what were the geopolitical particulars of the Spanish case? The political agreement between the United States and Franco's dictatorship of 1953 dispelled the few fears of a possible communist advance in the Iberian country. Even before, worries about the expansion of this ideology in Spanish territory had been very limited, given the repressive nature of the Franco regime. At that time, Spain was not among the priority geographical areas of the FF. Starting from that general framework, this chapter will try to explain the motivations, methods, and discourses of the FF in the Spain of the 1960s and 1970s. It will delve into the details of what happened, contrasting the unpublished documentation found in US archives with Spanish sources.

The Ford Foundation in Developing Spain

The rhythms and intensity of the cultural and ideological Cold War in Spain were different from that of the larger European environment. In the late 1950s, there was a series of transformations that could presage a situation of greater political instability in the coming years: the opening of the economy to external forces, growth in population, internal and external migration, tourism, and so forth. An uncertain panorama translated into the question, "After Franco, what?"—especially as Franco grew older. In other words, the social hotbeds of developing Spain would become a scenario, sui generis because of its European link but not at all different from that of developing countries in other latitudes. In fact, since the end of the 1950s the FF had begun progressively to move from Europe to Southeast Asia, Latin America, and Africa.[6] Thus, it is not surprising the landing of the FF in Spain occurred precisely in 1959.

The same year, the FF's Latin American[7] and Caribbean Program was launched, shortly after the victory of the Castro revolution (Calandra 2011: 11), that geopolitical event in the "backyard" of the United States that, together with the Soviet Union's launch of Sputnik I, the first artificial satellite, might increase the attractiveness of the communist option (Delgado Gómez-Escalonilla 2015: 18). The putting into orbit of that satellite "shook the confidence of Americans in their absolute technological supremacy." In response to that challenge, the US government began to inject more funds into aeronautical research: "Organizations like the National Science Foundation also channeled increasing amounts of money into defense programs" (Mëhilli 2014: 295). Although Ford had not had its own programs in Spanish territory before, its ambitious philanthropic projects were known. The press reported the enormous quantities delivered, with an appreciative tone. For example, in 1956, one of the most important newspapers in the country explained that the FF had donated more than $200 million to American hospitals and made similar bequests for educational improvements.[8]

The initial connection was established with the Sociedad de Estudios y Publicaciones (SEP), which was dependent on Banco Urquijo. This body comprised an array of intellectuals, mostly connected with Catholic liberalism, inclined toward closer ties with the United States (De Santisteban 2009: 162–69). In the summer of 1959, a group of Spanish intellectuals, including among others Pedro Laín, José Luis Aranguren, and Julián Marías, met in France with Shepard Stone (Berghahn 2001), director of international affairs of the FF, who explained to them how to channel official aid through the SEP. The programs financed by Ford in Spain ultimately consisted of a humanities seminar; an economic research seminar; and training, research, and planning activities to promote the economic and social modernization of Spain (De Santisteban 2009: 172ff.).

At the time, the spread of the "American ideal of modernization" became important in the design of Washington's foreign policy (Martín García 2015: 40). In quest of "native missionaries" for that modernizing creed, the Department of State deployed several initiatives for public relations and the training of human capital in Spain, most notably the Foreign Leaders Program (Delgado Gómez-Escalonilla 2012). The launch of the Fulbright Program in 1959 followed a similar logic (Delgado Gómez-Escalonilla 2009). For the leaders program, the procedure consisted of three-way cooperation: US diplomats suggested candidates; American universities, research centers, and enterprises received them, partly with funds from the FF; and several US nongovernmental institutions worked out the logistics.[9] One of the habitual handicaps in the selection of Spaniards, both for the Foreign Leaders Program and for Fulbright, had been their shaky knowledge of English, a linguistic barrier that compounded the difficulty in transferring knowhow from abroad. One of the gurus of the American informal empire, the economist Walt Rostow (1960), had been warning of this (Ish-Shalom 2006). Albeit slowly, the message was penetrating into Spanish educational circles. One of the points where local needs converged with the priorities of the FF was on the teaching of English.

In the '40s and '50s, the presence of this language in the classrooms of Spain had been diminished. Among the fundamental obstacles were the rigidity of the curriculum, the greater appeal that French still held, the lack of resources as compared to other countries, and cultural pride.[10] At the start of the '60s, the Fulbright Commission, the University of Madrid, and the Institute of Languages at Georgetown

University began coordinating their efforts to facilitate the takeoff of English teaching. They signed an agreement for improved English instruction in Spain with financial help from the FF.[11] In the years that followed, summer courses and seminars were organized and materials were purchased for sound and recording laboratories.[12]

In the early 1960s, only two of Spain's universities were training teachers of English, but a decade later, this program was offered at more than a dozen universities.[13] The steady efforts made by American public diplomacy, especially through the Fulbright Commission, along with a greater sense of its importance on the part of Francoist leaders and the financial push of the Ford Foundation, formed a secure base from which the teaching of English in Spain could take off (Martín García and Rodríguez Jiménez 2015).

In the late 1960s, the FF faced a period of internal turmoil. In 1967, the magazine *Ramparts* revealed that the Congress for Cultural Freedom had received funds from the CIA, a revelation that also tainted the Ford name. In an attempt to regain the lost prestige, the new FF president, McGeorge Bundy, did some internal restructuring, redirecting most of the funding of the international department to higher education and research.[14] The priorities of this and other US philanthropic organizations now increasingly shifted from Europe to Southeast Asia, Latin America, and Africa, partly because of the aforementioned scandal but also partly because the Western European bloc had a stable socioeconomic situation compared with other parts of the world.[15] As noted, the Spanish case was an anomaly in the European context; it had its own rhythms. Despite these storm clouds, the FF continued to cast a positive image in large Spanish sectors. Financial support was provided to projects of various kinds; besides the English teaching projects, for example, money went to archaeological digs. The Spanish press amplified the echo of these donations in the Iberian country, also telling what was being invested in others countries.[16]

Among the organizations inclined to strengthen ties with the FF was the Hispano-American Cultural Association. Chaired by Julio Rodríguez Villanueva, this association invited Frank H. Bowles, director of the Ford Education Program, to lecture on "Trends in Higher Education in the United States." The daily paper *ABC* praised the importance given to education in the United States, calling it the mirror in which Spaniards should look at themselves to lead the country's urgent transformations. But those "lessons," which for some inspired desires to emulate the American model, were for others just one more example of *Yankee cultural imperialism*.[17] In the discourse on who were or had been the most powerful figures in the world, the names of FF leaders tended to come up. An article in Spain titled "Power in Washington," for example, mentioned: "John F. Kennedy, McNamara, and McGeorge Bundy, the current president of the Ford Foundation, appear to us in the full dimension of power."[18] At that time, the Spanish press also reported on Bundy's diplomatic maneuvering as a facilitator of the meeting between Soviet leader Alexis Kosygin and US President Lyndon B. Johnson.[19]

The Ford Foundation in the Twilight of Francoism

If a turning point in the FF's work in Spain were to be found, it would be late 1968. From then until the early stages of the post-Franco transition, the foundation's presence in Spain's educational and political spheres increased, compared to the previous period. In October of that year, Peter Fraenkel, the new *hombre de la Ford* (Ford man) in Spain, traveled throughout the Iberian Peninsula. Raised in Bolivia, where his family had fled from the Nazi persecution, Fraenkel graduated in 1942 from the American Institute of La Paz and dedicated much of his life to managing programs of technical and educational assistance abroad. His profile fits well with the model of the committed "informal diplomat" described by Dino Knudsen (2016), and sagaciously applied by David Corrales Morales (chapter 5) to explore Ricardo Díez-Hochleitner's mission in Spain.[20]

When he arrived in Spain, Fraenkel had two decades of experience behind him, especially in Peru, Colombia, Bolivia, and Ecuador. But he also carried some prejudices with him; he sometimes fell into "observer of the tribe" syndrome (Aróstegui 2000); other times, his assessments were accurate. In his first report, Fraenkel held nothing back in critically describing the Spanish educational system. He saw extraordinary rigidity in both the content and the instructional methods. He also decried that the Spanish university was more concerned with preserving the past than with bringing itself into the modern age.

One of the most salient characteristics of Spaniards, he found, was that of individualism, a perceived hindrance to working collaboratively and committing to broad long-term goals: "They are inordinately dependent on individuals and their respective personalities." This situation appeared in both public and private companies, creating a serious problem: "There is not much assurance, therefore, of long-term continuity." For all this, he warned his superiors on the other side of the Atlantic: "We should apply caution in anything we may do in Spain. We must know the individuals with whom we work—before working with them! This takes time—anywhere, but more in Spain than in other places. Thus spend time, before money!"[21]

In sum, the FF did not do anything casually. Its leaders wanted to know where and for what their donations were going. Fraenkel drafted an extensive memorandum detailing the pros and cons. Among the former, and apart from the goals previously discussed (educational modernization, ideological anchorage with Europe, improvement of English teaching, etc.), it was noted that collaboration with Spanish universities would have an influence on the many students from Latin America who enrolled in them.[22]

One of the barometers used by the FF to measure the degree of modernization of the Spanish university and its comparison with Europe was checking the degree to which American studies courses were being introduced. In the first months of 1969, the scene was not very encouraging, partly because of the "competing, and more logical, attraction of Latin American Studies." The report left some room for hope. Even so, he warned: "It is a long-term problem, however, whose solution will come about only to the extent and the speed with which Spain enters the political and intellectual society of mid-twentieth century Europe."[23]

Alongside that general assessment, Fraenkel made some specific observations, for example, on the evolution of the English teaching program led by Robert Lado of Georgetown University.[24] Here again, Fraenkel was quite critical: he suggested the possibility of canceling the agreement with this university, at least if that professor was still in charge.[25] For *el hombre de la Ford*, the flaws in Lado's leadership had deep roots—"for reasons which are, in part at least, explainable in terms of history!"[26] It was attributable, in other words, not so much to his previous work experience in the United States as to identity issues. "After all, Lado was born in Spain—and the habit of report writing, I am confident, is not a natural component of the Spanish blood!"[27]

For Fraenkel, therefore, a profound change in the Spanish cultural background was necessary. It is interesting to see how such observations were similar to those expressed by the missionaries of Americanness in other latitudes. For example, Nino Maritano and Antonio H. Obaid, in charge of evaluating technical assistance programs and American educational cooperation in Latin America, argued: "Before they get anywhere, Latin Americans need a true cultural breakthrough to modify their traditional value concepts on work, civic responsibility, gracious living, ostentatious idleness and what is truly noble or dehumanizing" (1963: 88).

Both authors thought there were many traits of the "traditional Spanish social character" that the Latin American nations had inherited to such a degree that they were hindrances for the creation of the modern, dynamic, and egalitarian model advocated by President Kennedy's Alliance for Progress. Thus, they believed, the noble American efforts were stranded on that archaic cultural plateau. The desired modernization, therefore, required a substantial change in the Latin American mentality that reflected "the values and psychology of the Western North Atlantic world, that are consistent with a global capitalist economy" (Maritano and Obaid 1963: 42; Pearce 2001; Taffet 2007). The apathy and resistance to the Protestant work ethic could only be altered from the bottom up, starting at the lowest educational levels.

Where Spain was concerned, meanwhile, by the late 1960s political relations between Washington and Madrid were growing turbulent. The Ministry of Foreign Affairs, with Fernando María Castiella at the helm, had been pulling back on the rope for some time to rebalance the geostrategic balance between both nations, which had been tilted toward the US side since the signing of the 1953 military agreements (Delgado Gómez-Escalonilla 2003). It was a strategy that in the end brought about Castiella's fall from power, principally because of Franco's fear that the friendship with the American power had been broken. However, the policies of the new foreign minister, López Bravo, did not differ much from those of his predecessor (Pardo 2005; Powell 2007; Viñas 2003).

In the negotiations, the Spanish ministry wanted the United States to collaborate in educational reform as a counterweight to the US military presence in Spain. In its initial plan, very high figures for external contributions were discussed, about $40 million per year—a total amount that was expected to make a significant leap forward in the modernization of Spanish administrative and educational structures (although the figures ultimately submitted came to less than 30 percent of that amount). The proposed sum would be paid in part by the US government and partly by institutions such as the World Bank and the FF (Delgado Gómez-Escalonilla 2009: 79). The amounts suggested were very significant, considering, for example, that the Fulbright Program received only $55,000 in its first year of operation and that the total budget for the academic year 1963–1964 came to $400,000, which represented the highest amount for any year of that decade.[28]

In the early 1970s, Minister of Education Villar Palasí wrote to Peter Fraenkel soliciting his advice.[29] There were other parties to the communication: Ricardo Díez-Hochleitner, the true brain of the reform effort led by Palasí, and Kenneth Holland, president of the Institute of International Education, based in New York. Since the start of the century, this private organization had implemented numerous programs of technical assistance and educational cooperation.[30] Now it would be done in Spain, with financial assistance from Ford. Fraenkel served as the go-between.[31] Shortly after, he was proposed as an "international observer" of the Fulbright-Spain Commission.[32] His name and the notoriety of the project sponsored by Ford were featured prominently in the Spanish press.

The Centro Nacional de Investigaciones para el Desarrollo de la Educación (National Research Center for the Development of Education—CENIDE) would have to be a key player in the Villar Palasí–Díez-Hochleitner educational reform plan. The BOE defined its mission in these terms: "to coordinate the tasks of the Institutos de Ciencias de la Educación (Institute of Education Sciences—ICEs) and contribute, through the realization of their own programs, to the renovation of our educational system."[33] In a beginning phase, ICEs were built in Barcelona, Granada, Madrid, Salamanca, Santiago, Valencia, Valladolid, and Zaragoza, and in later years other institutes in Barcelona, Palencia, Seville, and Valencia. The World Bank also collaborated with training scholarships abroad (Corrales Morales 2016).

The goal of this network of centers was for the advances of research on educational theory and pedagogy to be incorporated as soon as possible into the processes of teacher training, with the ultimate goal of improving the educational system. A fluid dialogue with reciprocal feedback should be established between the CENIDE and the ICEs. The former would start the dialogue by indicating action guidelines and priorities and nurturing the process with materials; the latter would respond with data on implementation, the stumbling blocks encountered, and so forth. In short, it was intended to make educational research more rigorous, orderly, and in line with the latest trends developing in other countries. Although European influences were important (Fernández Soria 2005), the United States was to play a special role as the beacon.

This complex and ambitious undertaking was financed by the FF. So far, and considering the sources readily available, it is not easy to determine the exact amount paid by the foundation. Although there are discrepancies between the figures examined, it appears to have been approximately $500,000.[34] It was a modest sum, but significant when compared, for example, with the amount that nurtured the

Fulbright Program, previously cited. *ABC* reported on that generosity, noting that the FF had contributed $400,000 (about 28 million pesetas) for the training of ICE faculty.[35] For its part, *La Vanguardia Española* indicated that the breakdown would be 23 million pesetas in scholarships for educators and the remaining 5 million for the work of the consultants of the ICEs and that of CENIDE.[36]

The job of selecting candidates for those training scholarships fell to a committee made up of Spanish educators and foreign advisers. Fraenkel was one of the permanent members; local representation varied, depending on where the preliminary tests were conducted. Among the members coming from the ministry were José Manuel Paredes Grosso (general secretary of CENIDE) and Emilia Ruiz Campuzano (head of its Office of International Programs). After a first screening in the regional centers, each preselected candidate had to undergo a personal interview with the National Committee in the CENIDE headquarters.[37]

One of the final requirements was command of the training host country's language (in most cases English, though a few of the grantees were sent to France or Germany). Despite the aforementioned progress experienced in the teaching of English in Spain, the situation still had its problems. Quite a few candidates were discarded on this basis or had to undergo intensive courses before leaving. With his peculiar style, sometimes scarcely diplomatic, sometimes sarcastic, Fraenkel had already informed his superiors in New York about this matter: "I keep hearing of the tremendous interest in Spain in learning English—and I am amazed to find how scarce is the number of those who really master that language . . . English language competence may be even much lower than in Peru—to say nothing of countries like Chile or Mexico."[38]

Another of Fraenkel's constant concerns was that the selection process should be as transparent and objective as possible.[39] The Ford man accompanied his reports with flowery comments on the Spanish character—not very far, of course, from the usual descriptions made by Hispanists or foreign travelers (Kagan 2002). For Fraenkel, Spanish culture was "an extraordinary mix of emotions of pride and passion, of sensitivity and harshness, of individualism and authoritarianism, of 'anarchy and hierarchy,' of spontaneity and formalism, of inward-directed nationalism and a sense of the world-at-large." In the face of the pending reforms, even more serious for Fraenkel was the contradictory behavior of the Spaniard, which made it difficult to coexist with his own compatriots. And the worst problem was that the (proud, one can infer) Spanish character made it almost a chimera that "a

Spaniard acknowledges the receipt of advice from another Spaniard; how much more so, to accept it from a foreigner!"[40]

The Ley General de Educación y Financiamiento de la Reforma Educativa (General Law of Education and Financing of the Educational Reform) was an ambitious project whose doses of self-criticism—almost the first admissions to imperfection to come out of the Franco government—were in themselves worthy of praise. Its formulation and style brimmed with enthusiasm, arguably a bit overdone: "Educational reform is a peaceful and silent revolution, but the most effective and profound way to achieve a more just society and an increasingly human life."[41] Although in the articulation of this law it was affirmed grandiloquently, "where there's a will, there's a way," what was certain was that the money initially envisioned for this effort was far from materializing. Would these gaps in the local budget be filled with foreign funds? To what extent would the aid financed by Ford and other foreign institutions contribute to modernization of Spain's educational system?

All of this is part of a more complex puzzle, which will have to be completed in the future with examination of other initiatives developed through private channels. For example, Ford did not just channel funds through the aforementioned public initiatives; it also financed private projects, in collaboration with UNESCO. Such was the case with several San Estanislao de Kostka schools inaugurated in Spain at the start of the '70s.[42] It will also be necessary in the future to delve into some of the personal relationships between the actors involved. The records consulted make clear the harmonies and tensions involved. Personal feelings, differences of opinion over standards and criteria, and sometimes prejudices affected the processes of launching educational reform. Not in vain has the historiography of recent years been paying more attention than before to the importance of emotions in history (Keys 2011; Plamper 2015).

In that sense, it seems the Ford man in Spain got along well with Ángeles Galino Carrillo, one of the outstanding figures of the Spanish educational world of the last century. A promoter of various projects of innovation and pedagogical renewal, Galino held several positions in the Ministry of Education at several stages: General Director of Secondary and Professional Education, General Director of Educational Planning, President of the Board of CENIDE, etc. (Ruiz Berrio and Flecha García 2007). Fraenkel and Galino maintained a steady correspondence on the functioning of the various educational reform programs in which the FF collaborated.[43]

Fraenkel was not only concerned with educational matters. As a representative of Ford's interests on the Iberian Peninsula, he also informed his superiors in New York about legislative changes concerning Spanish industry, specifically the automobile industry. This happened at the beginning of 1973: "Ford Motor Company is reported to be awaiting decisions on a number of important issues, to be reached by the Ministry of Industry during the next two to three months."[44] It will be useful to explore in the future whether he intervened actively on behalf of the FF before the leaders of other ministries, apart from his more visible work in education, or if he was simply a messenger between the two shores of the Atlantic. Some of the recurring themes of Fraenkel's reports were the rigor and transparency of the candidates' selection processes, as well as follow-up on their progress in the program. Regarding the first issue, he transmitted this concern to New York in July 1972: "The pressures to embrace mediocrity are increasingly powerful! But I am confident that we shall succeed again in adhering to our criteria of selection." That would seem to imply the Ford representative felt pressured in some instances to favor some candidates over others, disregarding the necessary impartiality.[45]

That summer, Fraenkel also reported on the political situation in Spain and the uncertainties that loomed on the horizon with the dictator's advanced age.[46] It was an atmosphere of doubts that did nothing but increase after the assassination of the president of the government, Luis Carrero Blanco, in December 1973 at the hands of the terrorist group ETA. Where higher-level relations were concerned, it seems Ford's representative had better harmony with Minister of Education Cruz Martínez Esteruelas (January 1974 to December 1975) than with his predecessor, Julio Rodríguez Martínez. A member of Opus Dei, the latter was appointed in June 1973 and dismissed only six months later. His brief tenure, along with such eccentricities as his changing of the school calendar, earned him the ironic nickname "Julio the Brief."[47]

According to Fraenkel, in the final stretch of the Franco regime, the implementation of educational reforms was hampered by political turbulence and especially by the lack of continuity in projects, as well as personality conflicts and other problems. Barely concealing his consternation, he wrote to his superiors, "As a result of recent shifts in government appointments, the CENIDE is being totally reorganized." Apart from the institutional changes, the Ford delegate was worried about losing contacts that he considered valuable: "In all likelihood, however, Emilia [Ruiz Campuzano] will survive, at least on a part time basis."[48]

Fraenkel's previous warnings about the difficulty of advancing in education without a medium or long-term vision seemed to be coming true. The concern he expressed with reference to Spaniards in 1968 should be remembered: "They are inordinately dependent on individuals and their respective personalities," which he saw as a hindrance to "long-term continuity."[49] The lack of innovative agendas and openness to change, regardless of who was at the helm, did not help either; and the lack of collaboration between departments of the same university was not very encouraging. Fraenkel lamented the occurrence of that latter phenomenon at the University of Santiago de Compostela. This institution had received funds from Ford for the acquisition of material that could be used by several departments. However, Fraenkel complained, one of the professors had monopolized the donation, preventing its use by colleagues from other divisions.[50]

But it was not all negative. The Ford reports actually exuded a rather optimistic tone when talking about participants in training programs abroad: "Without doubt the most important contribution of the program for years to come is in the development of personnel who through their careers will train others to be better teachers." Such improvement in the training of education professionals would heighten the prospects for encouraging the talents of thousands of students. In sum, "our returned Fellows, most of them with advanced degrees, provide the multiplier effect for our grant and assure its reasonably lasting impact."[51]

At the twilight of Franco regime, Fraenkel's continuance as an adviser on educational modernization was perhaps needed most. However, six years after his arrival in 1968, some of his superiors demanded his return to New York. From Spain's side of the Atlantic, Minister of Education Martinez Esteruelas tried to fight that decision and to obtain extraordinary funds to extend Fraenkel's stay in Spanish territory, "a wish concurred in by the new American Ambassador to Spain, Admiral Horacio Rivero."[52] Shortly thereafter, Luis de Guzman, Managing Director of the Foundation of the Technological Institute for Postgraduates, also showed an interest in retaining Fraenkel's consulting services in Spain.[53]

The FF showed its gratitude for these expressions of interest and appreciation toward one of its most reputable men. However, the original decision was not reversed, so ultimately Frankel returned to the United States. This move is best understood as part of the broader FF strategy of moving to other latitudes. The European countries had merited the priority attention in the previous decades; in the mid-1970s, there were other geographical areas of concern. We can also not rule out that Fraenkel's mission in Spain was mediated by the economic timetables of the car company. Recall that Fraenkel sometimes transmitted information related to changes in industrial legislation. In April

1973, Minister of Industry José María López de Letona announced that the Ford Motor Company would open a factory in Almussafes, Valencia.[54] The plant, which boasted the most up-to-date available technology, was officially inaugurated in October 1976 by King Juan Carlos and the president of the company, Henry Ford II.[55]

A Provisional Balance Sheet

What has been presented here is only part of the puzzle, which will undoubtedly be complemented by future research. A more extensive study of the varied ramifications of this international largesse is pending, as new sources come to light. Even so, some conclusions can be advanced, albeit provisionally. The interest of the FF for the socioeconomic and political evolution of Spain began at the end of the 1950s and increased in the final stretch of the Franco regime.[56] Initially, one of the main objectives was to alleviate the great shortcomings in the speaking of English that most Spaniards had. Knowledge of this language was considered one of the first steps toward facilitating the transfer of knowledge and know-how.

Although at times showing his prejudices and stereotypes, Fraenkel's assessments accurately identified, in general terms, the deficiencies that hampered the modernization of education in Spain: lack of a tradition of teamwork, personality variables, rigidity in the curriculum, lack of English skills, etc. As a member of the committee of observers from the Fulbright Commission, he received firsthand complaints from American compatriots who were doing research and/or teaching stays in Spanish classrooms. Among the most prominent: pedagogical systems with doctrinaire orientations toward memorizing data rather than putting the knowledge to practical use, and a perpetual lack of resources. He also noted glaring shortcomings in knowledge about Spain in the United States, even in university environments.[57]

In seeking to evaluate the real impact of this "philanthropic patronage," it is important, simultaneously, not to lose sight of the perceptions of the recipients of that aid. While for fair proportion of the Spanish population looked to the United States as a beacon in the transformation of Spain, others considered the American influence harmful. The manifestations of anti-Americanism did not cease in the final stretch of the Franco regime. In fact, quite the contrary was the case.[58] As Volker Berghahn has correctly pointed out, "Foundations enjoyed a better comprehension and opinion among European public opinion than Washington policy makers" (1999: 419). Even so, there was no shortage of critics of the "cultural-ideological imperialism" that transmitted the philanthropic project. But hostile critics were not the only bane of the Ford man's existence in Spain. The difficulties that this reputable international consultant faced while maneuvering through the labyrinthine Spanish bureaucracy, trying to be heard by the decision makers, are a prime illustration of the limits of international educational and cultural transfers.

Finally, the lack of awareness on the part of the Spanish authorities about the need for investing their own funds to go beyond international philanthropy was an obstacle. This was a common complaint of FF representatives in other countries, for example, Brazil. From that country comes an interesting report, one of whose main conclusions can probably be extrapolated to what happened in many other scenarios:

> One lesson the Foundation has learned in these years is that change does not come only from above, but should be stimulated and fostered from below. The importance of the support the Foundation provides for grassroots movements and actions are not so much in the direct benefit it provides for a few groups, but on the demonstration effect these experiences can have for the whole country. (Schwartzman 1993: 193)

Acknowledgments

This work was supported by the Ministry of Economy and Competitiveness of Spain under the research project titled "La modernización del sistema educativo y científico español en su dimensión internacional (1953–1986)" (HAR2014-58685-R).

Francisco Rodríguez-Jiménez obtained his PhD from the University of Salamanca and won the award for best dissertation. He went on to work as a postdoctoral researcher at the Weatherhead Center for International Affairs at Harvard University and as a Fulbright Visiting Scholar at George Washington University. Currently, he is a professor at the University of Extremadura and serves as an executive committee member of the Global and International Studies Think Tank at the University of Salamanca. He contributes regularly in the media, mainly with op-eds in *Americracia,* a blog of *El Mundo*. His research focuses primarily on US public diplomacy and the Cultural Cold War (Spain–United States–Latin America), but he has also explored the relationship between anti-Franco labor unions and their American counterparts; the "American Woman Model" reception in Spain; the details of the Fulbright Program; and American historians and Spanish historiography. He recently coedited *US Public Diplomacy and Democratization in Spain: Selling Democracy?* (2015), *El Portugal salazarista frente a la democracia* (2016), *Estrategias de diplomacia cultural en un mundo interpolar* (2015), *¿Mujeres sabias? Mujeres universitarias en España y América Latina* (2015).

Notes

1. "The purpose of philanthropy itself is to promote the welfare, happiness, and culture of mankind" (Bremner 1960).
2. "At times, it appeared as if the Ford Foundation were simply a government delegation on matters involving international cultural propaganda. The Foundation had a broad agenda of covert actions in Europe, acting side by side with the Marshall Plan and with CIA agents. The architects of the cultural policy of the Foundation at the end of World War II were in perfect tune with the political imperatives that sustained the dominance of United States on the world stage. At times, it seemed as if the Ford Foundation was simply a government delegation on issues related to international cultural propaganda" (Stonor 2001: 198).
3. "Funds and Foundations," 19 May 1959; Birmingham to Director, FBI "Funds and Foundations," 28 October 1959. https://archive.org/search.php?query=Funds%20and%20Foundations.
4. "Philanthropy expresses certain postulates of American life, notably decentralized responsibility and voluntary action. American society has established a diversified pattern of separate educational systems, resting for financial support upon governmental and private sources" (Lashner 1976: 529).
5. "The Free University's Request for Funds from the Ford Foundation," 20 April 1958, Record Group 59, Board Foreing Scholarship—Plans and Development, 1955–60, Box 44, National Archive and Records Administrations (NARA); "American Studies in German Universities," 22 October 1951, American Studies Association Archive, Library of Congress. For the events in Spain at this time, see Rodríguez-Jiménez (2010).
6. "The Ford Foundation's Activities in Europe," March 1968, R.001986/-DF, Ford Foundation Archives (FFA).
7. Yet, and as Quesada (chapter 9) and Snider (chapter 8) mention, some American universities and the Ford Foundation itself had started exploring ways of cultural or educational cooperation with their Latin America counterparts some time before.
8. "Cuando la filantropía es caridad," *ABC*, 5 May 1956.
9. "Expediente Guy Bueno," Meridian Archive, Washington, DC. I am grateful to Susan Cabiati, Director of the Meridian, for her enormous help with the finding of this information.

10. "Report on the USIS English Teaching Program," 29 January 1957, RG 59, BFS-Plans and Development, 1955–60, Box 45, NARA.
11. "Gerald J. Campbell to Joseph M. McDaniel Jr.," 17 December 1965, R.1083/66-48, FFA.
12. "Robert Lado to Mr Matthew Cullen, Ford Foundation," 29 October 1964; and "The English Program in Spanish Universities by Robert Lado," June 1966, R-4574/ 62-42, FFA.
13. "Ford Foundation Program for English Teaching in Spain," 31 May 1973, R.1083/66-48, FFA.
14. The connection between the Ford Foundation and the Congress for Cultural Freedom—renamed the International Association for Cultural Freedom—did not completely end. It took, however, several different measures to avoid criticism.
15. "The Ford Foundation's Activities in Europe"; "The Ford Foundation Strategy toward Western Europe," March 1972, R.009033, FFA.
16. "Las subvenciones de la Fundación Ford," *ABC*, 23 January 1965; "Cinco mil elefantes," *ABC*, 29 March 1966.
17. "Ford Foundation under Attack," 10 July 1970, RG 59, 1970–73, Box 387, NARA.
18. Joseph Kraft, "El poder en Washington," *La Vanguardia Española*, 10 July 1969.
19. "Johnson ¿y Kosygin?" *La Vanguardia Española*, 12 December 1968.
20. Peter A. Fraenkel papers, 1940–1983, bulk 1959–1976, http://webapp1.dlib.indiana.edu/findingaids/view?doc.view=entire_text&docId=InU-Ar-VAD0090.
21. "Spain: Trip Report—Peter Fraenkel," 19 November 1968, R-4574, Box 62-42, I, FFA.
22. "Peter Fraenkel to F. Champion Ward," 10 November 1969, R-2281/70-305, FFA.
23. "Survey of American Studies, 1968," R-1956/61-41, FFA.
24. "Emilio Lorenzo to Peter Fraenkel," 8 January 1969; "Robert Lado to Fraenkel," 15 December 1969; and "Moselle Kimbler to F.F Headquarters," 20 April 1970, R.1083/66-48, FFA.
25. "Peter Fraenkel to Mr Howard Swearer," 18 February 1969, R.1083/66-48, 649, I, FFA.
26. "Peter Fraenkel to Mr Howard Swearer," 3 May 1969, R.1083/66-48, 649, I, FFA.
27. "Peter Fraenkel to Mrs Moselle Kimbler," 14 November 1972, R.1083/66-48, FFA. In this series of letters, the tone is similar, for example, in those dated 3 October 1972, 28 September 1972, and 31 May 1972.
28. "Commission for Educational Exchange between the United States of America and Spain. Annual Program Proposal," 11 February 1969, Box 54/10519, Archivo General de la Administración.
29. "Villar Palasí to Peter Fraenkel," 27 January 1970, R-2281/70-305, FFA. And in the same collection, another document, untitled, related to the agreement between the FF and the ministry, 28 May 1971.

30. For more details on FF financing of various universities and research centers after World War II, see Hammack and Anheier (2013): 75ff.
31. "FF to Mr. Kenneth Holland," 15 June 1970, R-2281/ 70-305, FFA.
32. "Actas de la Comisión Ejecutiva de la Comisión Fulbright-España," 13 October 1971, Box 7, Archivo de la Comisión Fulbright-España (ACFE).
33. *Boletín Oficial del Estado* 295 (10 December 1969): 19.183–19.184.
34. "Educational Modernization and Reform in Spain," 1 January 1969, R-2281/70-305, FFA.
35. "Proyecto de convenio entre el Ministerio de Educación y Ciencia y la Fundación Ford," *ABC*, 19 January 1970.
36. "Donación de 28 millones de pesetas de la Fundación Ford a la Reforma Educativa," *La Vanguardia Española*, 15 October 1970.
37. "Preselección de becarios para formación de personal docente e investigador en el extranjero," *La Vanguardia Española*, 30 October 1971.
38. "Peter Fraenkel to Robert Lado," 25 November 1970; "Ramón Bela to Robert Lado," 23 June 1970; "Ramón Bela to Robert Fraenkel," 1 April 1970; and "Emilio Lorenzo to Peter Fraenkel," 24 June 1970, R.1083/66-48, FFA.
39. "Peter Fraenkel to Robert Lado."
40. "Peter Fraenkel to FF Headquaters," 28 May 1971, R-2281/ 70-305, FFA.
41. Ley 14/1970, "General de Educación y Financiamiento de la Reforma Educativa," *Boletín Oficial del Estado* 187 (6 August 1970): 12525–12546.
42. "El Colegio San Estanislao de Kostka 'El Castillo'," *ABC*, 4 October 1972. On the work of UNESCO toward improvement of education, see Dorn and Ghodsee (2012).
43. "Angeles Galino to Peter Fraenkel," 27 January 1973, R-2281, Box 70-305, FFA.
44. "Peter Fraenkel to Mr Edward J. Meade," 16 January 1973, R-2281, Box 70-305, FFA; "Report on a Trip to Spain and Portugal, by Peter Fraenkel," 3 December 1976, R-5640, Box 76-185, FFA.
45. "Fraenkel to Edward J. Meade," 7 June 1973. R-2281, Box 70-305.
46. "Comments on Some Recent Developments in Spain," 12 July 1973, R-2281, Box 70-305, FFA; "Actas de las reuniones del Comité Supervisor del Programa de Cooperación Cultural NMA," 24 January 1973, Box 32, ACFE.
47. "Fraenkel to FF Headquarters," 15 January 1974, R-2281, Box 70-305, FFA.
48. "General Correspondence: Fraenkel to Patricia Bain Mills," 22 January 1974, R-2281, Box 70-305, FFA.
49. "Spain: Trip Report—Peter Fraenkel."
50. "Peter Fraenkel to Mr. Peter Ruof: Grant Evaluation Report," 4 June 1974, R. 1083, Box 66-48, FFA.
51. "Peter Fraenkel to President John W. Ryan," 23 July 1974, R-2467, Box 74-447, FFA. "Robert Lado: Grant Evaluation Report," 18 March 1974, R.1083, Box 66-48, FFA.
52. "Fraenkel to FF Headquarters," 1 June 1974, R-2467, Box 74-447, FFA.

53. "Luis de Guzman to Julius A. Stratton," 21 April 1976, R-2467, Box 74-447, FFA.
54. "The Ford Foundation Strategy toward Western Europe."
55. "La Ford, a Valencia," *ABC*, 27 April 1973; "El Rey inauguró la factoría Ford en Almusafes," *ABC*, 26 October 1976.
56. "Peter Fraenkel to Mr. Peter Ruof: Grant Evaluation Report"; "Report of the Agreement between the Ministry of Education & the Ford Foundation," 26 January 1973, R-2281/70-305, FFA; "Peter Fraenkel to Cruz Martínez Esteruelas," 30 April 1975, R-2467/ 74-447, FFA.
57. "Peter Fraenkel to Cruz Martínez Esteruelas"; "Spanish Fulbright Commission: Minutes of the Meeting," 7 March 1974, 5, Box 7, ACFE. "Peter Fraenkel to FF," 13 March 1975, R-2467, Box 74-447, FFA.
58. "Demonstrations in Spain against US Action in Cambodia," 23 May 1970, RG 59, Subject Numeric Files, 1970–73, Box 2598, NARA; "Damage to USIS Library in Madrid," 7 October 1972, RG 59, Subject Numeric Files, 1970–73, Box 378, NARA.

References

Augier, Mie. 2011. *The Roots, Rituals, and Rhetorics of Change: North American Business Schools after the Second World War*. Stanford, CA: Stanford Business Books.

Aróstegui, Julio. 2000. "El observador en la tribu (Los tratadistas extranjeros y la historia española)." *Historia Contemporanea* 20: 3–29.

Barjot, Dominique, dir. 2002. *Catching Up with America: Productivity Missions and the Diffusion of American Economic and Technological Influence after the Second World War*. Paris: Presses de l'Université De Paris-Sorbonne.

Bremner, Robert H. 1960. *American Philanthropy*. Chicago: University of Chicago Press.

Berghahn, Volker. 1999. "Philanthropy and Diplomacy in the American Century." *Diplomatic History* 23 (3): 393–419.

——. 2001. *America and the Intellectual Cold Wars in Europe*. Princeton, NJ: Princeton University Press.

——. 2012. "Turntables or Transatlantic Two-Lane Turnpikes?" In Krige and Rausch 2012: 261–270.

Calandra, Benedetta. 2011. "La Ford Foundation y la 'Guerra Fría Cultural.'" *Americanía* 1: 8–25.

Chorev, Nitsan. 2012. *The World Health Organization between North and South*. Ithaca, NY: Cornell University Press.

Corrales Morales, David. 2016. "'Helping the Implementation of the Reform': Los préstamos del Banco Mundial y su impacto en la educación de la infancia española (1970–1972)." In *El factor internacional en la modernización educativa, científica y militar de España*, ed. Lorenzo Delgado

Gómez-Escalonilla, Pablo León Aguinaga, Oscar J. Martín García, and Esther M. Sánchez, 197–218. Alicante: Biblioteca Virtual Cervantes.
Cull, Nicholas. 2008. *United States Information Agency and the Cold War*. Cambridge: Cambridge University Press.
Dorn, Charles, and Kristen Ghodsee. 2012. "The Cold War Politicization of Literacy: Communism, UNESCO, and the World Bank." *Diplomatic History* 36 (2): 373–398.
De Santisteban, Fabiola. 2009. "El desembarco de la Fundación Ford en España." *Ayer* 75 (3): 159–191.
Delgado Gómez-Escalonilla, Lorenzo. 2003. "¿El amigo americano? España y Estados Unidos durante el franquismo." *Studia Historica: Historia Contemporánea,* 21: 231–276.
——. 2009. *Viento de poniente: El Programa Fulbright en España, 1958–2008*. Madrid: Comisión Fulbright España-LID.
——. 2012. "Objetivo: atraer a las élites: Los líderes de la vida pública y la política exterior norteamericana en España." In *Guerra Fría y Propaganda: Estados unidos y su cruzada cultural en Europa y América latina*, ed. Antonio Niño and José A. Montero, 235–277. Madrid: Biblioteca Nueva.
——. 2015. "Modernización y 'Globalismo Nacionalista.'" *Historia y Política* 34: 13–26.
Ekbladh, David. 2009. *The Great American Mission: Modernization and the Construction of an American World Order*. Princeton, NJ: Princeton University Press.
Engerman, David C. 2007. "Bernath Lecture: American Knowledge and Global Power." *Diplomatic History* 31 (4): 599–622.
Gemelli, Giuliana, and Roy Macleod, eds. 2003. *America Foundations in Europe: Grant-Giving Policies, Cultural Diplomacy and Trans-Atlantic Relations, 1929–80*. Brussels: Peter Lang.
Gienow-Hecht, Jessica C. E., and Mark C. Donfried. 2010. *Searching for a Cultural Diplomacy*. New York: Berghahn Books.
Fernández Soria, Juan Manuel. 2005. "Influencias europeas en la política educativa española del siglo XX." *Historia de la educación: Revista inter-universitaria* 24: 27–37.
Hammack, David C., and Helmut K. Anheier. 2013. *A Versatile American Institution: The Changing Ideals and Realities of Philanthropic Foundations*. Washington, DC: Brookings Institution Press.
Ish-Shalom, Piki. 2006. "Theory Gets Real, and the Case for a Normative Ethic: Rostow, Modernization Theory, and the Alliance for Progress." *International Studies Quarterly* 50 (2): 287–311.
Kagan, Richard L. 2002. *Spain in America: The Origins of Hispanism in the United States.* Urbana: University of Illinois Press.
Keys, Barbara. 2011. "Henry Kissinger: The Emotional Statesman." *Diplomatic History* 35 (4): 587–609.
Knudsen, Dino. 2016. *The Trilateral Commission and Global Governance: Informal Elite Diplomacy, 1972–82*. New York: Routledge.

Krige, John, and Helke Rausch, eds. 2012. *American Foundations and the Coproduction of World Order in the 20th Century*. Göttingen: Vandenhoeck.
Lashner, Marilyn A. 1976. "The Role of Foundations in Public Broadcasting, Part 1: Development and Trends. *Journal of Braodcasting* 20 (4): 520–547.
Loescher, Gil. 2008. *The United Nations High Commissioner for Refugees (UNHCR)*. New York: Routledge.
Maier, Charles. 2006. *Among Empires: American Ascendancy and its Predecessors*. Cambridge, MA: Harvard University Press.
Maritano, Nino, and Antony H. Obaid. 1963. *The Alliance for Progress: The Challenge and the Problem*. Minneapolis, MN: Denison.
Martín García, Óscar J., and Francisco Rodríguez Jiménez. 2015. "The Engaging Power of English Language Promotion in Franco's Spain." *Contemporary European History* 24 (3): 415–433.
Martín García, Óscar J. 2015. "Una utopía secular: La teoría de la modernización y la política exterior estadounidense en la Guerra Fría." *Historia y política* 34: 27–52.
Mëhilli, Elidor. 2014. "Technology and the Cold War." In *The Routledge Handbook of the Cold War*, ed. Artemy Kalinovsky and Craig Daigle, 292–304. London: Routledge.
Pardo, Rosa. 2005. "España y EE.UU. en el tardofranquismo: las relaciones bilaterales durante la presidencia de Nixon." *Historia del Presente* 6: 11–41.
Parmar, Inderjeet. 2012. *Foundations of the American Century: The Ford, Carnegie and Rockefeller Foundations in the Rise of American Power*. New York: Columbia University Press.
Pearce, Charles. 2001. *Kennedy, Rostow, and the Rhetoric of Foreign Aid*. East Lansing: Michigan State University Press.
Plamper, Jan. 2015. *The History of Emotions: An Introduction*. Oxford: Oxford University Press.
Powell, Charles. 2011. *El amigo americano: España y Estados Unidos—De la dictadura a la democracia*. Barcelona: Galaxia Gutenberg.
Risse-Kappen, Thomas. 1994. "Ideas Do Not Float Freely: Transnational Coalitions, Domestic Structures, and the End of the Cold War Reviewed Work." *International Organization* 48 (2): 185–214.
Rodríguez-Jiménez, Francisco J. 2010. *¿Antídoto contra el antiamericanismo? American Studies en España, 1945–69*. Valencia: Universitat de València.
——. 2016. "Trade Unionism and Spain-US Political Relations, 1945–53." *Ventunesimo secolo* 38: 96–124.
Rostow, Walter W. 1960. *The Stages of Economic Growth, a Non-Communist Manifesto*. Cambridge: Cambridge University Press.
Ruiz Berrio, Julio, and Consuelo Flecha García. 2007. "Conversación con . . . Ángeles Galino Carrillo." *Historia de la Educación: Revista Interuniversitaria* 26: 519–538.
Stonor, Frances. 2001. *La CIA y la Guerra Fría Cultural*. Madrid: Debate.
Scott-Smith, Giles. 2008. *Networks of Empire: The US State Department's Foreign Leader Program in the Netherlands, France, and Britain 1950–1970*. Brussels: Peter Lang.

Schwartzman, Simon. 1993. "Educating the Ford Foundation." In *A Fundaçao Ford No Brasil*, ed. Sergio Miceli, 182–198. Sao Paulo: Sumaré.
Taffet, Jeffrey. 2007. *Foreign Aid as Foreign Policy: The Alliance for Progress in Latin America*. New York: Routledge.
Viñas, Ángel. 2003. *En las garras del águila: Los pactos con Estados Unidos, de Francisco Franco a Felipe González (1945–1995)*. Barcelona: Crítica.
Waters, Robert Anthony, Jr., and Geert van Goethem, eds. 2013. *American Labor's Global Ambassadors: The International History of the AFL-CIO during the Cold War*. London: Palgrave Macmillan.

Chapter 4

Educational Transfer and Local Actors

International Intervention in Spain during the Late Franco Period

Mariano González-Delgado and Tamar Groves

International Organizations as a Frame of Reference for Analysis of Educational Policies during the Late Franco Period

The years following the period encompassing the two world wars were characterized by widespread reflection on how to prevent the world from entering such belligerent times again. Among the fields tasked with helping achieve that objective, education was seen as an especially well-positioned institution (Moody 2014). As recently pointed out by Karen Andreasen and Christian Ydesen (2015), internationalization policies in education were intended to promote the idea that education could generate the construction of peace and international reconciliation. Along those lines, many educational theorists, teachers, and political actors in the Western societies introduced these ideas into their new agendas for intervention. However, policies focused on fostering international cooperation did not focus exclusively on promoting peace. In parallel with that goal and closely connected, the stability and economic growth of the various developing countries also came to play a part in the objectives of the multilateral education agencies (Mundy 2006).

The ideas for economic development involved efforts by the Western countries to foment the construction or expansion of national systems of education in those places that still showed deficits in this area. In the political framework created by the Cold War during the 1950s and 1960s, education soon became part of the strategic policies of international organizations to promote economic growth in developing countries and, to a certain extent, to stop the international spread of communism (Dorn and Ghodsee 2012). In relation to this dimension, modernization theories simultaneously became conjoined with this goal (Lindo-Fuentes and Ching 2012). The objective was to stop the escalation of those social, cultural, and political discontents that were rising in Latin America, Asia, Africa, and some Western European countries. This would convince Western countries that the way to solve such problems within these regions had to be through economic aid, military training, technical assistance, and the expansion of human capital (Alacevich 2011). In this sense, the best way to promote the wealth of such countries and avoid the aforementioned social conflicts would be through their educational institutions (Boel 2016).

Beginning in the 1950s, these ideas were increasingly the focus of discourse within international organizations dedicated to the educational sphere (Jones and Coleman 2005). The union that arose between the context of the Cold War and the theories of modernization produced in the ambit of educational multilateralism a broad reflection on the direction that educational policies and pedagogical practice should take on a global level (Fuchs 2014). Seen in this light, education would be a perfect ally to achieve the ultimate goal of social stability through economic growth and development (Delgado Gómez-Escalonilla 2015). In this way, several policies of educational intervention that were initially intended for the eradication of illiteracy and the diffusion of knowledge about different cultures soon came to take on a more economistic character (Giton 2016).

Educational policies of this nature also exerted a notable influence on Francoist Spain (Terrón 2013). It is true that, during the first years of the dictatorship, the imported pedagogical models had an ambivalent presence within the Spanish educational system (Pozo Andrés and Braster 2006). Even so, after the 1950s, numerous pedagogical proposals were introduced that had originated in the various forums of international cooperation—for example, projects sponsored by UNESCO such as adult education, popular education, programmed instruction, and health education (González-Delgado and Groves 2016, 2017; Terrón 2015). Also worth mentioning are the mediation and intervention carried out since the 1960s by the Organization for Economic Cooperation and Development (OECD), the Ford Foundation, and two of the most important suborganizations of the UN for economic modernization: the World Bank and the United Nations Development Program (Delgado Gómez-Escalonilla 2016).

The purpose of this chapter is to analyze and contextualize, in a concise manner, the main educational policies that were stimulated by the international organizations during the late Franco years. More specifically, it seeks to establish a historical journey through the educational initiatives that were intended to be promoted by local actors through the connections and the work they developed with multilateral agencies during this time—all with the aim of demonstrating that some of the main educational policies of the later Franco years can be understood more precisely if they are framed within a perspective that situates them in the context of the phenomena of internationalization and modernization in the latter half of the twentieth century.

This is not to suggest this research ignores the mediation that local actors can exercise in these educational transfers. This reality is revealed in a recent article about the modification of Finnish curricular policy (Sivesind et al. 2016). However, those authors point out that this same local institutional independence can play a favorable role in these policies. In this sense, educational transfer does not occur exclusively from a hierarchical position on the part of international organizations. As Joseph Watras (2010) has shown, such organizations try to create an important network with local actors to facilitate the implementation of their educational perspectives. This means, in some cases, the import process unfolds directly (Omolewa 2007; Adas 2009; Goodman et al. 2009). In others, the international bodies may run up against the mediations of the national context and have to modify the initial idea that they wanted to develop (Phillips and Ochs 2004; Popkewitz 2013). The transnational educational discourses "can be advantageous to examine and understand local and national points of view" (Sivesind and Wahlström 2016: 276). Therefore, the introduction and development of certain educational policies in the Franco dictatorship need to be understood as an international process in which local actors played an important role in the establishment or modification of them.

The Roots of International Educational Organizations in Francoist Spain

Among the historical events that marked the opening of General Francisco Franco's Spain to the outside world were the bilateral agreements signed with the United States in 1953. To be sure, these agreements to establish military bases in Spain were made in an awkward and contradictory context. The United States was presenting itself to the world as the promoter of the open society and liberal democracy in its race to check the geopolitical growth of the Soviet Union during the Cold War. At the same time, the geopolitical situation occasioned by the Cold War allowed for the justification of such agreements with the Iberian nation from a military and economic perspective. The result would be not only the installation of military bases in Spain but also a series of economic aid packages aimed at improving the economic development of this European country (León-Aguinaga 2012).

To that end, a series of human capital exchange and training programs were initiated with the objective of improving certain elements of Spain's administrative structures such as economy, education, and army. Leading cadres of the state apparatus, as well as military officers, technicians, educational specialists, media officers, and students, began to receive various types of training in the United States (Álvaro Moya 2011). This institutional approach helped make modernization theory a commonplace within the Francoist leadership (Martín García 2015) and to set Spain on a course toward the embrace of some economic liberalization measures (Cebrián Villar 2004; Cebrián Villar and López 2016). In this context, the administration of the Spanish state undertook, under the tutelage of the United States, a course of opening contact with international organizations. The new political space established by the agreements of 1953 resulted in the entry of Spain into the United Nations in 1955. A few years later, in 1958, it would also be linked to the World Bank and to the International Monetary Fund (Cavalieri 2014). On the other hand, as far as education was concerned, as Spain also began its journey with UNESCO as early as 1953. This aspect allowed the dictatorship to enter international circles of technical and educational modernization (De Puelles Benítez 2009).

As of February 1953, the Spanish National Commission for Cooperation with UNESCO began to operate through a royal decree published that same month by the Spanish Ministry of the Presidency. In it, the Spanish state undertook to ensure at the national level "compliance with the agreements taken by the General Conference of UNESCO."[1] The president of that commission would also be the Minister of Education, then Joaquín Ruiz-Giménez. Just the following year, the Working Group on Education was formed, and with it the work of pedagogical importation began to move. This is not to imply the Spanish pedagogical field was hitherto unfamiliar with the educational debates that were going on internationally. The Francoist educational elite (the San José de Calasanz Institute of Pedagogy, and the Spanish Pedagogy Society) had carried on institutional and intellectual relations with European and American educational centers since the beginning of the dictatorship (Groves and González-Delgado 2017). However, only with the entry of UNESCO into Spain in 1953 would multilateral cooperation and educational transfer discourses be formally channeled through the framework of international organizations so as to facilitate the development of such educational models locally.

UNESCO's first such contributions to Spain, by means of the National Commission, centered on publishing reports and bibliographies, awarding exchange and training scholarships, sending experts, compiling lists of pedagogical journals, and drawing up technical reports on the educational situation in Spain. At the same time, the National Commission was in charge of distributing to the main Spanish educational training centers (universities) the publications that UNESCO was generating from Paris to promote its ideas among the member states. Good examples of these were the periodicals that dealt with the most innovative ideas in education, such as *The UNESCO Courier* and the *Revista de Información*. Moreover, technical reports about the major programs of the international organization should be highlighted (Oliveros 1978). In fact, the first works of the National Commission were characterized by efforts to socialize the UNESCO strategies designed around the Programme of Fundamental Education, an aspect that would be accelerated in 1956 through the Major Project of Education in Latin America, which had been approved at the New Delhi Conference that same year.[2]

This trajectory was also realized through Spain's own institutional infrastructures for education. In the same years as Spain began working within UNESCO, the main educational journals in the country tried to reach the educational intellectuals and the teachers themselves. The objective was to launch the first models of intervention of the education program and to make known UNESCO's ideas. This aspect could be observed with the rapid publication of a series of articles of a promotional and didactic nature in *Revista de Educación* and *Bordón: Revista de Orientación Pedagógica*. Indeed, as early as 1952, the *Revista de Educación* launched an article that tried to explain the collaboration that was going to be established with the international organization (Perdomo García 1952).[3] In 1957, *Bordón* published a piece titled "Lecturas del maestro en colaboración con la UNESCO" (The teacher's readings in collaboration with UNESCO). Through a series of articles written by Spanish and foreign authors, it attempted to introduce improvements in teachers' reading and writing techniques (García Hoz 1957; Lauwerys 1957). The purpose was, without doubt, to try to improve teaching practices and begin to implement in Spain the adult literacy and education projects that had been developed in the Programme of Fundamental Education, an effort that other Spanish technocrats sought to promote through the *Revista de Educación* (Maíllo 1953, 1954).

The processes of educational transfer were not limited to the publication of technical or prescriptive articles. During these years, various works of authors connected with UNESCO were also published, presenting other theories about the importance of seeking new teaching-learning approaches. Arguments about the importance that educational TV and radio could have when promoting and improving literacy were also common within the pages of the *Revista de Educación* (Bousquet 1958) and *Bordón* (Ögren 1958). However, one of the UNESCO projects that had the greatest influence in the Spanish pedagogical field during these first years was the revision of textbooks for the teaching of social sciences. The proposal to revise the approaches used by textbooks from other countries grew out of an agreement reached in Puerto Rico in 1954 between the Spanish National Commission and the French National Commission (Oliveros 1978), and involved promoting the UNESCO program on "international understanding" in Spain (Lauwerys 1953). To this end, a report of recommendations was issued,[4] and these ideas were echoed in the Spanish educational journals.[5] The objective was to avoid distortion in the historical and geographical representation of neighboring countries and to try to inculcate principles of peace so as to reach international understanding through education (Kulnazarova and Ydesen 2017).

This type of campaign represented the first attempts within the Spanish pedagogical field to promote new models of educational policy in an international framework. Even so, the proposals focused more on undertaking modest transformations, and from a technical rather than political vision. The presence of some difficulties of an institutional nature should also be noted. As we have seen, the processes of importation and international influence were launched from the university level. During the 1950s, the teacher-training schools were not an integral part of university life. As Juan Mainer (2009) has indicated, the distance in those years between academic pedagogy and teaching was remarkable. This made for a wide gap between the two cultures and difficulty with propagation of the commitment to modernize the Spanish educational system through the recommendations of international organizations.

This did not mean the educational transfer process stalled or stagnated at this point. As a result of the Cold War context, the dictatorship had entered into the ambit of the international organizations and, under their recommendations, into a determined bid to propel economic development as guided by the blueprint of modernization theories. One way to try to overcome this isolation between educational cultures and to undertake the great modernizing objective was the creation of the Centro de Documentación y Orientación Didáctica de Enseñanza Primaria (CEDODEP). This center for teacher training and improvement was founded in 1958, its main intention being the "technical improvement of this level of education, as well as pre-, circum-, and post-school activities, and those of literacy and fundamental education."[6] CEDODEP had among its initiatives an effort to promote the educational ideas of the Programme of Fundamental Education. This aspect should not surprise us at all: CEDODEP was an initiative of Joaquín Tena Artigas, who at that time was General Director of Primary Education and had been the Deputy Secretary of the Spanish National Commission of UNESCO during its first years (Oliveros 1978: 58).

From the moment of its inception, CEDODEP functioned as a training institution in which direct collaboration with UNESCO was notable. From here, and within the framework of the Major Project of Education in Latin America, CEDODEP developed several specialized courses on teaching in one-room schools. The aim was to examine the Spanish school situation and introduce numerous proposed techniques to help improve literacy and boost student enrollment (CEDODEP 1968a). On the other hand, the work of educational transfer did not stop at this point. CEDODEP also sought to disseminate and implement international educational models through the main publications that were created within that institution and that reached all schools. *Vida Escolar* was a prime example. From its first issues, the journal published articles focused on offering information and methodological support relative to the main educational priorities of UNESCO. In the second issue, for example, we find articles that review some of UNESCO's publications (Gray 1957), as well as some proposals about the teaching of history and school hygiene.[7]

The Pedagogical Implications of Spain's Integration into International Networks

Notwithstanding, the influence of the international organizations and the attempts to modernize the Spanish educational system did not involve the promotion of teacher training alone. Economic development soon became the priority within which the future of the Spanish educational system would be framed. This new stage in the role of international organizations emerged at the dawn of the 1960s. In both the political and economic spaces, as well as the educational field, the efforts at securing various processes of institutional modernization were substantial. Indeed, the stabilization plan of 1959 was intended to create the conditions for planned development from 1962 to 1973, a process in which the educational system was to play a fundamental part (Martín Izquierdo 1991).

This relationship, which flowed directly out of the theories of development and human capital, fully involved the educational system in the process of achieving the economic objectives of the country. For its part, the collaboration between the Spanish government and international bodies such as the International Monetary Fund served to carry forward the modernizing project undertaken by the technocrats (Delgado Gómez-Escalonilla 2015: 119). In the field of education, there was close collaboration between UNESCO and the OECD. Starting in the late 1950s, UNESCO consolidated a strategy based on direct collaboration with nation-states. As early as 1956, the Program of Participation in the Activities of the Member States was created, giving a huge impetus in this direction. That element would be reinforced in 1959 with the creation of the UN Special Fund for Development. These two initiatives served as a basis for the implementation of more ambitious actions of the organization in the following decade and created a clear link between education and development (Monclús and Saban 1997: 84–92). An example of this was the creation in 1963 of the International Institute for the Planning of Education, whose objective was to help UNESCO's member states establish links between the ministers of education and the economic planning services.[8]

That last aspect bore particular importance for education in Spain. The OECD, constituted in 1961, undertook to initiate different activities related to improving the socioeconomic conditions of the less developed countries of Europe. The Mediterranean Regional Project was an example of this. Launched in 1963 for Spain, Portugal, Italy, Yugoslavia, Greece, and Turkey, its purpose was to study the training needs in each of these countries. The objective was to improve human resources and thereby promote development. Each country that participated in the project prepared a national report, published by MEN-OECD (1963); Spain's was titled *Las necesidades de educación y el desarrollo económico social de España: Proyecto Regional Mediterráneo*.

Thus, throughout the 1960s, clear policies could already be observed in the direction called for by such organizations. As early as 1961, CEDODEP published a new journal titled *Notas y Documentos* to transmit the main educational theories that were being generated in the international arena. The first issue opened with an article by Joaquín Tena Artigas (1961) titled "Economy and Education." That work was just a short preliminary report on the main ideas of The OECD Mediterranean Regional Project, but a year later, this same journal (together with the *Revista de Educación*) launched an expanded summary of the intentions of the project for the Spanish educational community. Under the title "Spanish Education in Economic Development," the Spanish educational authorities were urged to work on "teaching planning" to achieve "the strategy of economic development." As expressed by the World Bank and OECD, "the connection between education and economic development is so important that the Report would not be complete without some reference to this matter." The theories of human capital were bursting with force in the educational objectives of the Iberian country. For these international organizations, it was therefore essential not only to invest a fixed amount of money in "primary education," "scientific research," "technical education at the middle level," and "adult education"; its objective was to impress on the Spanish government that it must "pay the necessary attention to investment in human resources, given that the supply of qualified labor will be an important factor in determining the rate of economic growth."[9]

In other words, the ultimate purpose of the report was not merely to improve the educational structure in general: "it is not the only important thing." Fundamentally, around this process, the best "quality" standards should be sought.[10] From that point on, various works began to appear, stressing the need to put the prescribed recommendations into practice. Many authors, both Spanish and foreign, began to promote the importance of connecting professional and technical training with the new realities of development that were being opened. The *Revista de Educación* began a series of publications in which it insisted that "the main agent of economic development is man" and that "the better prepared you are, the better your performance will be and the better that development" (Ressing 1962: 110).

Indeed, this discourse that the international organizations had opened would also have its propagation during the 1960s in the curricular policy itself. One of the proposals whose implementation was attempted with much force was programmed instruction. This model was introduced in Spain through an initiative launched by UNESCO to improve literacy processes and make them converge with economic development. To this end, a paper titled "Report on the Meeting of Textbook Editors"[11] stressed the necessity of including programmed instruction as a technique that could eradicate illiteracy more effectively while also bringing about the modernization of the school systems in relation to economic growth. A short time later, the first article in Spain on this particular topic appeared. It was a translation of a report that Arthur Lumsdaine (1962), professor of education at the University of California, Los Angeles, first wrote as a paper for the first UNESCO meeting held in Paris in March 1962 on new methods and techniques of education. In this piece, the American author pointed out the novel effects that programmed instruction could bring to bear on improving teaching and learning conditions. As a new curricular method based on behaviorism, programmed instruction offered the advantage of improving student learning and eradicating illiteracy more easily. This new perspective was also supported by its supposed superiority as a way to accelerate the acquisition of knowledge and productive skills of students. With this, it was assumed that greater and more effective economic development could be achieved (UNESCO 1962: 6).

These ideas involving education, development, and programmed instruction soon caught on among the Spanish educational specialists themselves. From 1963 on, several authors affiliated with Spain's leading educational institutions began to theorize about the need to introduce programmatic models in the classroom (Moreno 1963). There seemed to be no doubt that programming could help improve student performance, establish immediate control over it, and promote self-directed and individualized learning. Manifestations of this type would be repeated with force in the various articles that appeared more and more in journals such as *Vida Escolar* (De la Orden 1964), *Bordón* (Moreno 1966a), *Escuela Española* (Lorente 1964), *Revista de Educación* (Fernández Huerta 1963), *Educadores* (Ventosa 1965), and one of the best-known educational encyclopedias in Spain during that time: the *Diccionario de Pedagogía Labor* (Fernández Huerta 1964).

In parallel, CEDODEP promoted the move toward new curricular policies, going beyond the promotion of programmed instruction. Other proposals appeared on the scene that, similarly, were inserted into the modernizing paradigm. Educational TV, for example, emerged as another great curricular model to promote the growth of the country's human capital as it was doing in Latin American countries like El Salvador and Brazil (see chapters 7 and 8). For this, CEDODEP undertook several important activities that went beyond the publication of articles in *Notas y Documentos* and *Vida Escolar*. In 1966, special teaching guides on the use of programmed instruction (Moreno 1966b) and audiovisual techniques (Navarro Higueras 1967) were published as cyclostyled booklets. The following year, publications and seminars proliferated, and titles appeared like *Audiovisual Media in School* (*Los medios audiovisuales en la escuela*) (Navarro Higueras 1967), *School Organization: Foundations for Building Your Program* (*Organización escolar. Bases para la construcción de su programa*) (Moreno 1967), *Ideas for the Introduction of Audiovisual Techniques in School* (*Ideas en orden a la introducción en la escuela de las técnicas audiovisuales*) (CEDODEP 1968b), *Audiovisual Technology and Education* (*Tecnología audiovisual y educación*) (CEDODEP 1969), and, in collaboration with Radio y Televisión Española, *School Television in Spain, 1967–1968* (La Televisión Escolar en España, 1967–1968) (CRE 1968). All these included multiple articles on the importance of the new teaching techniques and how to put them into practice. We must also add the large number of communications on these issues that were brought to the Third National Congress of Education held in Salamanca in 1964. The very title of that conference, "The Spanish School System in Relation to Its Economic and Social Needs," allows us to understand where so much of the interest in programmed instruction and educational TV was ultimately rooted (Fernández Huerta 1965).[12]

The rapid reception of these new curricular approaches and the types of publications that came out about them in Spain should not surprise us. Indeed, UNESCO had been promoting programmed instruction and educational TV in other regions of the world right along. Shortly after the appearance of the articles by Arthur Lumsdaine, Peter Kenneth Komoski, and David Cook in the Spanish arena,[13] Komoski himself (director of the African Division of UNESCO for this theme) had prepared a report on the Programmed Instruction Workshop in Nigeria (Komoski and Gustafson 1963). This project, promoted by UNESCO and the Ford Foundation, aimed at improving the economic development of West African countries through the introduction of the aforementioned perspectives on curriculum. However, UNESCO's efforts did not focus exclusively on this region. Other reports with the same objective were prepared for other African countries (Von Recum 1963), for the Middle East (Green and Hartley 1963), and for Latin America (Bergvall and Joel 1964). Similarly, educational TV was extended as another of the curricular models that could improve literacy efforts and increase economic growth in developing countries. As was the case with programmed instruction, attempts to expand TV as a curricular element also got underway in Pakistan (Cassirer and Duckmanton 1960), Israel (Cassirer and Duckmanton 1961), American Samoa (Schramm 1967), and El Salvador.[14] UNESCO itself tried to accelerate the process with the publication in different languages of several pieces on educational TV in the magazine *The UNESCO Courier* (Cassirer 1966). Both orientations were built, in this international framework, as the curricular models that best represented "modernization" in the educational field.

UNESCO was not the only international institution that promoted the new development initiatives in Spain. Since the second half of the 1950s, the Spanish government had signed a series of agreements with American Social Aid to implement a food distribution program. These programs involved several plans of action including proposals on health education in Spanish schools. Starting in the 1960s, health education initiatives would increase in Spain through agreements signed with the World Health Organization, the Food and Agriculture Organization of the United Nations, and the United Nations Children's Fund (Turner 1966). In relation to the purposes of international organizations, food support programs were transformed into a series of planning efforts within schools to direct nutritional objectives toward their own economic development (Terrón et al. 2017).

In parallel, the United States, through the US Information Agency (USIA), tried to popularize in Spain some of the latest educational proposals that were produced in the United States in the 1960s. For this, the USIA used two magazines geared toward the Spanish cultural and university elites, *Atlántico* and *Facetas*. With them, the agency aspired to "help the thinkers of the two countries find common points of view" (Reid 1956: 5). The purpose of both magazines was to influence and generate support among the intellectual elites for America's own model of social, cultural, economic, and educational development. Both magazines featured articles that spoke of the benefits of the American educational and political systems. One could find descriptions there of the most ambitious projects of educational TV in the United States[15] and the democratic improvements that anticipated the movement toward a "technetronic" society: "pragmatic," "participatory," and "progressive" (Brzezinski 1969: 38–41).[16]

However, the enormous amount of information that came from the international organizations could not just be transferred in the abstract into the schools. A series of theoretical tools were needed with which to carry out these processes of educational transfer. In that regard, comparative education had to play a fundamental role. Since the second half of the twentieth century, UNESCO had notably promoted the field of comparative education. The aim was to study and transfer the best educational examples and introduce them within the framework of national pedagogical discourses (Altbach 1991). To that end, Spanish educational authorities also followed the advice of international organizations. It was thus not unusual to find, within the pages of Spanish educational journals, articles on the importance of knowing the systematic study of other educational systems around the world. In this context appeared the first articles by Pedro Roselló (1961) and Juan Tusquets (1969) about the theory of educational currents.

The expansion of the ideas thus far described had their correlates in the educational policies of the Franco dictatorship. We refer to the predominance of the views put forth in "Cuestionarios Nacionales de Enseñanza Primaria" in 1965. Devised by CEDODEP, it was structured in certain aspects under the developmental principles of the aforementioned international organizations. In the preamble it insisted, time and again, on the need to renew the Spanish educational system and adapt it to "to the different spheres of life as a response to the speed of development and the application of scientific knowledge." [17] In relation to this argument, the best way to acquire this principle in practice would be through the inclusion of the "psychodidactic arguments," the "experimental investigations," the "studies of comparative education" and, ultimately, pass "from the Questionnaire to the Program."[18]

In this respect, Spain did not come across as an educational island. It was one of the countries within the orbit of the various international organizations' strategic plans to increase literacy, economic development, and technological modernization through the expansion of educational systems. The initiating of the different educational policy proposals in Spain, therefore, did not originate as a mere pedagogical tool in the abstract. In fact, it had its origin in the need for improvement of human capital that the educational cooperation agencies had identified as a chief concern for Western societies. They sought to achieve, with new technical supports, the improvement of employability and the modernization of productive structures, and to prevent Spain from lapsing into certain policies of Eastern European countries. In the end, it was about offering a solution to social problems—poverty, unemployment, inequality, and educational deficiencies—through technical elements.

The Creation of New Educational Institutions and the Strengthening of Relations with the International Organizations

It is true that the imported pedagogical proposals had played an important role in Franco's educational policy during the first half of the 1960s. The "Cuestionarios Nacionales de Enseñanza Primaria" of 1965 constituted clear proof of this. However, the institutional ties forged between Spain's educational administration and the international organizations would undergo a greater process of unification at the end of this decade. The open institutional framework did more than facilitate the renewal of certain elements of the economic structure and the division of labor (Puig Raposo and Álvaro Moya 2004). At this point, it is worth mentioning a new twist with respect to the measures undertaken to modernize the Spanish educational system: these measures were accompanied not only by important loans and economic transfers but also by strategic support through international advisers.

The way international organizations and Spain's own Ministerio de Educación y Ciencia (Ministry of Education and Science—MEC) found to keep pace with the impetus and acceleration of economic growth by way of the educational system was the creation of the Centro Nacional de Investigaciones para el Desarrollo de la Educación (National Research Center for the Development of Education—CENIDE). In actuality, CENIDE was an institution promoted by the international organizations. Although the Royal Decree for its creation dates from 1969,[19] it was not until 1971 and 1972 that the plan of operations with the United Nations Development Program (UNDP) was approved and signed, respectively, to provide the institution with stronger political support. With funding of $1,227,838, it was a tripartite creation promoted by UNDP, UNESCO, and the MEC. Called SPA 19, it functioned as a subproject for the assistance that the Spanish government needed for the country's economic development. The creation of CENIDE was part of a broader plan whose other project titles included "Telecommunications," "Educational Television," "Air Pollution in the Bilbao District," and "Scientific Study of Water Resources in the Canary Islands." The plan was divided among the three productive sectors—primary, secondary, and tertiary—within which CENIDE's ultimate objective would be to promote the "human resources subsector".[20]

To achieve this objective, the CENIDE/ICEs network was established as a federative entity responsible for coordinating the Institutos de Ciencias de la Educación (ICEs) around a "triple responsibility of research, training and experimentation."[21] These goals would be developed through a series of seminars to be held at CENIDE's own headquarters and at designated ICE sites within the network. Toward the stated goals of "obtaining the highest possible return" from the education system and converting this aspect into "a preliminary matter of urgent relevance" (Alberti et al. 1970: 5), a significant number of courses, teacher training seminars, and technical research projects were launched. Within this branch of activities, undoubtedly, the promotion of programmed instruction, the pedagogical retooling of the various school subjects, and the crown jewels of educational technology—educational TV and computer-assisted instruction (CAI)—stood out as primary.[22]

In this manner, CENIDE began importing educational models with the support of various international consultants. This was the main formula used to accelerate the research activities within the center and to realize the goals of educational modernization. Perhaps the most characteristic example of CENIDE's own spirit was the creation of a closed circuit educational TV system between 1969 and 1971. In December 1969, the director of the Centre d'Electronique of Massey, J. Comiran, wrote a letter to Jacques Bousquet of UNESCO's Advanced Training Program in Spain. The purpose of this letter was to begin to develop a closed-circuit educational TV program such as had been proposed to CENIDE by the international bodies.[23] This project was framed within the UNESCO plan to promote teacher training and educational research through educational TV and film. With an approximate budget of $17,187 donated by the World Bank, the Ministry of Education initiated the start-up of the project. A few months later, Bousquet met with the Spanish publisher Vicens Vives to prepare a report on the instructional possibilities of the EVR System for Educational TV. In this confidential report, the technical characteristics of the EVR system were explained. The report also indicated that the model described "would allow us to place in the hands of the Ibero-American countries such an important advance in the media and education, that we do not hesitate to qualify as one of the advances that will revolutionize the 1970s."[24] The result was a recommendation from Bousquet to the General Technical Secretariat of the MEC to hurry up and "order and install the appropriate closed-circuit TVs as soon as possible."[25]

The following year, the CENIDE/ICEs network went to work on this task and organized several research and teacher training courses involving "active TV," "micro-instruction," "creation of educational cassettes," and "suitable tapes."[26] During this time, in collaboration with CENIDE, a Bachillerato Radiofónico (Radio Baccalaureate) curriculum was updated, with the processes of teaching and learning carried out through educational radio and TV educational courses.[27] However, the expansion of these new educational models also needed the support of international experts. For that reason, another project that the CENIDE/ICEs network coordinated as a means promoting the development of teaching and the training of human capital was the exchange/invitation of consultants from UNESCO. In a financing program designated SPA19.04.93[28] and supported by funds from UNDP, the arrival of consultants in various specialties was planned between 1969 and 1972. Most of those being tapped were involved in research on issues related to educational innovation, a concept that at the time was considered synonymous with programmed instruction, educational television and, above all, CAI. The weight of that last component among the interests of the institution was increasingly evident.

In a familiar pattern, the push for CAI in Spain came to be exerted by the international organizations themselves. This program was part of a broader structural remodeling initiative of CENIDE. In the CENIDE/ICEs network's first phase of evaluation, known as the SPANED19 project, the UNESCO experts were concerned about "the unequal influence of the consultants" and the "difficulties of the ICEs in sending their staff to Madrid to attend the training seminars."[29] They were bothered by the centralized model that CENIDE had fallen into, an issue that "diverges a lot from the recommendations presented first by the CENIDE-ICE system in 1970." According to this argument, the experts opined that the center was convenient but should evolve toward "a relatively small coordinating body" and not function as a "super-ICE at the national level" of "hypertrophic expansion."[30] This report resulted in the restructuring of CENIDE into a new institution called the Instituto Nacional de Ciencias de la Educación (National Institute of Education Sciences [INCIE]) but also the promotion of a more narrowly defined form of educational model focused on CAI. In fact, among the recommendations proposed for the new INCIE/ICEs network, there was no longer any type of program focused on promoting curricular policies aimed at combating illiteracy. In 1972, experts indicated Spain "should pay particular attention to the implementation of the CAI project as a nationwide task."[31]

It is no surprise that, during these years, the perspectives on how to modify the educational system to achieve greater economic development had such a tone. As we have seen, the Iberian country tried to follow the different guidelines regarding the introduction of new technologies in the educational field promoted by international organizations. In this sense, Spain was constituted as another one of the countries that functioned as a testing ground of international politics. However, the reformist spiral into which the Spanish educational system had entered was not over. The foreign consultants who were involved at the ministerial level during this time urged the government to proceed with introducing educational reform of a structural nature. The International Committee for Educational Reform, which had operated since the late 1960s, had now become aware of the various problems that afflicted the Spanish educational system. Despite all the initiatives that were carried out, problems related to infrastructure, teacher training, and teaching and learning processes could still be seen in the Spanish classrooms. The day of the Ley General de Educación (General Education Law—LGE) had dawned. With it came efforts to obtain, once and for all, the realization of the educational modernization plan that had been birthed at the start of the 1950s. Nevertheless, the creation of the LGE represents a historical event in its own right that needs to be dealt with separately.

Conclusions

In the second half of the twentieth century, after getting past the aftermath of World War II and entering the dawn of the Cold War, the Western world saw in economic development and education the antidotes to the spread of revolutionary ideas and social instability. The international organizations that were created to increase cooperation and collaboration became important agents in this process of economic and social modernization. In this era, globalization as we know it today was still in the process of being configured. However, in the educational field the development of transnational education policies as we know them today could already be observed.

This study has endeavored to analyze the Spanish case. It inspires special interest due to the particular position that the Iberian country occupied with respect to the international dynamics that emerged after World War II. Spain came to be an example of a country that was within the orbit of the US education policies and that, under its assistance, initiated a series of reforms linked to the objectives set by international organizations. Despite being a country in the grip of a dictatorship, the international agreements that were signed promoted the introduction of the most current ideas in education. Perhaps the most important examples of this dynamic can be seen in the creation of CEDODEP, the proposals regarding programmed instruction, educational TV, and the creation of the CENIDE/ICEs network. But we must also emphasize the efforts to implement these reforms through the various seminars and visits of specialists that were arranged, as well as the significant sums of money that were received for the promotion of the various educational projects. However, the new international political alliances also ensured, in a paradoxical way, that the country itself would actively participate in the making of the educational policies that the international organizations were devising for Latin American countries such as Colombia, El Salvador, and Argentina (see chapters

7–10). Spanish specialists thus played a strong role in the design of the educational programs of the international organizations that were being applied in other developing countries.

This chapter presents an interesting case study on how transnational education policies were shaped within international organizations and subsequently penetrated into national contexts. In the Spanish case, this process provides a new theoretical framework to reinterpret the most important reform in the history of education in Spain in the twentieth century: the 1970 LGE. While this chapter does not analyze in detail the international influences on the elaboration of the LGE, it does study the path leading up to it, as developed by the Francoist educational administration. In this sense, this chapter opens a new theoretical framework that integrates the international perspective in detail and that can contribute to a new interpretation of this reform.

Acknowledgments

This work was supported by the Ministry of Economy and Competitiveness of Spain under the research project "La modernización del sistema educativo y científico español en su dimensión internacional (1953–1986)" (HAR2014-58685-R). We would like to express our gratitude to the Comisión Nacional Española de Cooperación con la UNESCO and in particular to Eva Balsera Porris, Victoria de la Serna Ramos, Carmen Pinar, and Virginia González Martínez for their help and support in the consulting of different archival materials.

Mariano González-Delgado is Lecturer in History of Education at the Universidad de La Laguna. He has worked at the University College London Institute of Education and Uppsala University as a visiting fellow. He has published several articles on history of textbooks in Spain, the international influences on curriculum in the late Francoism, and historiographical educational in Spain in different international journals such as a *History of Education, History of Education and Children's Literature*, and *Revista Mexicana de Investigación Educativa*. His main interests and topics of research focus on curriculum history and textbooks, history of teachers and teaching, and contemporary history of education.

Tamar Groves is Senior Lecturer in the Department of Education Sciences, and Associate Dean for International Relations of the Teacher Training College at University of Extremadura. She obtained her PhD from Tel Aviv University and the Universidad Nacional de Educación a Distancia in 2010 (awarded with a prize) and published a book based on her dissertation, *Teachers and the Struggle for Democracy in Spain* (2014). She coauthored *Tradición e innovación en la educación europea en los siglos XIX y XX: los casos de España y Portugal* (2018) and *Social Movements and the Spanish Transition* (2017), and coedited books such as *Performing Citizenship: Social Movements across the Globe* (2015) and *Women and Knowledge* (2018). In addition, she has published in leading international journals such as the *Journal of Social History, European History Quarterly, Paedagogica Historica: International Journal of the History of Education, War and Society*, and *History of Education*. Her main fields of interest are citizen education, educational social movements, international education, and women and higher education. Currently, she is collaborating with the Peace Research Institute Oslo in a project on Societal Transformation in Conflict Contexts working on educational grassroots initiatives in Asia, Africa, and the Middle East.

Notes

1. Royal Decree of 20 February 1953, establishing the Spanish National Commission of UNESCO.
2. This aspect can be observed, for example, with UNESCO's attempt to create a Training Center for Rural Teachers (Centro de Formación de Maestros Rurales) in Spain to modernize literacy processes and Latin American education systems. "Nota para la Secretaria de la Comisión Nacional de Cooperación con la UNESCO a efectos de la próxima reunión del comité ejecutivo. Asunto: Formación de maestros de escuelas rurales," 7 June 1955, Box 459/1, Archivo de la Comisión Nacional Española de Cooperación con la UNESCO (ACNEC-UNESCO). It is true that the Spanish Ministry of National Education rejected the UNESCO proposal. The "modest financing of $5,000" offered by the aforementioned agency, as well as a series of institutional limitations such as the lack of a "Fundamental Education Center" in Spain, limited the start-up of the project. "Formación de maestros de escuelas rurales," 4 July 1955, Box 459/1, ACNEC-UNESCO. However, this does not mean the Iberian country rejected the idea of being the country that channeled UNESCO's plans on rural education to Latin America. Spain would act as a country of educational transfer to this region, especially in relation to teachers' training (Maíllo 1960). More information can be found in chapters 7 and 8.
3. The appearance of an article by UNESCO in the pages of the *Revista de Educación* in 1952 may seem strange. However, Spain was invited to

UNESCO as an observer in 1951 before becoming a full member. For this reason, some articles related to UNESCO's work in those years can be found in the main educational journals (Oliveros 1978: 31–41).

4. "Conversaciones Unesco franco-españolas para la revisión bilateral de los Manuales de Historia organizadas por las Comisiones Nacionales de la Unesco de España y Francia," *Revista de Educación* 149 (1962): 135–145; "Correspondencia de entrada y salida de la Comisión Nacional con la Comisión Nacional de Francia sobre: Revisión de manuales de historia y geografía: 1960–1998," Box 58/1, ACNEC-UNESCO.
5. "En torno a la enseñanza de la Geografía (Reproducción de unos capítulos del folleto número VII de la serie 'La UNESCO y su programa' (año 1950), titulado 'La enseñanza de la Geografía al servicio de la comprensión internacional')," *Bordón* 39 (1953): 689–698.
6. Royal Decree of 25 April 1958, creating the Centro de Documentación y Orientación Didáctica (Center for Documentation and Educational Guidance).
7. "Sobre la enseñanza de la historia," *Vida Escolar* 45 (1959): 7–57.
8. Its first director was Philip H. Coombs, who was employed as an adviser for educational issues in the Kennedy administration and affiliated with the Ford Foundation (Dorn and Ghodsee 2014; Ossenbach and Martínez Boom 2011: 692).
9. "La educación española en el desarrollo económico," *Notas y Documentos* 5 (1962): 6–15, here 6.
10. Ibid., 9.
11. "Informe sobre la reunión de editores de libros de texto organizada por la Unesco," *Notas y Documentos* 1 (1961): 12–18.
12. Further analysis on the origin and evolution of programmed instruction and educational TV in Spain can be found in González-Delgado and Groves (2017) and Ossenbach and Groves (2013).
13. "En relación con la enseñanza programada," *Notas y Documentos* 5 (1962): 5–41.
14. For further explanation of the evolution of educational TV in UNESCO and its relationship with the theories of modernization, see Lindo-Fuentes (2009) and chapter 7.
15. "Alas Pedagógicas," *Atlántico: Revista de Cultura Contemporánea* 24 (1963): 21–23.
16. We thank Óscar Martín García for sharing his insights on this particular topic and on the role played by the USIA and the magazines *Atlántico* and *Facetas* in Spain.
17. "Cuestionarios Nacionales de Enseñanza Primaria," *Vida Escolar* 70–71 (1965): 2–96, here 2.
18. Ibid., 5.
19. According to Jacques Bousquet (1972: 155), a UNESCO technician specialized in educational TV who since the creation of CENIDE also ran the Advance Training Program (ATP) in Educational Planning and Management in Spain, "The CENIDE/ICE network has received, since

October 1969, the technical assistance of UNESCO under the Special Fund of the United Nations."

20. "Country and Intercountry Programming. UNDP assistance requested by the Goverment of Spain," p. 15. ACNEC-UNESCO, Box 75/Carpetilla 1.
21. "Decreto de creación del CENIDE": 35, Box 75/1, ACNEC-UNESCO.
22. "Formación y perfeccionamiento del profesorado de los ICEs," Box 61765, Records of CENIDE, 1969–1976, Archivo Central de la Secretaría de Estado de Educación (ACSEE).
23. "Carta de J. Comiran a Monsieur Bousquet Secretaría General Técnica. Ministerio de Educación," Box 61765, Records of CENIDE, 1969–1976, ACSEE.
24. "Informe sobre el Sistema EVR y sus posibilidades para la enseñanza. Estrictamente confidencial," Box 61765, Records of CENIDE, 1969–1976, ACSEE.
25. "Carta de J. Bousquet ATP CENIDE vía J. Manuel Paredes Secretario General CENIDE a Ilmo. Sr. Pedro Segú y Martín Secretario General Técnico del MEC," 30 March 1970, Box 61765, Records of CENIDE, 1969–1976, ACSEE.
26. "Informe de J. Bousquet, ATP UNESCO a Ilmo. Sr. Secretario Denetal Técnico. Asunto: Circuito cerrado de TV para la formación del profesorado en el CENIDE. Anexo IV," 1971, Box 61765, Records of CENIDE, 1969–1976, ACSEE.
27. "Memoria e Informe sobre el Bachillerato Radiofónico y el Instituto a Distancia," Madrid, September 1970, Box 61728, Records of CENIDE, 1969–1976, ACSEE.
28. "SPA.019.4.93: Plan de Operaciones España—Centro Nacional de Investigaciones para el desarrollo de la Educación," Box 61709, año: 1972–1979, "Proyectos y programas de la UNESCO," Archivo General de la Administración.
29. "Asistencia al Centro Nacional de Investigaciones para el Desarrollo de la Educación, Madrid. (Proyecto SPANED-19). Informe de la Misión de Inspección," September 1972: 8, Box 75/1, ACNEC-UNESCO.
30. Ibid., 19
31. Ibid., 23.

References

Adas, Michael. 2009. *Dominance by Design: Technological Imperatives and America`s Civilizing Mission*. Cambridge, MA: Belknap Press.

Alacevich, Michele. 2011. "The World Bank and the Politics of Productivity: The Debate on Economic Growth, Poverty, and Living Standards in the 1950s." *Journal of Global History* 6 (1): 53–74.

Alberti, Bernardo, Luis Martínez, José Manuel Paredes, Ángeles Quiralte, Emilia Ruiz, and Pilar Torres. 1970. "El CENIDE y las investigaciones sobre educación." *Revista de Educación* 209: 5–14.

Altbach, Philip G. 1991. "Trends in Comparative Education." *Comparative Education Review* 35 (3): 491–507.

Álvaro Moya, Adoración. 2011. "Guerra Fría y formación de capital humano durante el franquismo. Un balance sobre el programa estadounidense de ayuda técnica (1953–1963)." *Historia del Presente* 17: 13–25.

Andreasen, Karen Egedal, and Christian Ydesen. 2015. "Educating for Peace: The Role and Impact of International Organizations in Interwar and Post-War Dabish School Experiments, 1918–1975." *Nordic Journal of Educational History* 2 (2): 3–25.

Bergvall, Pär, and Nahum Joel. 1964. *UNESCO Pilot Project for New Methods and Techniques in Physics Teaching in Latin America*. Paris: UNESCO.

Boel, Jens. 2016. "UNESCO's Fundamental Education Program, 1946–1958: Vision, Actions and Impact." In Duedahl 2016: 153–167.

Bousquet, Jacques. 1958. "Televisión y educación." *Revista de Educación* 73: 35–38.

——. 1972. "El Centro Nacional de Investigaciones para el Desarrollo de la Educación." *Perspectivas* 0: 155–159.

Brzezinski, Zbigniew. 1969. "La edad tecnetrónica." *Facetas* 2 (4): 38–52.

Cassirer, Henry R. 1966. "Television for the Pre-school Child." *The UNESCO Courier* 19: 4–11.

Cassirer, Henry R., and T. S. Duckmanton. 1960. "Educational Television in Pakistan." Report of a UNESCO mission, 4–23 October. WS/0961.113.

——. 1961. "Educational Television in Israel." Report of a UNESCO mission, 31 May–27 June.

Cavalieri, Elena. 2014. *España y el FMI: La integración de la economía española en el sistema monetario internacional, 1943–1959*. Madrid: Banco de España.

Cebrián Villar, Mar. 2004. "La Regulación Industrial y la transferencia Internacional de Tecnología e España (1959–1973)." *Investigaciones de Historia Económica* 3: 11–42.

Cebrián Villar, Mar, and Santiago M. López. 2016. "La dimensión internacional de las transformaciones en la política científica y el cambio técnico." In Delgado Gómez-Escalonilla et al. 2016: 233–261.

Centro de Documentación y Orientación Didáctica de Enseñanza Primaria (CEDODEP). 1968a. *El Centro de Documentación y Orientación Didáctica: Diez años de actividades (1958–1968)*. Madrid: Ministério da Educação e Ciência.

——. 1968b. *Ideas en orden a la introducción en la escuela de las técnicas audiovisuales*. Madrid: CEDODEP.

——. 1969. *Tecnología audiovisual y educación*. Madrid: CEDODEP.

CRE (Comisión de Radiotelevisión Educativa). 1968. *La Televisión Escolar en España, 1967–1968*. Madrid: RTVE and Dirección de Enseñanza Primaria.

De la Orden, Arturo. 1964. "La enseñanza programada." *Vida escolar* 63–64: 15–17.

De Puelles Benítez, Manuel. 2009. *Modernidad, republicanismo y democracia: Una historia de la educación en España, 1898–2008*. Valencia: Tirant lo Blanch.

Delgado Gómez-Escalonilla, Lorenzo. 2015. "Modernizadores y tecnócratas: Estados Unidos ante la política educativa y científica de la España del Desarrollo." *Historia y Política* 34: 113–146.
——. 2016. "Estados Unidos, ¿Soporte del franquismo o germen de la democracia?" In Delgado Gómez-Escalonilla et al. 2016: 263–307.
Delgado Gómez-Escalonilla, Lorenzo, Ricardo Martín de la Guardia, and Rosa Pardo Sanz, eds. 2016. *La apertura internacional de España: Entre el franquismo y la democracia (1953–1986)*. Madrid: Sílex.
Dorn, Charles, and Kristen Ghodsee. 2012. "The Cold War Politicization of Literacy: Communism, UNESCO, and the World Bank." *Diplomatic History* 36 (2): 373–398.
Duedahl, Poul. 2016. *The History of UNESCO: Global Actions and Impacts*. London: Palgrave Macmillan.
Fernández Huerta, José. 1963. "Textos didácticos revolucionarios." *Revista de Educación* 54 (157): 57–64.
——. 1964. "Enseñanza programada." In *Diccionario de Pedagogía Labor*, vol. 1, ed. Víctor García Hoz, 346–347. Madrid: Editorial Labor.
——. 1965. "Técnicas de enseñanza y organización." *Revista Española de Pedagogía* 23 (91–92): 541–549.
Fuchs, Eckhardt. 2014. "History of Education beyond the Nation? Trends in Historical and Educational Scholarship." In *Connecting Histories of Education: Transnational and Cross-Cultural Exchanges on (Post)Colonial Education*, ed. Barnita Bagchi, Eckhardt Fuchs, and Kate Rousmaniere, 11–26. New York: Berghahn Books.
García Hoz, Víctor. 1957. "Las lecturas del maestro en función de su tarea." *Bordón* 70: 367–376.
Giton, Céline. 2016. "Weapons of Mass Distribution: UNESCO and the Impact of Books." In Duedahl 2016: 49–72.
González-Delgado, Mariano, and Tamar Groves. 2016. "Influencias extranjeras en la formación continua del profesorado en el segundo franquismo." In *La formación del profesorado: Nuevos enfoques desde la teoría y la historia de la educación*, ed. Miguel Ángel Martín-Sánchez and Tamar Groves, 51–64. Salamanca: FarenHouse.
——. 2017. "La enseñanza programada, la UNESCO y los intentos por modificar el currículum en la España desarrollista (1962–1974)." *Espacio, Tiempo y Educación* 4 (2): 73–100.
Goodman, Joyce, Gary McCulloch, and William Richardson. 2009. "'Empires Overseas' and 'Empires at Home': Postcolonial and Transnational Perspectives on Social Change in the History of Education." *Paedagogica Historica* 45 (6): 695–706.
Gray, William S. 1957. *La enseñanza de la lectura y la escritura*. Paris: UNESCO.
Green, Edward J., and James Hartley. 1963. "Final Report on UNESCO/UNRWA Ramallah Workshop on Programmed Instruction." Ramallah, Jordan, 22 June–1 August. WS/1163.35.
Groves, Tamar, and Mariano González-Delgado. 2017. "Chocando contra la cultura escolar: Las paradojas de la importación pedagógica en la España

del desarrollismo." In *El factor internacional en la modernización educativa, científica y militar de España*, ed. Lorenzo Delgado Gómez-Escalonilla, Pablo León Aguinaga, Óscar J. Martín García, and Esther M. Sánchez, 129–151. Alicante: Biblioteca Virtual Miguel de Cervantes.

Jones, Phillip W., and David Coleman. 2005. *The United Nations and Education Multilateralism, Development and Globalization*. New York: Routledge.

Kulnazarova, Aigul, and Christian Ydesen. 2017. "The Nature and Methodology of UNESCO's Educational Campaigns for International Understanding." In *UNESCO without Borders: Educational Campaigns for International Understanding*, ed. Augil Kulnazarova and Christian Ydesen, 3–12. London: Routledge.

Komoski, P. Kenneth, and H. W. Gustafson. 1963. "Final Technical Report to UNESCO and the Ford Foundation on the Programmed Instruction." Institute of Education, University of Ibadan, Nigeria, 12 July–23 August. WS/0963.36/ED.

Lauwerys, Joseph A. 1953. *History Textbooks and International Understanding: Towards World Understanding*. Paris: UNESCO.

——. 1957. "Definición y finalidad de la lectura de carácter profesional." *Bordón: Revista de pedagogía* 70: 377–386.

León-Aguinaga, Pablo. 2012. "Faith in the USA: El mensaje de la diplomacia pública americana en España, 1948–1960." In *Guerra Fría y propaganda: Estados Unidos y su cruzada cultural en Europa y América Latina*, ed. Antonio Niño and José A. Montero, 197–234. Madrid: Biblioteca Nueva.

Lindo-Fuentes, Héctor. 2009. "Educational Television in El Salvador and Modernisation Theory." *Journal of Latin American Studies* 41 (4): 757–92.

Lindo-Fuentes, Héctor, and Erik Ching. 2012. *Modernizing Minds in El Salvador: Education Reform and the Cold War, 1960–1980*. Albuquerque: University of New Mexico Press.

Lorente, Gabriel. 1964. "Un nuevo auxiliar del maestro: Las máquinas de enseñar." *Escuela Española* 1289: 1199–1201.

Lumsdaine, Arthur A. 1962. "Máquinas de enseñar y enseñanza programada." In *Nuevos métodos y técnicas de educación*, 32–37. Paris: UNESCO.

Maíllo, Adolfo. 1953. "Los problemas de la Educación popular." *Revista de Educación* 4 (11): 256–261.

——. 1954. "Objetivos y métodos de la educación fundamental." *Revista de Educación* 8 (22): 91–94.

——. 1960. "Los centros de Orientación Didáctica y el perfeccionamiento de los maestros en ejercicio." In *Proyecto Principal de Educación UNESCO / América Latina Boletín Trimestral* vol. 2 (7): 89–104.

Mainer, Juan. 2009. *La forja de un campo profesional: Pedagogía y didáctica de las Ciencias Sociales en España (1900–1970)*. Madrid: CSIC.

Martín Izquierdo, Héctor. 1991. *Educación y desarrollo económico en España*. Valladolid: Secretariado de Publicaciones de la Universidad.

Martín García, Óscar J. 2015. "Una utopía secular. La teoría de la modernización y la política exterior estadounidense en la Guerra Fría." *Historia y Política* 34: 27–52.

MEN-OECD. 1963. *Las necesidades de educación y el desarrollo económico-social*. Madrid: Ministerio de Educación Nacional and OECD.

Monclús, Antonio, and Carmen Saban. 1997. *La escuela global: La educación y la comunicación a lo largo de la historia de la Unesco*. Mexico City: Fondo de Cultura Económica.

Moody, Zoe 2014. "Transnational Treaties on Children's Rights: Norm Building and Circulation in Twentieth Century." *Paedagogica Historica* 50 (1–2): 151–164.

Moreno, Juan M. 1963. "Enseñanza Programada ¿Qué es la programmed instruction?" *Bordón* 115: 130–152.

——. 1966a. "Sentido profundo del Programa Escolar." *Bordón* 142: 227–241.

——. 1966b. *Presentación de la enseñanza programada*. Madrid: CEDODEP.

——. 1967. *Organización escolar: Bases para la construcción de su programa*. Madrid: CEDODEP.

Mundy, Karen. 2006. "The Evolution of Educational Multilateralism from 1945 to 2005." In *Bildung International: Historische Perspektiven und aktuelle Entwicklungen*, ed. Eckhardt Fuchs, 181–199. Würzburg: Ergon-Verl.

Navarro Higueras, Juan, ed. 1967. *Los medios audiovisuales en la escuela*. Madrid: CEDODEP.

Ögren, Gustaf. 1958. "La enseñanza del inglés por la radio en las escuelas elementales suecas." *Bordón* 78–79: 425–436.

Oliveros, Ángel. 1978. *XXV años de la Comisión Nacional Española de Cooperación con la UNESCO*. Madrid: UNESCO and Ministério da Educação e Ciência.

Omolewa, Michael. 2007. "UNESCO as a Network." *Paedagogica Historica* 43 (2): 211–221.

Ossenbach, G., and T. Groves. 2013. "Entre la mitificación y la crítica: el cine y los medios audiovisuales en la escuela primaria en España en el tardofranquismo y la transición, 1958–1982." *Cahiers de civilisation espagnole con contemporaine* 11: 1–12.

Ossenbach, Gabriela, and Alberto Martínez Boom. 2011. "Itineraries of the Discourses on Development and Education in Spain and Latin America (circa 1950–1970)." *Paedagogica Historica* 47 (5): 679–700.

Perdomo García, José. 1952. "La cooperación intelectual en la Unesco." *Revista de Educación* 2 (5): 167–175.

Phillips, David, and Kimberly Ochs. 2004. "Researching Policy Borrowing: Some Methodological Challenges in Comparative Education." *British Educational Research Journal* 30 (6): 773–84.

Popkewitz, Thomas S., ed. 2013. *Rethinking the History of Education: Transnational Perspectives on Its Questions, Methods, and Knowledge*. New York: Palgrave Macmillan.

Pozo Andrés, María del Mar del, and J. F. A. Braster. 2006. "The Reinvention of the New Education Movement in the Franco Dictatorship (Spain, 1936–1976)." *Paedagogica Historica* 42 (1–2): 109–126.

Puig Raposo, Núria, and Adoración Álvaro Moya. 2004. "La guerra fría y los empresarios españoles: la articulación de los intereses económicos de

Estados Unidos en España, 1950–1975." *Revista de Historia Económica: Journal of Iberian and Latin American Economic History* 22 (2): 387–424.
Reid, John T. 1956. "Presentación." *Atlántico: Revista de Cultura Contemporánea* 1: 5–6.
Ressing, Luis. 1962. "La preparación para las enseñanzas técnicas y el desarrollo económico." *Revista de Educación* 143: 111–113.
Roselló, Pedro. 1961. "La teoría de las corrientes educativas." *Notas y Documentos* 1: 19–25.
Schramm, Wilbur. 1967. "Educational Television in American Samoa." In *Case Studies for Planners*, 11–57. Paris: UNESCO.
Sivesind, Kirsten, and Ninni Wahlström. 2016. "Curriculum on the European Policy Agenda: Global Transitions and Learning Outcomes from Transnational and National Points of View." *European Educational Research Journal* 15 (3): 271–278.
Sivesind, Kirsten, Azita Afsar, and Kari E. Bachmann. 2016. "Transnational Policy Transfer over Three Curriculum Reforms in Finland: The Constructions of Conditional and Purposive Programs (1994–2016)." *European Educational Research Journal* 15 (3): 345–365.
Tena Artigas, Joaquín. 1961. "Economía y Educación." *Notas y Documentos* 1: 3–8.
Terrón, Aida. 2013. "La profesionalización del magisterio en el tecnofranquismo: Entre los valores eternos y la ciencia verdadera." *Innovación educativa* 23: 25–45.
——. 2015. "La educación sanitaria escolar, una propuesta curricular importada para la escuela española del desarrollismo." *Archivos Analíticos de Políticas Educativas* 23 (19): 1–17.
Terrón, Aida, Josep M. Comelles, and Enrique Perdiguero-Gil. 2017. "Schools and Health Education in Spain during the Dictatorship of General Franco (1939–1975)." *History of Education Review* 46 (2): 208–223.
Turner, Clair E. 1966. *Planning for Health Education in Schools*. London: Longman and UNESCO.
Tusquets, Juan. 1969. *Teoría y práctica de la Pedagogía Comparada*. Madrid: Magisterio Español.
UNESCO. 1962. "Nuevos métodos y técnicas en educación." *Notas y Documentos* 4: 3–13.
Ventosa, José M. 1965. "Enseñanza programada." *Educadores* 35: 951–956.
Von Recum, Hasso. 1963. "Conference on the Methodology of Human Resources Formation in Development Programmes: Rationalization of Teaching and Learning." Frascati, 24–28 June. UNESCO/SS/PP/It/10, WS/0663.84.
Watras, Joseph. 2010. "UNESCO's Programme of Fundamental Education, 1946–1959." *History of Education* 39 (2): 219–237.

Chapter 5

Much Ado about Nothing?

Lights and Shadows of the World Bank's Support of Spanish Aspirations to Educational Modernization (1968–1972)

David Corrales Morales

In October 1971, taking advantage of the recent visit to Spain of Robert S. McNamara as president of the World Bank, Joan Farga published an article in a special issue of *Cuadernos para el Diálogo*, in which she denounced the use of this international entity as an instrument of the US government at the service of its "imperialist cause." Reflecting the animosity that prevailed in certain sectors of Spanish society toward the American power, Farga (1971: 15–16) regarded the institution's interest in financing various educational projects as a mere attempt to safeguard the future activity of US private capital, as well as to push the introduction of North American methods in the field of education. This commentary, as well as the context in which it was framed, allows us to pose a series of questions based on the interconnection of issues as wide as the role of various organs in the international sphere, the link between the United States and the World Bank, and outside support for the educational reforms promoted by Spanish technocrats in the late 1960s. These issues have emerged from the relatively new approaches to the history of international relations, which involve examining the Cold War from a transnational and global perspective (Pardo 2015: 148–149).[1]

Amid a climate of growing tension with the Soviet Union, the discourse of modernization "made in the USA" was meant to steer the aspirations for progress that were emerging in some developing countries in the early 1960s and to ensure a liberal order under the domination of the American power. To this end, it was essential to establish cooperative ties with other international actors to support this mission (Ekbladh 2009: 8–9). As a result, several international organizations, many having a notable American presence, adopted some of the scientific objectives and criteria on which this theoretical—and ideological—construction rested. One of those agencies that financed programs to promote economic growth in various regions was the International Bank for Reconstruction and Development, commonly known as the World Bank, where US hegemony was fully manifested in its capital and decision-making capacity.[2] As an illustration of that reality, 27.42 percent of the economic contributions received by member countries in the fiscal year 1970 came from the United States, which retained 24.53 percent of the voting power at that time.[3] The US presence was also evident in the World Bank's staff, most notably with the appointment in 1968 of McNamara, former Secretary of Defense during the presidential terms of John F. Kennedy and Lyndon B. Johnson, as president of the agency.

With this appointment came a significant shift in the policy of the financial institution, characterized primarily by a greater amount of attention paid to poverty in the Third World and by a progressive increase in loans dedicated to the field of education. While in 1968 the bank had allocated $29.1 million to this latter pursuit, in 1972 the figure reached $160 million (UN 1968: 971; 1970: 773). Although increasing the amount of skilled labor in developing countries as a way to boost their economic growth continued to be a priority for the executive directors of the agency, endeavors such as the promotion of experimental approaches to primary education began to take on greater weight. It was a trend that emerged as the result of a new discourse that, following the lead of the United Nations Educational, Scientific and Cultural Organization (UNESCO), regarded the educational sphere as an integrated system whose different elements served a common purpose, for which reason the objectives to be pursued needed to be diversified (Jones 2006: 105–107). However, as happened with the actions of North American and other multilateral actors in Asia and Latin America in the heat of modernization theory, the principles that governed the funded projects collided with the dynamics of the host societies, limiting their impact on more than a few occasions (Staples 2006: 181). While international assistance for educational reforms in countries such as South Korea or Brazil was not exempt from selective adaptation of some of the tendered projects to serve the interests of the current regime, these changes were received in other countries like El Salvador with some skepticism, and even animosity, on the part of the faculty.[4]

Taking as a point of reference the search for an external support to guarantee implementation of the Ley General de Educación (General Education Law—LGE) of 1970 in Spain's period of waning Francoism, this chapter examines the negotiation and subsequent impact of the loans granted by the World Bank in the late 1960s and early 1970s. This research rests on three main axes: the figure of Ricardo Díez-Hochleitner as the principal intermediary between the Francoist government and various international actors, the planning process for the two agreements signed between 1970 and 1972, and the subsequent realization of the financed projects. In this way, it is intended to reflect how the educational framework allowed for the convergence of diverse internal and external forces, each moved by particular interests and circumstances. It was a situation that could lead to unforeseen consequences, as well as to failures associated with the financial assistance received from the World Bank.

Ricardo Díez-Hochleitner: The Role of Informal Governance Diplomacy in the Educational Context

From an educational perspective, the end of World War II gave way to the conception and construction of a complex network comprising a wide range of ideas, spheres of influence, organizational structures, and financial agreements in which numerous countries and international organizations had a stake (Jones 2006: 43). This phenomenon contributed to the establishment of what Phillip W. Jones (2006: 48) has called a "global architecture of education," that is, a nexus of interconnections at the transnational level that exerted a powerful influence on the educational systems of different countries in order to promote their modernization and economic growth. This process resulted mainly from the emergence of an epistemic community made up of numerous actors who shared the same interests, thought patterns, and research techniques in relation to the role of education in the development of society. In this manner, a wide network of experts and advisers emerged, going beyond their own national borders, to disseminate and put into practice the discourses of educational planning worldwide (Ossenbach and Martínez 2011: 686).[5]

Similarly, as a consequence of the growing process of integration of the international system since the late 1960s, reflected especially in the emerging weight acquired by various transnational organizations and multinational corporations, political authorities from different countries began reaching out to notables in the private sphere so that their national policies might benefit from the experience and contacts of these individuals. This tendency gradually increased the existence and effectiveness of a "parallel diplomacy" that sought, not only to increase the presence of some countries outside their own national borders but also to penetrate those spheres of influence where formal diplomacy itself was limited (Knudsen 2016: 11–13). When it comes to classifying this heterogeneous group of intermediate actors under a common label, "informal governance actors" is extremely useful. The coining of this term by the historian Dino Knudsen aims to get past the sense of a dichotomy between state and civil society that has dominated the historiography for decades and, as an alternative, to assume a notion of governance in which decisions such as the promotion of certain initiatives are the result of close collaboration between political authorities and various private actors (2016: 8–9).

The interrelation of these factors proves paramount to examining the search for international support in the implementation of educational reform in Spain, as exemplified by the role played by Ricardo Díez-Hochleitner. After completing his academic training in countries such as the Federal Republic of Germany and the United States, this Spanish economist expanded his ties with the outside world even further in 1956, when he was appointed general coordinator of Colombia's Ministry of Education, with the task of elaborating a five-year plan that would serve as a model for other countries in the region (1992: 263). After this first step, the Organization of American States appointed him coordinator of the First Inter-American Conference on Educational Planning, which took place in Washington in 1958.[6]

Due to the success of these initiatives, Díez-Hochleitner (1988: 482) began working as a specialist in educational planning and administration at UNESCO, where he promoted international conferences, technical assistance missions, and regional institutes for the development of teaching. This work dovetailed with his position as executive secretary of the commission in charge of preparing the "Ten-Year Education Plan for Latin America," a key piece in the program of the Alliance for Progress.[7] In 1963, the World Bank, influenced by the discourses on educational development that were by now permeating various international forums, created a Department of Investment in Education, whose direction would fall to Díez-Hochleitner himself. Throughout these years, the Spanish economist defended the role of education as a fundamental engine for producing the technical leadership required for the transformation of a society. Consistent with this belief, he arranged for funding for educational projects in many regions, linked in each instance to a socioeconomic development plan.[8]

Given the career of this noted individual, it is not surprising that the Francoist government made numerous requests for his support in the development and subsequent implementation of an educational reform with far-reaching national scope. Even so, apart from certain specific collaborations with the Spanish authorities,[9] Díez-Hochleitner's incorporation into the Ministry of Education and Science (MEC) did not occur until May 1968, when he was serving as director of UNESCO's Department of Planning and Financing Education. The insistence of José Luis Villar Palasí, the newly appointed minister, to René Maheu, director general of the international organization, ensured that Díez-Hochleitner would be granted the status of an international civil servant on secondment, eventually occupying the position of Technical General Secretary of the MEC (*ABC*, 24 May 1968, 73).

Because it would require strong external support to realize the aspirations for making the educational system an engine of transformation for the country's growth, Díez-Hochleitner went on to perform the vital function of mediator between the Spanish government and various international actors. This occurred in three different aspects. First was a steady increase of the Spanish presence in congresses and colloquia carried out in different countries, such as the Conference on Educational Planning (Paris, 1968). To this we must add the visits to foreign centers by some representatives of the university environment, many of which were financed by private foundations and international organizations.[10] Second was the holding of major national events that had serious implications for Spanish foreign relations. Beyond the inauguration of the First International Exhibition of Material and Techniques for Teaching (Valencia, 1969), one of the most important initiatives was the creation of the International Committee for the Reform of Education under the presidency of Gabriel Betancourt Mejía, who had held the positions of Minister of Education in Colombia and Deputy Director General of UNESCO.[11] Third, Díez-Hochleitner was instrumental in obtaining funding and technical assistance from multiple sources.

Alongside the Treaty of Friendship and Cooperation signed with the United States in August 1970, which included both a cultural-educational program and a scientific-technical one (see Delgado Gómez-Escalonilla 2010), the search for economic support to facilitate the modernization of Spanish education was a multifaceted venture. "I negotiated with my friends from the Ford Foundation and the United Nations Development Fund," Díez-Hochleitner explained in a letter. "I have also had several contacts with authorities of the French government and the German government."[12] Thus, at the end of the

1960s, a wide range of negotiations was underway for the purpose of acquiring foreign loans. Especially important were those conducted for several years with the World Bank.

Early Contacts with the World Bank and the Financing of a Beginning Education Project

Spain's integration into the international monetary system was strengthened after its admission to the Bretton Woods agencies in 1958, thus favoring a process of economic liberalization supported by the United States. After sending an evaluation mission that same year, the World Bank, chaired at that time by Eugene R. Black, published a report laying out the steps to take in the face of the bank's relations with the Franco regime. Although the mission saw value in the possible financing of future projects, such assistance was to be conditional on the implementation of a stabilization program by the Spanish government.[13] This requirement was achieved a year later with the passage of a set of measures that ended the autarkic policies of the dictatorship.[14] For this reason, at the start of the 1960s, the bank announced the incremental awarding of various loans aimed at sectors such as agriculture, industry, and transport, with the aim of promoting the modernization of Spanish society. In fact, by 1969, a total of $212.2 million had been granted.[15]

Where the educational field was concerned, with the exception of certain attempts in 1963 that were ultimately frustrated, the consultations directed toward a formal request for a first loan did not take hold until 1968, coinciding not only with the modernizing aspirations of Villar Palasí but also with the notable "political turn" of the body under the presidency of McNamara. In June of that year, Díez-Hochleitner suggested to several representatives of the Franco regime the need to obtain financial assistance from the World Bank as a way to ensure the transformation of the education system.[16] To that end, Minister of Finance Juan José Espinosa San Martín made use of the organization's annual meeting to request greater attention to this matter, in light of the initiatives that were being undertaken by the newly appointed Technical General Secretary of the MEC—Díez-Hochleitner—who had performed administrative functions for the World Bank. [17]

These beginning steps were followed by new proposals from the Spanish authorities—some of them coming in tandem with their present and future collaboration with the Inter-American Development Bank and the International Development Association—climaxing in the sending of a fact-finding mission in collaboration with UNESCO between October and November of that year.[18] At the conclusion of the expedition, the delegates issued a report favorably assessing a possible program of external financing focused on the restructuring of the education system.[19] For this reason, at the same time as distribution of the *White Paper on Education* began, the negotiations took on an increased momentum.[20] During the early months of 1969, the Francoist government came to perceive the growing interest that this project was generating in the World Bank, a perception driven home by two significant events. First, the Foreign Financing Office of the Ministry of Finance informed Díez-Hochleitner of the possible loan program approved by the institution for the next five years.[21] Although this information was confidential and was supposed to be officially ignored, the amount of money intended for the Spanish educational field reached $60 million, $10 million of which was earmarked for the first pilot loan. [22]

Then, in May, a visit was received from Munir P. Benjenk, Deputy Director of the bank's Department of Europe, Near East and North Africa, who took advantage of his meeting with Espinosa San Martín to address for the first time one of the most problematic issues of the negotiations: "I explained to the Minister that Spain fell into a special category of countries which posed a difficult problem for the Bank, in view of the fact that they had a relatively high per capita income and were developing very rapidly." Given the reluctance that some of the bank's financial contributors and executive directors felt toward financial assistance to Spain, this special category required the establishment of two necessary conditions for the granting of future credits: exclusive selection of those programs that would stimulate institutional changes, and search for complementary outside financing.[23] Efforts got underway to satisfy that latter point by opening dialogue with a widening range of actors, most notably the Eximbank, UNESCO, and the Organization for Economic Cooperation and Development. In 1969 and 1970, loans obtained in the international market came to $25 million and $76 million, respectively.[24]

Under these circumstances, the green light was given in July for the writing of a memorandum requesting a loan for educational use. The task of writing it fell to Díez-Hochleitner.[25] However, that same summer, the financial institution decided to ask UNESCO to undertake a preliminary mission and make a series of recommendations to the Spanish authorities before the plan was presented in the fall. Although the delegation later reported observing some deficiencies such as the need for greater coordination in the unit responsible for school buildings, as it happened, receipt of these remarks by the technical secretary general of the MEC only occurred after the loan request had been sent to Washington.[26] While the World Bank scrutinized the contents of the report sent before making a final decision on the financing—or not—of the proposed program, two events at the national level had a favorable impact on this first phase of the negotiations: the presentation of the draft of the LGE to the Francoist government, and the appointment of Díez-Hochleitner (1988: 272–276) as undersecretary of the MEC, before the political changes that took place after the "Matesa Case." So, encouraged—among other reasons—by the increasing prominence that one of the former directors of the institution in the MEC was acquiring as promoter of educational modernization, McNamara announced the sending of an evaluation mission, which represented a first step toward the drafting and subsequent signing of an agreement between both parties.[27]

Throughout the first months of 1970, a Spanish delegation led by Díez-Hochleitner met several times with representatives of the financial institution with the intention of drafting a future agreement. One of the concessions obtained by the newly appointed deputy secretary of the MEC was the consent of the international organization that the economic aid would not be conditional on approval of the LGE, which was being debated in the Cortes Generales at that time.[28] Notwithstanding, the difficulties that endangered the finalizing of the agreements were not minor. Proof of this was the Ministry of Finance's desire for the amount of the loan to help to reduce the budgetary allocation earmarked for the educational field for the 1970–1971 biennium. This intended measure aroused suspicions in Villar Palasí and Díez-Hochleitner, who strongly opposed such a decision, considering its application would transmit a bad image abroad and limit the scope of educational reform.[29]

With just a few weeks left before the signing of the agreement, McNamara sent a detailed report to all the executive directors of the entity with the purpose of setting out the terms of the loan, which was to become the first World Bank loan for primary education.[30] The reason for this change from the usual policies of the organization was the experimental nature of the program, as it was a good opportunity to gain experience before implementing similar initiatives in developing countries, as some Francoist leaders had maintained.[31] The pilot project consisted mainly of the construction and equipping of nineteen Educación General Básica (Basic General Education—EGB) centers, twenty secondary schools, and eight Institutos de Ciencias de la Educación (Institutes of Educational Sciences—ICEs), which were especially concentrated in the Galician regions in order to contribute to the so-called Plan Galicia de Educación.[32] To this must be added materials directed to the Centro Nacional de Investigaciones para el Desarrollo de la Educación (National Research Center for the Development of Education—CENIDE), as well as the sending of specialists and technical advisers.[33] Although the agency's contribution exceeded the estimate unofficially made in April 1969, it financed only $12 million of the $24 million budgeted for the implementation of the plan.[34]

Finally, on 30 June 1970, J. Burke Knapp, vice president of the World Bank, and Santiago Argüelles y Armada, Spain's ambassador in Washington, signed the agreement.[35] The form of payment, one of the most hotly debated aspects coming up amid the earnest efforts of the Ministry of Finance to get the loan dispensed quickly, worked favorably to the interests of the financial institution. According to the terms, the Spanish state had to advance all of the expenses of the program, and the world organ, after justifying such payments, would proceed to reimburse half in the form of the loan.[36] It was also agreed to create an administrative unit, associated with the MEC, in charge of managing the educational project to ensure its success. Despite the importance of the event, the grant of credit got scant notice from the Spanish press (*La Vanguardia Española*, 1 July 1970, 22; *Diario de Madrid*, 1 July 1970, 10). The agreement was later mentioned in the *Boletín Oficial del Estado* (BOE) of 23 October, followed by the publication of its general conditions and terms in the *BOE* of 11 November. By then, the LGE had been approved in the 28 July Plenary Session of the Cortes Generales and been sanctioned by Francisco Franco on 4 August. This legislation was born with a lack of economic resources for its implementation, for which reason a new round of negotiations was launched that same year to obtain another loan from the World Bank.

"Two Is Better Than One!" Persuasive Maneuvers for a New Loan from Mr. McNamara

Díez-Hochleitner was well aware of the need and expedience of more outside credit for the modernization of the education system. For this reason, capitalizing on the last round of contacts in Washington before the signing of the first agreement, the MEC undersecretary presented the leaders of the bank with the outline of a second project: "The proposal," he reported, "was very well received . . . and I am very hopeful that, without much delay, we will reach the signing of a new loan agreement in the amount of 60 million dollars." Contrary to the initial optimism that so intoxicated the Spanish authorities, the truth is that numerous problems were endangering this second initiative. In the first place, tensions were rising between the Ministry of Finance and the MEC. The staff of the latter department continued to show their dissatisfaction with the stipulation made earlier that loans obtained from abroad had to be deducted from the investments budgeted in the Development Plan. According to Villar Palasí, this rule was of serious detriment, not only limiting the renovations in the field of education but also putting foreign aid at risk.[37] Second, numerous internal difficulties—especially economic constraints, as well as delays in the launching of certain projects—continued to impede implementation of the LGE, which is why the aid granted in June did not start to show results until the beginning of 1971.[38] A third factor was the reluctance of the president of the World Bank, who warned Laureano López Rodó, minister and commissioner of the Economic and Social Development Plan, that the conditions surrounding the granting of loans to Spain could vary as a result of decisions made by some of the executive directors, who were informed of Spain's ongoing processes of development: "Spain . . . could borrow in capital markets at commercial rates. The Bank was lending at concessionary rates to those countries which could not borrow in the commercial markets."[39]

Faced with this situation, Díez-Hochleitner, in collaboration with several government officials, launched two initiatives to lay the foundations for a second educational agreement. First, taking advantage of the trip made by Prince Juan Carlos de Borbón to the United States in January 1971, they arranged a meeting with McNamara, which was also attended by the deputy secretary of the MEC (*La Vanguardia Española*, 29 January 1971, 6). It should be noted in this connection that the prince, who had been designated successor to Franco in 1969, was valued by the US authorities at that time as the option of change that entailed the least risk for Spain once the dictator died, an aspect of vital importance to preserve their interests in that country (Delgado Gómez-Escalonilla 2016: 295). The harmony between the prince and McNamara played a favorable part days later when Díez-Hochleitner began to discuss the financing of a second project in the offices of the World Bank.[40]

Second, after much persistence, the Spanish leaders managed to get the president of the World Bank to visit the country at the end of April (*ABC*, 18 March 1971, 67).[41] The main purpose of the trip was to learn firsthand the limitations of Spanish development in order to have a better picture of what the future contributions of the organization might be (*Diario Madrid*, 28 April 1971, 13).[42] For three days, McNamara had conferences with various officials of the regime, inspected the Livestock Development Agency in Seville, and met with a large group of Catalan businessmen at Barcelona's Chamber of Commerce, Industry and Navigation.[43] At the conclusion of his eventful itinerary, he did not hold back from showing his admiration for the transformations carried out over the past few years, appraising this process of modernization as a "miracle," brought about by the efforts exerted by Spanish society (*Diario Madrid*, 1 May 1971, 5).[44]

This trip played a decisive role toward the future granting of a second loan for education reform in Spain. Beyond a meeting with the Minister of Education and Science, the World Bank president held meetings with representatives of several universities, who highlighted the main problems to be resolved—especially teacher training.[45] The situations laid bare by some of these personalities contributed to McNamara's reaffirming his willingness to keep on supporting education reform, not only with economic contributions dedicated to the building and equipping of infrastructures but also with greater technical assistance (*La Vanguardia Española*, 2 May 1971, 7). It undoubtedly gave a fresh boost to contacts between both parties, which began to materialize weeks later with the visit of Díez-Hochleitner to the United States and the subsequent sending of an evaluation mission to Spain.[46]

A long negotiation process began in May of that year and lasted until April 1972. During the opening discussions, representatives of the bank and a Spanish delegation—headed once again by the undersecretary of the MEC—reached an agreement of principle whereby one of the demands made from the outset was satisfied: all proposals directly related to the EGB were eliminated from the project.[47] This decision presupposed an important change with respect to the objectives pursued by the World Bank years earlier. This new turnaround was the result of the reluctance that the granting of more economic aid to Spain was continuing to engender among the executive directors of the organization, who were aware of both the growing development of the Spanish nation over recent years and the continuing delays that the pilot project was still experiencing. This way, World Bank approval was made contingent on the selection of a series of specific initiatives aimed at promoting socioeconomic transformations in a short period of time.[48] However, to this explanation must be added another previously stated factor: the close relationship between this banking institution and the US government.

From the start of the 1970s, this connection became increasingly evident from the budget cuts to the bilateral aid programs in the United States that resulted from the military intervention in Vietnam and the inflation that was afflicting the country at that time. Given the criticism being directed at personalities like McNamara himself, President Richard M. Nixon established a commission headed by Rudolf A. Peterson, former president of the Bank of America, to find solutions to this situation.[49] Following the presentation of a final report by that committee, the Nixon administration replaced the current bilateral foreign assistance system with one of a multilateral nature. While it is true that this decision stemmed from an interest in maintaining the support of Congress for international aid, the White House also tried to avoid the resentment of American power that prevailed in some countries.[50] Due to this new orientation, the US contribution to the World Bank increased to $123 million in 1972, which coincided with the gestation period for the second educational loan in Spain (UN 1972: 773).

This factor, as well as its maintenance of technical control of the financial institution, increased the political influence of the United States in this organization at the beginning of the 1970s. It was a situation that favored a convergence of interests and objectives between the US government and the World Bank when promoting the modernization of certain countries (Ekbladh 2009: 253). In the Spanish case, the interest of the bank's directors in those initiatives linked to higher education and vocational training relegated the activities aimed at primary education to a lower-tiered level. In other words, the priority lay in those projects focused on the production of short-term human capital in order to promote structural and political changes in Spanish society, an aspect that was largely linked to the orientation of the US administration toward preparing for Spain's post-Franco era (Delgado Gómez-Escalonilla 2006: 296–297).

With the conditions imposed by the World Bank during the negotiations accepted, J. Burke Knapp, vice president of the agency, and José Vilarasau Salat, representative of Spain's Ministry of Finance, met in Washington on 21 June to sign a second agreement, which was published in the 5 August *BOE* (*ABC*, 23 June 1972, 41). The plan included the construction and equipping of thirty-nine high school institutes, thirty-seven vocational training centers, an agricultural engineering school in Palencia, a polytechnic university in Barcelona, and four ICEs aimed at teacher training, among which were included the facilities of three experimental centers in Seville. Though a higher loan had been initially envisioned, the financial institution granted $50 million of the $152.5 million budgeted for the implementation of that plan, which was scheduled to go into effect on 15 September.[51] However, as had been the case with the pilot program, several difficulties arose that ended up limiting fulfillment of the plan's objectives in the short and medium term.

Between Mirage and Reality: Materialization of the Funded Projects

Despite the strong support given by the World Bank to the modernization of the Spanish educational system, on 25 February 1975, the Franco government pulled out of both agreements. At that time, the bank had only disbursed $472,000 of the $12 million designated by the first agreement, while the amount agreed to in the second one remained frozen.[52] To understand the decision of the Spanish authorities, it is necessary to examine not only those specific difficulties that emerged in the execution of the programs being financed but also an array of side problems that had been present from the start and had managed to hinder the development of those plans.

One of the principal objectives associated with the pilot project was the construction and equipping of primary and secondary schools. Despite the fact that the new buildings intended for construction would not even be adequate to meet the demand for classroom space in Spanish territory, they were earmarked for purely experimental purposes. For example, those EGB centers were intended to offer a curriculum that would include practical fields (agriculture, crafts, industrial arts, etc.) within the compulsory educational program, with the intention that the students, once they had completed their years in school, could choose either extension of their general studies or professional career training.[53]

In any case, the constant haggling over the design and construction of these facilities caused numerous delays, on top of which occurred disputes among political leaders and a lack of coordination among the Spanish departments. In 1972, Manuel Utande, director of the administrative unit responsible for World Bank programs, complained that the Council of Ministers had not yet approved the legal creation of these schools.[54] Although the situation seemed to improve some months later with the launching of an international competition for projects and works, the fact is that at the height of 1975 none of the buildings provided for in either agreement, which would have included high school institutes as well as the much-touted ICEs, had been built.[55]

Where the budget for the CENIDE equipment was concerned, the list of equipment and materials presented by this institution never had the approval of the international organization, which showed substantial reluctance to see a large part of the money allocated to the launching of that project, a computer-assisted teaching program. That unwillingness had been present from the negotiations of the first agreement, on grounds that the viability of this initiative was not entirely guaranteed: "The Bank felt . . . that the proposed computer was too advanced, and that Spain was probably not ready for computer-assisted instruction."[56] Similarly, the obstacles imposed by the Spanish administrative system made it difficult to hire advisers and technical assistants, for which reason an agreement with UNESCO was established: that body would assume that function with the understanding that the Franco regime would subsequently reimburse the amounts advanced plus 14 percent of those amounts for administrative expenses.[57]

Amid that discouraging backdrop, one of the few successful measures derived from the agreements signed was a scholarship plan for foreign students, whose processing and management fell to the International Programs Office of CENIDE. These grants, which were intended for the training of teaching and research staff over a period of four to twelve months, exceeded at that time those paid by the United Nations Development Program or the Ford Foundation.[58] However, notwithstanding the positive impressions shown by some representatives of the World Bank during the initial years of implementation, after the signing of the second loan, some sharp differences emerged regarding the system for selection of beneficiaries: "The balance of candidates under the first project was predominantly in favor of languages and liberal arts studies rather than science and mathematics as we had wished—this, despite our repeated mutual protests."[59] For that reason, after 1972, the financial institution demanded a new administrative procedure to give itself greater control.

In addition to the setbacks that occurred amid the attempts to carry out the two approved projects, the cancelation of the World Bank loans was occasioned by three issues of wide scope. The first involved the deficiencies displayed by the administrative unit responsible for the management of the programs, which was separated from the regular services of the MEC by request of the Spanish leaders. That arrangement isolated this body by preventing efficient coordination with other departments, while impeding some of those departments' more experienced personnel from being assigned to that unit. These problems were exacerbated by the body's constant managerial changes and the suspicions that its work was arousing within the Franco regime itself.[60]

Second, a deceleration was occurring in the implementation of the educational reform program, reflected several different aspects.

Although public investment in education had increased since the early 1960s, in mid-1972, World Bank representatives were complaining this item only occupied 11.2 percent of central government expenditures.[61] For his part, Díez-Hochleitner (1988: 276), exhausted by the fierce internal opposition to the LGE and by the continuous impediments to its application, submitted his resignation as deputy secretary of the MEC that same year and took a new position as consultant to the World Bank. Undoubtedly, that decision contributed at least somewhat to the stagnation of many of the initiatives that were taking place thanks to external support. However, the main factor that led to the increasing paralysis of Spain's educational modernization was the appointment of Cruz Martínez Esteruelas as Minister of Education and Science in 1974. From that moment, rather than the experimental projects agreed to with the financial institution, the MEC chose to give its priority to an ambitious plan for the construction of schools (Mayordomo 1999: 33).

The third factor was the rigidity of the terms that the two agreements came with. As in other regions, the loans of the World Bank were conditioned to compliance with the so-called loan covenants, that is, a series of requirements related to broader issues that had to be met by the borrowers. From an educational perspective, these requirements allowed the international organization to indirectly influence countries' internal policies (Jones 2006: 99). In the Spanish case, these provisions began to be seen in the medium term as obstacles that hindered the flexibility with time, money, and objectives required to implement of the LGE. The interplay of all these elements ultimately led to the termination of the agreements of 1970 and 1972. Years later, the staff of the World Bank examined the failure of these initiatives in a report acknowledging having overestimated the goals to be achieved.[62] As was indicated in its conclusions, the conducting of a prior analysis aimed at evaluating the possible risks in the execution of both programs would have been key to helping zero in on goals more suitable to the circumstances of that moment.

Conclusions

The study of the planning and subsequent materialization of the World Bank's educational loans to Spain reflects a contradictory situation, where the dictatorship blocked the very thing it aspired to through various national impediments that hindered the stated objectives. The role played by Díez-Hochleitner as "informal governance actor" was exemplary of the interest of the Franco regime in gaining international support that, taking advantage of the hegemony of development discourses during those years, helped promote a transformation of the Spanish education system. In contrast to those interpretations that have emphasized the controlling nature of US leadership in the expansion of the principles of modernization, this case shows how the Spanish leaders were the main stakeholders in negotiating the granting of credits. To achieve this purpose, not only were numerous meetings organized with representatives of the World Bank, but the special condition of the country in those years—a midrange position between developed and underdeveloped nations—was used to highlight the benefits that the agency could obtain from it, especially the chance for experimentation for projects that could later be deployed in Latin America.

This last point, alongside the prominence that one of the bank's former directors had acquired in the MEC, aroused the interest of the institution, which decided—though not without certain conditions—to finance a preliminary project aimed at primary education. However, coinciding with an even greater increase in US hegemony in the bank's capital, due to the promotion of a multilateral system of foreign aid from Washington, that interest was modified in the second loan, which instead prioritized higher education and vocational training as ways to promote structural changes in the short and medium term. That shift of focus was not far from the interests of the US government, and its view toward preparation for the post-Franco era.

Despite the apparent success of the negotiations between the two parties, the fact is that by 1975 the two agreements had been canceled. Paradoxically, in light of the efforts made by the Francoist authorities and Díez-Hochleitner, that turn of events was the result of a set of obstacles present in Spain's own institutional structure. The lack of staff preparation, financial constraints, lengthy administrative processes, poor coordination among different departments, ministerial tensions, and different visions for implementation of the LGE all combined to torpedo the achievements. These circumstances ended up reducing both agreements to a mere pipe dream.

Acknowledgments

This work was supported by the Ministry of Economy and Competitiveness of Spain under research project "La modernización del sistema educativo y científico español en su dimensión internacional (1953–1986)" (HAR2014-58685-R).

David Corrales Morales has a bachelor's degree in History and a master's degree in Modern History. Thanks to a dissertation fellowship awarded by the Spanish government, he is now doing his PhD at the Institute of History of the Spanish National Research Council. He has published several articles in peer-reviewed journals such as the *Journal of Transatlantic Studies* or *Revista de Indias*, participating at the same time in international conferences in cities such as Athens, Plymouth, and Copenhagen. In addition, in the past few years, he has been a visiting scholar at Georgetown University (Washington, DC), the Johns Hopkins University SAIS (School of Advanced International Studies) Europe (Bologna), and the Roosevelt Study Center (Middelburg). His research interests include international relations, American cultural transfers, and the history of childhood.

Notes

1. Examples of these new directions include Immerman and Goedde (2013); Kalinovsky and Daigle (2014).
2. For more background on the origins of the World Bank and the subsequent evolution of its policies, see Alacevich (2009); Dorn and Ghodsee (2012); Sharma (2017).
3. International Bank for Reconstruction and Development (IBRD), "Memorandum Relating to the Financial Statements," 30 June 1970, Collection (10) 26.2, Box 54/12502, Archivo General de la Administración (AGA).
4. In addition to the contributions made by Héctor Lindo-Fuentes (chapter 7) and Colin Snider (chapter 8), some recent studies that have an impact on this issue are Lee (2017); Lindo-Fuentes and Ching (2012); Sang Chi (2008).
5. For more detail about the study of "networks" in the history of education, see Fuchs (2007).
6. Ricardo Díez-Hochleitner, "Educational Planning in Latin America," 28 June 1963, Folder 1651574, WB International Bank for Reconstruction and Development / International Development Association (IBRD/IDA), Records of Office of External Affairs (EXT), World Bank Group Archives (WBGA).
7. For an in-depth analysis of this initiative, which was promoted during the presidency of John F. Kennedy, see Taffet (2007).
8. "Statements of the Chief of the Education Division of the World Bank for National Radio of Spain (March 1963)," 9 June 1963, Folder 1651574, WB IBRD/IDA EXT, WBGA; Ricardo Díez-Hochleitner, interview conducted by Lorenzo Delgado Gómez-Escalonilla and David Corrales Morales, 8 June 2017.

9. One of these activities was the conference given at the National School of Public Administration in Alcalá de Henares in 1967 (see Díez-Hochleitner 1967).
10. Letter from Miguel Siguán Soler to Ricardo Díez-Hochleitner, 17 October 1969, Collection (5) 13, Box 55/03688, AGA.
11. "Informe final del Comité de Cooperación Internacional para la Reforma Educativa en España," 1969, Doc. 974, Archivo de la Fundación Nacional Francisco Franco.
12. Letter from Ricardo Díez-Hochleitner to Javier Irastorza, 14 October 1970, Collection (5) 1.18, Box 23307, Folder 1, AGA.
13. IBRD, "Report of Mission to Spain," 15 December 1958, Report EA90, WBGA.
14. For more about the Stabilization Plan of 1959, see Cavalieri (2014); Fuentes (1984); Sánchez (2006).
15. IBRD, "Report and Recommendations of the President to the Executive Directors on a Proposed Loan to Spain for an Education Project," 10 June 1970, Collection (5) 1.18, Box 23307, Folder 2, AGA.
16. Letter from Ricardo Díez-Hochleitner to Javier Irastorza, 14 October 1970.
17. Norman Horsley, "Office Memorandum: Mr. McNamara's Meeting with the Spanish Delegation to the Annual Meeting," 14 October 1968, Records of President Robert S. McNamara (RPRM), Contacts—Member Countries Files (CMCF), Folder 1771181, WB IBRD/IDA 03 EXC-10-4549S, WBGA.
18. By means of a memorandum of understanding signed in 1964 and amended in 1967, and thanks to the efforts of Díez-Hochleitner and Betancourt Mejía, the World Bank and UNESCO agreed to cooperate in the identification, preparation, and supervision of educational projects in different countries. IBRD, "Report of the Executive Directors to the Boards of Governors," 30 June 1970, Collection (10) 26.2, Box 54/12502, AGA.
19. Letter from José Luis Villar Palasí to Fernando María Castiella, 22 March 1969, Box 61727, Archivo Central del Ministerio de Educación (ACME).
20. The *White Paper on Education*, whose official title was *Education in Spain: Bases of an educational policy* (1969), was a critical report produced by the MEC on the Spanish educational system.
21. Confidential note from Fernando Benito Mestre to Ricardo Díez-Hochleitner, 21 April 1969, Collection (5) 1.18, Box 23307, Folder 1, AGA.
22. For practical reasons, all figures are expressed in dollars. While in November 1967 the exchange rate was set at 70 pesetas per dollar, in December 1971 it was established at 64.47.
23. Munir P. Benjenk, "Office Memorandum: Visit to Spain—Discussions with Finance Minister," 26 June 1969, RPRM, CMCF, Folder 1771181, WB IBRD/IDA 03 EXC-10-4549S, WBGA.
24. IBRD, "Report and Recommendation of the President to the Executive Directors on a Proposed Loan to Spain for a Second Education Project," 17 May 1972, Report P-1072, WBGA.

25. "Educational Project," July 1969, Collection (5) 1.18, Box 23310, Folder 47, AGA.
26. Letter from M. Dino Carelli to Ricardo Díez-Hochleitner, 7 August 1969, Collection (5) 1.18, Box 23307, Folder 1, AGA.
27. "Misiones previas (Previous missions)," 1970, Collection (5) 1.18, Box 23307, Folder 1, AGA.
28. Despite this concession, this loan could only take effect subject to the approval of the General Education Law by Franco.
29. Note from Juan Manuel Ruigómez Iza to Ricardo Díez-Hochleitner, 6 April 1970, Collection (5) 1.18, Box 23307, Folder 1 AGA.
30. IBRD, "Report and Recommendations of the President," 10 June 1970.
31. "Project Performance Audit Report: Spain First and Second Education Projects," 30 June 1977, Report 1657, WBGA.
32. Within the framework of educational reform, Educación General Básica was the name given to the compulsory primary school cycle, which consisted of eight courses of schooling that children ages six to thirteen had to complete. On the other hand, the Institutos de Ciencias de la Educación were oriented to educational research and to the training of teachers bound for the second cycle of EGB—sixth, seventh, and eighth grade—or to secondary education.
33. The CENIDE, created in 1969, was in charge of coordinating the educational research of the ICEs.
34. IBRD, "Report and Recommendations of the President," 10 June 1970.
35. The loan, at an annual interest rate of 7 percent, had a repayment term of twenty years, with a grace period of five. The semiannual installments for repayment of the loan were to begin on 15 August 1975 and end in 1990. "Loan Agreement (Education Project) between Spain and IBRD," 30 June 1970, Legal ISC Files, Loan 699 SP, WBGA; "World Bank Press Release No. 70/44," 1 July 1970, Collection (10) 26.2, Box 54/12502, AGA.
36. Report on the quantitative expansion of the education system, 1971, Folder 61765, ACME.
37. Letter from José Luis Villar Palasí to Laureano López Rodó, 6 November 1970, Collection (5) 1.18, Box 23307, Folder 1, AGA. Despite the importance given to education at the start, the Third Development Plan (1972–1975) ended up not fulfilling its goals in that area (see Ortega 1992).
38. Dieter Hartwich, "Office Memorandum: Spain—Your Meeting with Don Laureano López-Rodó," 13 November 1970, RPRM, CMCF, Folder 1771181, WB IBRD/IDA 03 EXC-10-4549S, WBGA.
39. Norman Horsley, "Memorandum for the Record: Meeting of the Spanish Minister of Planning with Mr. McNamara—Bank Lending Program for Spain," 14 January 1971, RPRM, CMCF, Folder 1771181, WB IBRD/IDA 03 EXC-10-4549S, WBGA.
40. Munir P. Benjenk, "Office Memorandum: Your Meeting with Don Juan Carlos de Borbón," 26 January 1971, RPRM, CMCF, Folder 1771181, WB IBRD/IDA 03 EXC-10-4549S, WBGA.

41. Robert S. McNamara to Alberto Monreal Luque, 8 March 1971, RPRM, Chronological Files, Folder 1771877, WB IBRD/IDA 03 EXC-10-4541S, WBGA.
42. Robert S. McNamara, "Remarks on Arrival in Spain," 27 April 1971, RPRM, Statements, Speeches and Interviews (SSI), Folder 1772440, WB IBRD/IDA 03 EXC-10-4547S, WBGA.
43. "Mr. McNamara's Visit to Spain," April 1971, RPRM, Travel Briefings, Folder 1772581, WB IBRD/IDA 03 EXC-10-4540S, WBGA.
44. "Toast to Minister of Finance of Spain," 30 April 1971, RPRM, SSI, Folder 1772440, WB IBRD/IDA 03 EXC-10-4547S, WBGA.
45. "McNamara's Visit to Spain: Summary of Discussions," May 1971, RPRM, CMCF, Folder 1771181, WB IBRD/IDA 03 EXC-10-4549S, WBGA.
46. O. H. Calika, "Spain: Second Education Project," 27 May 1971, RPRM, CMCF, Folder 1771181, WB IBRD/IDA 03 EXC-10-4549S, WBGA.
47. Note from the Secretary of the World Bank on the status of the negotiations regarding the second loan, 17 April 1972, Collection (5) 1.18, Box 23312, Folder 1, AGA.
48. Munir P. Benjenk, "Office Memorandum: Spain—Your Meeting with Don Enrique Fontana Codina," 9 March 1971, RPRM, CMCF, Folder 1771181, WB IBRD/IDA 03 EXC-10-4549S, WBGA.
49. Robert S. McNamara, "Address to the Conference on International Economic Development," 20 February 1970, Collection (10) 26.2, Box 54/12502, AGA.
50. "The White House to the Congress of the United States: Foreign Assistance for the Seventies," 15 September 1970; and Letter from Aurelio Valls to Gregorio López-Bravo, 25 September 1970, Collection (10) 26.2, Box 54/12685, Folder 327 (73), AGA.
51. IBRD, "Report and Recommendations of the President," 17 May 1972; Cost of project, 30 March 1972, Collection (5) 1.18, Box 23312, Folder 5, AGA. The loan, whose annual interest rate was 7.25 percent, had a repayment term of 20 years, with a grace period of five. The semiannual installments for repayment were to begin on 15 August 1977, and end on 15 February 1992.
52. "Project Performance Audit Report," 30 June 1977.
53. "World Bank Press Release," 1 July 1970.
54. Letter from Manuel Utande to the General Directorate of Educational Planning, 8 May 1972, Collection (5) 1.18, Box 23307, Folder 5, AGA.
55. Chronology of projects and works, January 1974, Collection (5) 1.18, Box 23308, Folder 18, AGA.
56. "Project Performance Audit Report," 30 June 1977.
57. Final report on technical assistance, February 1974, Collection (5) 1.18, Box 23308, Folder 22, AGA. It is striking that one of the most valued aspects of the educational program with the World Bank was technical assistance. Bank leaders reiterated on numerous occasions the quality of the specialists, the effectiveness of UNESCO's intervention, and the significant help being given for the objectives pursued.

58. Between 1971 and 1974, CENIDE had granted 122 scholarships, of which 53 had been financed by the World Bank. "Becas CENIDE para la formación de personal en el extranjero" (CENIDE Scholarships for the training of personnel abroad)," 1974, Collection (5) 1.18, Box 23315, Folder 24, AGA.
59. Letter from J. J. Stewart to Manuel Utande, 13 December 1972, Collection (5) 1.18, Box 23315, Folder 24, AGA.
60. "Project Performance Audit Report," 30 June 1977.
61. IBRD, "Report and Recommendations of the President," 17 May 1972.
62. "Project Performance Audit Report," 30 June 1977.

References

Alacevich, Michele. 2009. *The Political Economy of the World Bank: The Early Years*. Stanford. CA: Stanford University Press.

Cavalieri, Elena. 2014. *España y el FMI: La integración de la economía española en el sistema monetario internacional, 1943–59*. Madrid: Banco de España.

Delgado Gómez-Escalonilla, Lorenzo. 2010. "'After Franco, What?' La diplomacia pública de Estados Unidos y la preparación del posfranquismo." In *Claves internacionales en la Transición española*, ed. Óscar J. Martín García and Manuel Ortiz Heras, 99–127. Madrid: Catarata.

——. 2016. "Estados Unidos ¿Soporte del franquismo o germen de la democracia?" In *La apertura internacional de España: Entre el franquismo y la democracia, 1953–1986*, ed. Lorenzo Delgado Gómez-Escalonilla, Ricardo Martín de la Guardia, and Rosa Pardo Sanz, 263–307. Madrid: Sílex.

Díez-Hochleitner, Ricardo. 1967. *Política y financiación de la educación*. Alcalá de Henares: Escuela Nacional de Administración Pública.

——. 1988. "La reforma educativa de 1970: Su pequeña historia." In *Simposium internacional sobre Educación e Ilustración*, ed. Ulrich Herrmann Tubinga, 477–498. Madrid: Centro de Publicaciones del Ministerio de Educación y Ciencia.

——. 1992. "La reforma educativa de la Ley General de Educación de 1970: Datos para una crónica." *Revista de Educación* S1: 261–278.

Dorn, Charles, and Kristen Ghodsee. 2012. "The Cold War Politicization of Literacy: Communism, UNESCO, and the World Bank." *Diplomatic History* 36 (2): 373–398.

Ekbladh, David. 2009. *The Great American Mission: Modernization and the Construction of an American World Order*. Princeton, NJ: Princeton University Press.

Farga, Joan. 1971. "Miseria y dependencia de la investigación científica en España." *Cuadernos para el diálogo* 27: 11–16.

Fuchs, Eckardt. 2007. "Networks and the History of Education." *Paedagogica Historica* 43 (2): 185–97.

Fuentes Quintana, Enrique. 1984. "El Plan Nacional de Estabilización Económica de 1959, veinticinco años después." *Información Comercial Española* 612–613: 25–40.
Immerman, Richard H., and Petra Goedde, eds. 2013. *The Oxford Handbook of the Cold War*. Oxford: Oxford University Press.
Jones, Phillip W. 2006. *Education, Poverty and the World Bank*. New York: Sense Publishers.
Kalinovsky, Artemy M., and Craig Daigle, eds. 2014. *The Routledge Handbook of the Cold War*. London: Routledge.
Knudsen, Dino. 2016. *The Trilateral Commission and Global Governance: Informal Elite Diplomacy, 1972–82*. New York: Routledge.
Lee, Chee Hye. 2017. "The Way to Modernization: Language Ideologies and the Peace Corps English Education in Korea." *Education and Society* 35 (1): 63-80.
Lindo-Fuentes, H., and E. Ching. 2012. *Modernizing Minds in El Salvador: Education Reform and the Cold War, 1960-80*. Albuquerque: University of New Mexico Press.
Mayordomo, Alejandro. 1999. "Aproximación a tiempos y enfoques de la política educativa." In *Estudios sobre la política educativa durante el franquismo*, ed. Alejandro Mayordomo, 7–39. Valencia: Universidad de Valencia.
Ortega, Félix. 1992. "Las ideologías de la Reforma Educativa de 1970." *Revista de Educación* 1: 40–41.
Ossenbach, Gabriela, and Alberto Martínez Boom. 2011. "Itineraries of the Discourses on Development and Education in Spain and Latin America (circa 1950–70)." *Paedagogica Historica* 47 (5): 679–700.
Pardo Sanz, Rosa. 2015. "Las dictaduras ibéricas y el aliado americano en clave de modernización, 1945–75." *Historia y política* 34: 147–179.
Sánchez, Esther M. 2006. *Rumbo al Sur: Francia y la España del desarrollo, 1958–69*. Madrid: CSIC.
Sang Chi, James. 2008. "Teaching Korea: Modernization, Model Minorities, and American Internationalism in the Cold War Era." Ph.D. dissertation. Berkeley: University of California.
Sharma, Patrick Allan. 2017. *Robert McNamara's Other War: The World Bank and International Development*. Philadelphia: University of Pennsylvania Press.
Staples, Amy L. S. 2006. *The Birth of Development: How the World Bank, Food and Agriculture Organization, and World Health Organization Changed the World, 1945–65*. Kent, OH: Kent State University Press.
Taffet, Jeffrey F. 2007. *Foreign Aid as Foreign Policy: The Alliance for Progress in Latin America*. New York: Routledge.
UN (United Nations). 1968. *Yearbook of the United Nations, Vol. 22*. New York: UN Office of Public Information.
——. 1970. *Yearbook of the United Nations, Vol. 24*. New York: UN Office of Public Information.
——. 1972. *Yearbook of the United Nations, Vol. 26*. New York: UN Office of Public Information.

Chapter 6

US Foreign Policy toward Spanish Students

Youth Diplomacy, Modernization, and Educational Reform

Óscar J. Martín García

In the past two decades, a research body has presented the Cold War as a "clash of ideas and cultures as much as a military and strategic conflict" (Westad 2010: 13). From the beginning of this century, scholars in the fields of diplomatic and international history have contended that the bipolar struggle was also an ideological, psychological, and cultural competition for the hearts and minds of international public opinion (Gienow-Hecht 2010). Under the framework of bipolar cultural rivalry, the Americans and the Soviets both strove to channel the idealism and transformative potential that the youth possessed into their own political agendas. Leaders in Washington and Moscow felt that gaining the support and understanding of youth leaders represented an important resource in the East-West battle to steer historical change (Honeck and Rosenberg 2014: 233–239).

Drawing on this approach, different works on the cultural Cold War have shown that in the 1950s, the United States and the Soviet Union engaged in an intense ideological and propagandistic battle to control international organizations of young people and students (Kotek 1996; Koivunen 2017; Krekola and Mikkonen 2011; Paget 2003; Peacock 2012). Likewise, in recent years, growing historiographical interest in the "global sixties" has brought about the appearance of new work on youth and student revolts in Third World nations, in authoritarian contexts, and in countries at an intermediate stage of development (Brazinsky 2007; Christiansen and Scarlett 2013; Jian et al. 2018; Martín García 2018; Scott-Smith 2011; Slobodian 2011). Building on this bibliography, the objective of this chapter is to analyze from the point of view of the cultural Cold War the relationship between the United States and Spanish students during the 1960s and 1970s.

Focusing on the Spanish case, this chapter deals with the US diplomacy aimed at attracting youth and student leaders who might have a voice in the political future of their (developing) countries. The important role played by students in the social upheavals and anti-American demonstrations occurring in various (semi-)peripheral countries in the late 1950s and early 1960s increased US interest in the young leaders of such nations. In 1958, the tour of US Vice President Richard Nixon of various Latin American countries was received with strong acts of protest organized by youths and students. The revision of the bilateral treaty for defense between the United States and Japan in 1960 sparked vigorous student opposition in the Asian country. At the same time, students from South Korea carried out powerful demonstrations against US-backed President Syngman Rhee (Koda 2018: 402–403). Moreover, at the beginning of the 1960s the US National Security Council detected a "pervasive political malaise in Spain," especially among the younger generation.[1] The strategists of the US Department of State believed the political instability and student protests in these countries were because of the profound social transformation that was occurring in the developing world. The rising unrest among young people and students in various (semi-)peripheral nations was perceived by the US Foreign Service as the result of the "underlying economic, social and political problems which rapid social change and the thrust of national development force upon them."[2] In the same vein, US diplomats thought a new generation of leaders appeared to be emerging in the Third World in the context of accelerated and chaotic transformations and political turmoil that "accompanies the process of modernization."[3]

Such a situation of untimely development, political instability, and social dislocation could, as Roger Hilsman (Director of Intelligence and Research of the State Department) indicated in August 1962, be exploited by communist forces to manipulate impatience and youthful idealism. In the view of this counterinsurgency expert, such a threat was especially worrisome in developing and undemocratic countries, where unfamiliarity with liberal traditions hindered the sort of recognition and articulation of student demands that would close the doors to communist subversion.[4] A good example of this could be seen in Spain. In the 1960s, the Iberian country underwent profound economic and social transformations that made it, according to US official sources, "the most developed of the underdeveloped nations."[5] The rapid modernization of Spain highlighted the absolute necessity to reform the obsolete university structure of the country. University reform was one of the main demands of the emerging student movement. However, the student demands in favor of the modernization of higher education often clashed with the authoritarian nature of Franco's regime. The collision between the students' demands and the political immobility of the dictatorship gave rise to a fierce university conflict.

As we will see hereafter, during the 1960s, students in Spain staged strong protests that helped weaken the Franco regime (Carrillo-Linares 2015; Rodríguez 2015). Mobilization in Spanish universities was part of a transnational cycle of youth revolts that became a "constituting factor" in international relations during that decade (Klimke 2010: 235). In conformity with the student conflict increasing in intensity during the 1960s, there was an increase in expression of student hostility toward the United States. From the US perspective, this growing student anti-Americanism might threaten US military interests in a country of great geostrategic value in the framework of the Cold War. In this regard, the attitude of Spanish students toward the United States appeared to be similar to their peers from other developing countries. As was revealed by various surveys and opinion polls prepared by US official bodies during the first half of the 1960s, the youth leaders in the world's (semi-)periphery did not see the American colossus as an ally for achieving their dreams of development, justice, and freedom. On the contrary, they perceived the United States as a neocolonial power, the force propping up dictatorial regimes, the epitome of predatory capitalism, and the cause of their nations' underdevelopment.[6]

By means of the study of the Spanish case, this work intends to shed light on the US response to the student challenge in an authoritarian and developing country. To this effect, first an analysis of how the US officials perceived the growing signs of student disobedience promoted in Spanish universities by communist and left-wing organizations is carried out. Second, I will examine, on the one hand, the efforts of the Americans to win over the friendship and understanding of the Spanish student leaders through diverse programs of public diplomacy and, on the other hand, the reaction of these students in the context of 1968. Finally, the work addresses the US support of the General Education Law of 1970 as an intent to promote economic growth and contain student unrest in Spain. However, the US commitment to the modernization of the educative system in this country did not manage to neutralize the student protests or the growth in anti-American feeling in the Spanish campuses.

The United States and Spanish Students

As has already been seen in earlier chapters, Spain underwent a spectacular and unprecedented "economic miracle" during the 1960s, which led to important social and cultural changes. Such transformations were also notably seen in higher education. Throughout this decade, Spanish universities witnessed a spectacular increase in the number of students. In a few years, higher education centers, traditionally dedicated to the training of elites, became mass universities. Such an increase in students imposed strong pressure on the obsolete education system of the Franco regime, accentuating the problems of massification of the classrooms and other structural deficiencies. But it also meant a transformation in the social composition of the students because of the arrival in the universities of the children of the new middle classes (Hernández et al. 2007). Both factors facilitated the appearance and growth of anti-Franco student organizations with a high capacity to create a climate of permanent revolt that altered the academic, political, and cultural life of Spanish universities (Álvarez 2004; González 2009: Rodríguez 2009).

These student groups pushed academic demands for an end to the massification of the lecture theaters, criticizing the lack of halls of residence, exorbitant prices in university canteens and transport, teachers with low academic qualifications, and the rigid study plans. However, these demands were combined with others directed against the university institutions of the dictatorship. In this regard, it is important to note that the economic and social change that occurred in the country in the 1960s did not correspond with parallel political modernization. Despite the half-hearted official projects of associative, informative, and union opening which were implemented in the middle of this decade, Franco's regime maintained an eminently authoritarian and repressive character. Evidence for this was how the Spanish rulers treated the student discontent as a problem exclusively of public order, to which they replied with repression, without taking into consideration the imbalances suffered by an education system which was inadequate for a rapidly transforming society. As a result, the universities were converted into a continuous focus for response and student unrest which "substantially contributed to the wear and tear of the regime" of Franco (Hernández et al. 2007: 23).

During the 1960s, the student movement was mainly driven by the Spanish Communist Party and by other parties associated with the New Left, like the Popular Freedom Front. This was an anti-imperialist and pacifist group, inspired by the Cuban Revolution and the anti-colonial revolutionary movements. It took a very critical approach both to Soviet communism, as well as to US capitalism. From 1961 onward, its militants, along with communists and socialists, became one of the main fronts of student opposition to the dictatorship, called the Federación Universitaria Democrática Española (Spanish Democratic University Federation). As Manuel Lora Tamayo, Minister of Education at the time, recalls, the federation was the "organization which caused the incidents and events of greatest importance in the Spanish university." Among those incidents may be found numerous acts as a sign of protest against the Vietnam War. In fact, one of the main objectives of the federation was, according to the aforementioned minister, student awareness of "confrontation . . . with the financial and landowning oligarchy allied to the imperialist USA" (1993: 220–221).

In the Spanish campuses, small liberal groups, centrists, Christian democrats, and social democrats also operated. But their activity was very modest in a university in which Marxist ideas became increasingly attractive among students and intellectuals with great prestige in academic circles. At the height of 1967, even official publications recognized that "the current University has assimilated a Marxist culture, whether we like it or not" (Hernández et al. 2007: 216). So, it can be affirmed that the student opposition to Franco's dictatorship did not have so much of a liberal democratic orientation but more so a Marxist and revolutionary style, in which anti-capitalism and anti-Americanism were common ingredients (Antentas 2018; Carrillo-Linares 2015). As the US Embassy in Madrid in November 1968 indicated, "most student activists of Spain and a large share of their followers have some form of Socialist leanings and therefore reject the American experience as a monopolistic capitalistic economic system not wanted here."[7]

So, how did the American diplomats perceive the increase in student protest and the Marxist, left-wing, and anti-American influence in the higher education centers in Spain? Through the eyes of modernization, US officials interpreted the situation in Spanish universities as a symptom of the tensions and conflicts generated by the accelerated socioeconomic dynamics of the country. At the end of the 1960s, a memorandum from the US Department of State on national security indicated the economic boom of that decade had fueled the "revolution of rising expectations," the emergence of "political pressures," and the intensification of "demand for reform and social justice" in several groups, among which young people and students stood out.[8]

From the moment the first symptoms of economic and social change could be noticed, the US diplomacy began to detect expressions of dissent and disaffection at the universities. For example, already in the summer of 1960, official sources had pointed to the emergence of a new political generation, among which there was "increasing evidence of discontent with the present government, particularly among university groups."[9] In July 1963, the US Policy Planning Council remarked on the "active dissent among intellectuals and youth" seen in the country's universities.[10] In 1965, the US diplomatic corps took notice of a "growing restiveness among Spanish workers and students."[11]

From the American point of view, this rising student mobilization, driven mainly by communist and leftist organizations with an anti-American orientation, endangered two conditions considered by the Department of State as essential to preserve their defensive interests in Spain: (1) maintenance, for the short term, of the political stability of the Francoist dictatorship, and (2) a nonviolent and moderate post-Franco succession in the future that would facilitate the eventual establishment of a new government friendly to the United States. In this regard, from the end of the 1950s, the US officials highlighted that "significant difficulties could arise [between workers and students] to impede a peaceful transition into the post-Franco era."[12]

Notwithstanding these dangers, the US Foreign Service in Spain saw the mobilization of students not merely as a threat but also as a possible opportunity. From the modernizing perspective typical of American analyses, a social, technological, scientific, and industrial revolution was taking place in Spain, the result of which was the deterioration and erosion of traditional values and norms.[13] This sort of change caused social tensions that might be manipulated by communists, to be sure, but also opened new ways to seek to identify US interests "with the constructive aspirations of the important youth sector."[14] According to the US officials, the sweeping socioeconomic development of Spain was increasing the political, social, and cultural weight of sectors like those of the students and intellectuals. These circumstances could be taken advantage of by the United States for their own interests. As an important US Policy Planning Council report in 1963 stated:

> US policy should exploit the existing ferment among some intellectuals, both within and outside the universities, and the discontent of the more politically alert elements among youth . . . We should take advantage—continued the aforementioned report—of the shift within the Spanish universities toward increased influence of the younger generation and seek to reach the new Spanish intellectual elite.[15]

For the US diplomats, it was just as important to channel some of the unleashed effects of the impetuous social change (growing popular expectations, mass mobilization, social unrest) as to seize the opportunities derived from the modernization which brought Spain closer to the countries in its Western environment. As an official report observed in 1960, "as Spain moves out of its isolation, it is essential that its youth and leaders of the next five to ten years look to the United States as the source of guidance."[16] To that end, American officials felt it was necessary to convince Spanish students that, like them, the United States also stood "for dynamism and growth, for positive change and vitality."[17] In sum, despite the radical demands and actions, the protests in the universities were also seen by US strategists as a reflection of the desire of the Spanish youth to achieve greater levels of freedom, development, and well-being. The US diplomats thought the Spanish student revolt was hiding a yearning for prosperity and modernization that could be used by US diplomats as a lever to assert their own vision of historical and social change.

This official analysis of the Spanish case converged with the general US vision of the growing student disaffection in developing countries. US foreign policy makers thought that behind the discontent expressed in the universities of the Global South lurked a positive potential. Such restlessness could be channeled in a favorable direction if students were shown that the United States knew their problems, shared their same desires for social transformation, and was willing to cooperate with the progress of their nations. As Secretary of State Dean Rusk said in a letter sent in 1965 to all US embassies abroad, it was essential to convey to "politically conscious students" what "the United States is today, its goals and how they coincide with those of youth everywhere, its deep interest in the legitimate aspirations of youth in other lands for a better future, and its desire to help them to realize these aspirations in freedom."[18]

Thus, although student vigor seemed to have Marxist organizations capitalizing on it in the universities of many developing countries, US strategists believed "there is no reason why this youthful energy and enthusiasm cannot be captured for constructive purposes."[19] The key was not to confront or diametrically oppose students but rather to channel their expectations in a direction compatible with US interests. President John F. Kennedy himself thought, in the face of the growing hostility to the United States of students from different parts of the world, it was imperative "to harness the tremendous force that lies in their energy and idealism to deal in a responsible manner to some of the myriad of problems in a rapidly changing world."[20] How, then, to align the security objectives of the superpower with the demands for change of the students? How to channel their desires for economic, political, and social transformation toward the achievement of nonrevolutionary change? How to improve the image of the United States in the universities and to bring to Spain's students the American achievements in the fields of culture, economics, education, and science? How to ensure the student leaders perceived the United States not as an anti-communist guardian and supporter of Franco but as an ally in the modernizing of their country?

The US Machinery of Student Persuasion

In response to questions such as these, the Kennedy administration created the Inter-Agency Youth Committee (IYC) in April 1962 "to broaden our contacts and improve our relationships with young and potential leaders in the universities and intellectual circles."[21] The US president entrusted this committee with the task of deploying and coordinating programs abroad to attract those young people who were active and capable of influencing both the political future of their countries and the international sphere. To entice these young people, the IYC had the support of various government agencies, such as the United States Agency for International Development (USAID) and the Central Intelligence Agency. But especially relevant for this purpose was its collaboration with the United States Information Agency (USIA), the official agency in charge of transmitting to foreign audiences "an accurate image of the United States, particularly of its economic and social characteristics, to dispel ignorance and correct distortions."[22]

One of the main functions of the USIA was to deploy programs of public diplomacy aimed to seduce, by means of the diffusion of US values and ideas, influential sectors of the public opinion of other countries, such as institutional, media, intellectual, union, and student leaders (Cull 2008). The youth were already one of the "target groups" of the US foreign propaganda activities during the Eisenhower administration (Osgood 2006). But from 1962, the USIA intensified its work toward this sector. At the beginning of the 1960s, an official Task Force on Youth was concerned "that the apparent hostility of the young people of the world to the US results from our failure to convey to them an understanding of our national goals and the nature of our society" (quoted in Scott-Smith 2015: 24; see also Dizard 2004: 90). Consequently, the US policy makers considered it necessary for the

USIA to launch an informative, educational, and cultural offensive to show the youth and student leaders the advantages of the US economic and social system and its superiority over the Soviet model.

The deployment of the IYC, together with the increase in the youth activities of the USIA, reflected the new "emphasis on youth" that permeated US foreign policy since the early 1960s. In 1963, the IYC leaders sent instructions to more than a hundred embassies to establish sections dedicated to improving the image of the United States among the young people. That same year, the Embassy in Madrid established its own Youth Committee (YC), dedicated to identifying young leaders who could play an important role in Spain's present and future, to cultivate their contacts and promote activities aimed at increasing their interest in American society and culture (Martín García 2011).

As of 1963, the work of the YC and USIA's contingent in Spain, known as the US Information Service (USIS), in the youth sphere was focused on counteracting "frequent misunderstanding and criticism of US judgment and maturity in international affairs and the shallow knowledge of US policies and its governmental, economic and social institutions, especially in Spanish universities."[23] In the following years, the YC and the USIS directed several of its programs in Spain at opening channels of dialogue with those brightest and most active students who, according to the US field officers, would possibly become the "political leaders of influence when the present regime either turns over power to a new government or is removed."[24]

The YC and the USIS engaged in various public diplomacy activities aimed at winning the hearts and minds of young Spaniards. Among these activities, they emphasized (1) educational exchange programs; (2) conference cycles in colleges and universities; (3) library services and distribution of books, magazines, and other publications among student leaders and professors; (4) American cultural weeks (exhibitions, screenings, musical performances, theatrical performances, lectures) on university campuses; (5) English and American Studies courses; (6) activities for young people in the binational cultural centers of Madrid, Barcelona, and Valencia; and (7) radio broadcasts.

These programs were aimed at conveying to Spanish students the sophistication of American cultural values and the advances of that society in fields such as economics, technology, and science. US public diplomats used magazines, pamphlets, conferences, and exhibitions as an instrument to channel student expectations and energies toward the mission of national development in a "constructive," "responsible," and favorable direction to US strategic priorities. The US propaganda machine also made a notable effort to familiarize Spanish students with the ways of life of American students and with the advantages of the US educational system. The cultural and educational activities organized by the YC and the USIS tried to present US experience to Spanish student leaders as the best example to follow in order to achieve the modernization of their country in a nonviolent manner. The US youth program attempted to create, for young people and students, a psychological climate favorable to modernization "made in America" (Martín García 2018). However, US public diplomacy did not manage to obtain the support of the Spanish students, as was observed in the wave of agitation that shook the universities of the country between 1967 and 1969.

During this period, the Spanish campuses were submerged in a situation of disorder and crisis of authority (Ysás 2004: 15–16). In 1968, the same Francoist authorities recognized that the student movement represented an "extraordinary risk factor." It was precisely the student pressure that caused the resignation of the Minister of Education, the technocrat Manuel Lora Tamayo, in March 1968.[25] Around the same time, the US Embassy reported that most of the universities were in a state of "extreme turmoil" that could affect the stability of the Francoist government. But for the US observers, even more worrisome was the fact that such ripples also reflected a growing student rejection of the US presence in Spain.[26]

Already, in the summer of 1967, US Ambassador Angier Biddle-Duke had pointed out that "the growth of political activity in the universities" had been "accompanied by an apparent increase in criticism of the United States, with alleged US support to the Franco regime, civil rights issues, and US position in Vietnam, among the main specific targets."[27] A few months later, another official report highlighted the emergence in Spanish universities of "a rising chorus of opposition to the United States foreign policy, especially to the conduct of the war in Vietnam, and more critical comments on racial problems and on what some regarded as a breakdown of order and morals in the domestic body politic."[28] During the last third of the 1960s there was a notable increase in the number of student demonstrations and activities against the United States, including attacks on institutions related to US cultural permeation of Spain, such as the binational cultural centers of Madrid, Valencia, and Barcelona.

In the fall of 1968, the US Embassy once again recognized the increasing spread of anti-American sentiment in Spanish universities. According to a report prepared in September, in the previous months "students manifested their dissatisfaction with the presence of US military bases in Spain and our role in the war in Vietnam," two issues that had fueled "widespread opposition on the part of the students" against the foreign policy of the US government. In sum, the document concluded, the military alliance with Franco, the Vietnam War, and the internal problems in American society itself (racial violence, urban disturbances) had led many Spanish students to question the value system of American civilization.[29]

The demonstrations and disturbances in Spanish universities highlighted the inability of the United States to win students over. Students perceived the message of the superpower as a mere cosmetic coating used to hide its imperialist ambitions and its support for Franco. The cultural and educational activities carried out by the YC and the USIS did not counteract the adverse effects that US collaboration with the Franco dictatorship projected on student public opinion. In other words, Spanish university students judged the US government more by its actions than by its speeches. The art of public diplomacy failed to make up for an US foreign policy considered by many students to be illegitimate and lacking in moral authority (Martín García 2013: 326–29). In this regard, IYC Director Martin McLaughlin had warned as far back as 1965 that the identification of the United States with authoritarian governments in the developing world could decimate cultural and educational programs aimed at the youth sectors. That warning was confirmed in the global scenario of 1968, leading US officials to conclude that, as long as the geostrategic needs of the Cold War required the US to ally itself with the reactionary forces of the world's (semi-)periphery, any attempt to win students ideologically could be doomed to failure.[30]

A Change in Strategy

The unrest in Spanish universities between 1967 and 1969 was not a purely national phenomenon but was part of a global student revolt with a clear anti-imperialist and anti-capitalist component, which for Secretary of State Dean Rusk portended "very serious overtones" for the "foreign policy interests" of the United States.[31] The global student protests of 1968, coupled with the assassinations of Robert F. Kennedy and Martin Luther King Jr., the Vietnam War, racial problems, and violent urban unrest, sowed distrust in the United States as a symbol of the "Free World" and modernity (Gilman 2003: 79–80).

The late 1960s witnessed the crisis of American hegemony and the decline of the grand narratives of the Cold War. In this context, the radicalization and anti-Americanism that spread among the students considerably reduced the US capacity for maneuver and influence in the university environment. An August 1968 report of the IYC indicated that "our missions generally report that there is little the US can do on a short-term basis to defend itself against the consequences of student unrest."[32] In fact, any youth activity bearing the official seal of Washington ran the risk of being boycotted or of having counterproductive effects on the image of the superpower. The strong student rejection shown in various parts of the world convinced US officialdom of the impossibility of directly reaching the leaders of this sector. Given these circumstances, the IYC decided to keep a low profile and confine itself to analyzing the problems that underlay youth disaffection so as to anticipate future explosions of protest.[33]

Therefore, it may be asserted that the anti-Americanism and anti-imperialism that marked the cycle of protests in the late 1960s brought about a change in US strategy toward the youth and student sectors. US foreign policy makers decided to reduce the programs aimed at actively attracting students, who because of their intense politicization were no longer the objects of priority for US diplomatic attention. This new post-1968 US foreign policy toward students was also applied in the Spanish case. The US Embassy in Madrid reduced its programs and its contacts with those students who were considered effectively unwinnable for the American cause. Instead, US public diplomacy devoted greater interest to young professionals linked to the ruling classes and official circles. Given the difficulties in winning over disaffected sectors such as university students, the US official chose to strengthen its ties with the official sectors that constituted a community of support and political affinity with the United States. Thus, since the beginning of the 1970s, both the USIS and the YC stopped working with the student leaders and directed their persuasion toward the young bankers linked to the financial oligarchy, the new generations of technocrats, the new leaders of the Francoist single party, and the young conservative urban elites.[34] This new strategy was in tune with the spirit of the foreign policy of the new Republican administration, whose emphasis on the defense of stability and bipolar equilibrium on the old continent led to a reaffirmation of United States' commitment to its authoritarian allies (Schmitz 2006: 69–70).

However, despite this new fallback position, the US diplomats believed not all to be lost in the student field. Even account for the corrosive effect that the 1968 youth rebellion had had on US international prestige, the officials in Washington believed the events of that year had also brought with them an important opportunity for constructive change. The reason was that the student revolts had made many national governments mindful of the urgent need to reform their educational institutions. In the same vein, the IYC felt the student upheaval might represent a positive stimulus to the promotion of educational reforms that could prove favorable to US interests.[35] Along this line, the Student Unrest Study Group created by the Department of State to analyze the 1968 global phenomenon estimated that, although the unrest in the classrooms was being manipulated by subversive groups, many of the students' grievances, especially those related to the structural deficiencies of the educational systems, embodied "a legitimate demand and one that offers the greatest opportunity for action."[36] From the point of view of this working group, it was necessary to initiate an international movement of educational reforms, which should act on the underlying and structural causes of discontent in the universities, in order to depoliticize it and reduce the support for radical groups.[37] As a result, the US government set out to induce discreetly the implementation of educational reforms in other countries as a mechanism to promote economic development and contain the radicalization of youth. In addition, being involved in these reforms would allow the US Foreign Service to project a subtle, indirect, and long-term influence on foreign societies without drawing the ire of the students.

The application of these approaches to the Spanish case led to US support for the educational reforms that led to the Ley General de Educación (General Education Law—LGE) approved in August 1970 (Delgado Gómez-Escalonilla 2015a). For the US Embassy, assistance in this field represented "an exceptional opportunity to influence future generations of Spaniards and the global structure of society in a constructive manner and in accordance with our long-term political interests."[38] To this end, the US government collaborated between 1968 and 1970 with organizations such as UNESCO, the OECD, and the World Bank in the implementation of educational reform in Spain.

US officials had already been cooperating in the field of education with the Spanish government since the end of the 1950s with the objective of encouraging the expansion of the Spanish educational structures as the engine of economic development in the making (González Delgado and Groves 2017). Additionally, throughout the 1960s, US public diplomacy had promoted publications, talks, seminars, film screenings, and exhibitions in order to familiarize Spanish academic elites and students with the US educational system. In this way, educational changes in Spain were intended to follow the US model as the best guarantee to ensure national development. Not coincidentally, the promotion of education formed part of the three Development Plans encouraged by the technocratic sectors of the dictatorship between 1962 and 1973 (Milito Barone and Groves 2013: 137). The LGE was also carried out by the technocratic sectors of the Franco regime, who saw in the reform of the obsolete and archaic Spanish education system a way to support the survival of the dictatorship on a more modern basis. Such sectors sought to relegitimize the Spanish dictatorship by creating a modern and efficient education system, capable of promoting economic welfare and stability that would repair the decimated social foundations of the Franco regime (Ortega 1992: 39–43).

Spanish authoritarian technocrats signed onto the ideas about education and development connected with the theories of modernization and human capital (Milito Barone and Groves 2013: 135–36). They hoped educational reform based on the developmental and technocratic principles of such theories would contribute to reducing social antagonisms, encourage a gradual de-ideologization of the new generations, and boost the social hegemony of the moderate middle classes. As some of the principal technocratic leaders responsible for the educational changes in Spain put it, a "silent and peaceful" revolution from above was necessary to transform the old educational structures in an integral and orderly manner as the only alternative to the social upheaval from below.[39]

In this sense, Spanish technocrats promoted the LGE to reinforce the political stability of the Franco dictatorship at a time of deteriorating authoritarian rule. However, the implementation of this law in the summer of 1970 was met with strong resistance from students and professors. After a brief period of reflux in university protests between 1969 and 1971, the approval of the LGE reactivated student mobilization in Spanish universities during the last years of the dictatorship. The most politicized student organizations saw in the LGE an act of submission by Spanish rulers to the interests of "American imperialism." It was common for the propaganda of the leftist organizations to refer to LGE as the law of the *yanquis*. For the student opposition, this law represented an instrument of ideological control of the repressive local oligarchy in the service of American expansionist capitalism (Hernández et al. 2007: 311).

A good number of students and professors opposed the hierarchical nature of a reform they felt had been imposed from above without any attention paid to their opinions. They were opposed to the technocratic character of the LGE and advocated a model of educational democratization from below (Aguilar 2007: 28; Carbonell 1992; Groves

2012; Jiménez 2000; Milito Barone and Groves 2013). The situation of the Spanish educational world at the beginning of the 1970s seemed to resemble that of other developing countries where there was also strong resistance to educational reforms endorsed by the United States. In places like Brazil and El Salvador (Lindo-Fuentes and Ching 2012), while local technocratic elites enthusiastically accepted the recommendations of US experts and international agencies, students, and teachers mobilized in anger over their exclusion from participation in educational reforms.[40]

In Spain, the top-down nature of the educational reform, in the preparation of which the advice of international experts had been taken into account more than that of Spain's educational community, led to a notable increase in university protests. Thus, after 1971 and until the death of Franco in 1975, this law became the focus of dissatisfaction of large sectors of the university community. According to official sources, the 1971–1972 academic year was the most convulsive since 1968, the main cause of such intense student agitation being "the near-universal student (and faculty) opposition to the New Education Reform Law and the manner in which it is being implemented." In this context, rejection of the LGE became "almost an article of faith with Spanish university students and professors."[41]

Thus, although the LGE represented considerable modernization of the country's educational institutions, the authoritarian and technocratic nature of some of its parts, together with the slow, inconsistent, and distorted application of its most innovative elements, generated a strong student critique against it (Aguilar 2007: 32). Student mobilization against the university reforms in the first half of the 1970s only increased the American disrepute among the students—a hostility to the US power that by the middle of that decade had already spread into broad sectors of Spanish society (Alonso 2003: 6; Niño 2003: 14; Pardo 2003: 41–43). Thus, at the time of Franco's death in 1975, many Spaniards did not identify the "American friend" with democracy and prosperity but with the authoritarian order that was now coming to an end. As Lorenzo Delgado Gómez-Escalonilla concludes, "the lack of coherence between the democratic ideology and the entente with the Franco regime undermined the credibility of the United States' message and policy in Spain" (2015b: 202–203). This translated into a clear social rejection of the United States that, among other reasons, led the US government to take a step back and leave to its Western European allies the leadership role as the main guarantors of the international status quo in the face of the uncertain change of regime in Spain (Del Pero 2011; Varsori 2009).

Conclusion

In its intense rivalry with the Soviet Union, the United States favored the economic, social, cultural, and educational modernization of its authoritarian allies in the global (semi-)periphery. But in the tense ideological environment of the Cold War, social change and promises of development had the effect of mobilizing sectors such as youth and students, whose demands collided with the autocratic power of local dictators friendly with Washington, a fact that conferred to growing student unrest a clearly anti-American characteristic. A similar idea was expressed by Seymour Martin Lipset during a seminar on "Youth and Leadership in the Developing Nations" held in Washington in November 1966. This renowned theorist of modernization thought the US assistance to the growth of higher education in the developing countries was causing an increase in the leftist, revolutionary, and anti-American tendencies among the students. In the opinion of this academician and adviser to the US government, the combination of accelerated socioeconomic modernization and educational expansion represented a threat to US interests in these countries.[42]

In the same vein, a report by USAID written in 1968 warned of the fact that, although the US government had made great efforts to promote reforms favorable to educational progress in developing nations, the youth of these countries saw the superpower as an adversary: an enemy that, in collaboration with the local tyrants whom the students detested already, supported projects that did not involve their opinions or their participation.[43] In the face of the global student rebellion that took place that year, US officials were forced to recognize that, paradoxically, while the United States supported economic, social, and educational change in many parts of the world, its government was not identified by students as a force for progress. Therefore, as the Spanish case shows, US efforts to promote stability and prosperity in the developing world caused a rise in expectations and student demands that, when they ran into conflict with undemocratic political structures, soon became politicized and in opposition to local autocrats and their allies in Washington. It was largely a rebellion of the offspring of the emerging middle classes who benefited from the modernization processes but felt dissatisfied with the frustration of the political, social, and cultural expectations that such processes generated (Suri 2010: 471–477).

Acknowledgments

This work was supported by the Viera y Clavijo Research Program (University of La Laguna) and by the Ministry of Economy and Competitiveness of Spain under the research project "La modernización del sistema educativo y científico español en su dimensión internacional (1953–1986)" (HAR2014-58685-R). A few brief passages and some of the overall analysis in this chapter first appeared in Martín García (2018).

Óscar J. Martín García is currently a tenure-track researcher in the Ramón y Cajal Program in the Department of Political History, Theories, and Geography of the Universidad Complutense de Madrid. His professional career as a social and diplomatic historian began in 2003. Since then, his investigation has focused on two different lines of inquiry: social movement studies and international history. Within this second field, he has specialized on the United States and United Kingdom's soft power, public diplomacy, and foreign policy toward the Iberian dictatorships during the Cold War. On these topics, he has authored various articles in refereed journals such as *Contemporary European History*, *Cold War History*, and *Contemporary British History*. He has recently coedited—with Rósa Magnúsdóttir—the volume *Machineries of Persuasion: European Soft Power and Public Diplomacy during the Cold War* (2019).

Notes

1. "National Security Council Report," NSC 6016/1, 5 October 1960 (quoted in Landa et al. 1993: 786).
2. "Report on the Work of the Inter-Agency Committee on Youth Affairs," 1963, Record Group (RG) 306, US Information Agency, Subject folders, Box 121, US National Archives and Records Administration (NARA).
3. "Emphasis on Youth: Reaching and Influencing Rising Young Leaders," 1965, RG 353, Inter-Agency Youth Committee, General Records, 1959–1973, Box 1, NARA.
4. "Communist Exploitation, Short of Violence, of Transitional Societies," 10 August 1962, Roger Hilsman Papers, Series 2, Subject Files, 1961–64, Box 6, John Fitzgerald Kennedy Presidential Library.
5. "USIS Country Plan for Spain, FY 1962," 7 March 1962, RG306, Office of Research, Foreign Service Dispatches, 1954–1965, Box 4, NARA.
6. "The Role of USIA Media in the Emphasis on Youth Policy," 7 January 1965, RG353, General Records, 1959–1973, Box 11, NARA.

7. "Student Unrest," 28 November 1968, RG59, Department of State, Central Foreign Policy Files, 1967–1969, Political and Defence, Box 2489, NARA.
8. "US Policy toward Spain," 16 January 1970, National Security Council Files, Institutional Files, Meeting Files (1969–1974), NSC Meetings, Box H-41, Richard Nixon Presidential Library.
9. "Comments on Authoritarian Regimes Receiving US Assistance," 6 June 1960, RG59, Bureau of European Affairs, Country Director for Spain and Portugal, 1956–1966, Box 5, NARA.
10. "The Succession Problem in Spain," 17 July 1963, RG59, Policy Planning Council, Planning and Coordination Staff, Subject Files, 1963–73, Box 16, NARA.
11. "Talking Points for Leddy-Ball Meeting," 8 November 1965, RG59, Bureau of European Affairs, Country Director for Spain and Portugal. 1956–1966, Box 2, NARA.
12. "Inspection Report USIS Spain," 29 May 1959, RG306, Inspection Reports and Related Records, 1954–62, Box 8, NARA.
13. "USIS Country Plan for Spain, FY 1962."
14. "Some General Observations on United States Policy towards Spain," 25 June 1965, RG59, Bureau of European Affairs. Country Director for Spain and Portugal, 1956–1966, Box 2, NARA.
15. "The Succession Problem in Spain," 17 July 1963, RG59, Policy Planning Council, Planning and Coordination Staff, Subject Files, 1963-73, Box 16, NARA.
16. "Annual Report on Educational Exchange Activities in Spain for FY 1960," July 29, 1960, RG59, CU, Policy Review and Coordination Staff, Country Files, 1955–66, Box 30, NARA.
17. "Student Unrest."
18. "Emphasis on Youth."
19. "Interdepartmental Meeting on Youth," 17 March 1962, RG353, General Records, 1959–1973, Box 5, NARA.
20. Words of John F. Kennedy, quoted by the US Ambassador to Spain, Angier Biddle-Duke, during a conference in 1965. "Visit of Ambassador and Mrs. Duke to Barcelona," 15 November 1965. RG59, Central Foreign Policy File (CFPF), Education and Cultural Exchange, 1964–1966, Box 402, NARA.
21. "Study of progress, Problems and Potential," 14 November 1963, RG306, Subject folders, Box 121, NARA.
22. "Report on the Work of the Inter-Agency Committee on Youth Affairs."
23. "Country Assessment Report—USIS Spain 1961," 15 February 1962, RG306, Office of Research, Foreign Service Dispatches, 1954–1965, Box 4, NARA. On the work of the USIS in Spain during the Franco era, see, among others, Delgado Gómez-Escalonilla (2010), Niño and Montero (2012), León (2009), Rodríguez-Jiménez (2010).
24. "USIS Country Plan for Spain, FY 1961," 25 June 1960, RG306, Office of Research, Foreign Service Dispatches, 1954–65, Box 4, NARA.

25. This Minister was replaced in his post by another technocrat, José Luis Villar Palasí, who had previously participated in the US student exchange programs and had connections with the United States. Villar Palasí drove profound reforms in the Spanish education system, which gave rise to the famous *Ley General de Educación* (General Education Act of 1970), which will be analyzed in the following section.
26. "Barcelona University Student Protest Movement Further Disarmed by Communist Division," 5 April 1968, RG59, Central Foreign Policy Files, 1967–1969, Political and Defence, Box 2491, NARA.
27. "Comments on the Spanish Student Scene," 26 July 1967, RG59, Central Foreign Policy Files, 1967–1969, Political and Defence, Box 2491, NARA.
28. "US Policy Assessment," 9 May 1968, RG59, Central Foreign Policy Files, 1967–1969, Political and Defence, Box 2493, NARA.
29. "Student Unrest," 28 November 1968, RG59, Central Foreign Policy Files, 1967–1969, Political and Defence, Box 2489, NARA.
30. "Emphasis on Youth."
31. "For Ambassador to Secretary," 24 May 1968, RG353, General Records, 1959–1973, Box 6, NARA.
32. "Comments on the Field on Youth and Student Unrest," 16 August 1968, RG353, General Records, 1959–1973, Box 6, NARA.
33. "General Action Recommendation on Student Unrest," 1968, RG353, General Records, 1959–1973, Box 6, NARA.
34. "Impact of Youth and the US National Interest: Mission Youth Program—American Embassy," April 1, 1970, RG59, Central Foreign Policy Files, 1970–1973, Political and Defence, Box 2597, NARA.
35. "Report on the Student Unrest Study Group," 17 January 1969, RG353, General Records, 1959–1973, Box 9, NARA.
36. "General Action Recommendation on Student Unrest."
37. "Comments on the Field on Youth and Student Unrest."
38. "The Educational and Cultural Exchange Program with Spain," 27 October 1969, Group IX, Box 240, Archive of the Bureau of Educational and Cultural Affairs.
39. Quote from Minister of Education José Luis Villar Palasí, in De Pueyes (1992: 13); see also Díez Hochleitner (1992: 268).
40. "General Action Recommendation on Student Unrest"; "World-Wide Youth and Student Unrest," 1969, RG353, General Records, 1959–1973, Box 8, NARA.
41. "Spanish Student Unrest and University Situation," 19 April 1972; and "Spain: A Troubled Academic Year Ahead?" October 27, 1972, RG59, Subject Numerical Files, 1970–1973, Culture and Information, Box 397, NARA.
42. "Youth and Leadership in the Developing Nations," 15 November 1966, RG306, Office of Administration, Historical Collections, Reports and Studies, 1953–1998, Box 3, NARA.
43. "The AID Program and Student Unrest," 26 December 1968, RG353, General Records, 1959–1973, Box 1, NARA.

References

Antentas, Josep Maria. 2018. "1968 and the Spanish State: The Year in Its Context." Verso blog, 19 June. https://www.versobooks.com/blogs/3890-1968-and-the-spanish-state-the-year-in-its-context.

Aguilar, Raúl. 2007. "El despliegue de la Universidad Autónoma de barcelona entre 1968 y 1973: De fundación franquista a motor del cambio democrático en Cataluña." *Cuadernos del Instituto Antonio de Nebrija* 10: 13–199.

Alonso, Carlos. 2003. "Miradas torcidas: Percepciones mutuas entre España y Estados Unidos." *Documento de Trabajo del Real Instituto Elcano* 22: 1–36.

Álvarez, José. 2004. *Envenenados de cuerpo y alma: La oposición universitaria al franquismo en Madrid (1939–1970)*. Madrid: Siglo XXI.

Brazinsky, Greg. 2007. *Nation Building in South Korea: Koreans, Americans, and the Making of a Democracy*. Chapel Hill: University of North Carolina Press.

Carbonell, Jaume. 1992. "De la Ley General de Educación a la Alternativa de Escuela Pública: Algunas notas introductorias sobre los movimientos sociales en el sector de la enseñanza." *Revista de Educación* S1: 237–225.

Carrillo-Linares, Alberto. 2015. "Universidades y transiciones políticas: El caso español en los años 60–70." *Espacio, Tiempo y Educación* 2 (2): 49–75.

Christiansen, Samantha, and Zachary Scarlett, eds. 2013. *The Third World in the Global 1960s*. New York: Berghahn Books.

Cull, Nicholas. 2008. *The Cold War and the United States Information Agency: American Propaganda and Public Diplomacy, 1945–1989*. Cambridge: Cambridge University Press.

Delgado Gómez-Escalonilla, Lorenzo. 2010. "'After Franco, What?' La diplomacia pública de Estados Unidos y la preparación del post-franquismo." In *Claves internacionales en la transición española*, ed. Óscar Martín García and Manuel Ortiz, 99–127. Madrid: Los Libros de la Catarata.

——. 2015a. "Modernizadores y tecnócratas: Estados Unidos ante la política educativa y científica de la España del desarrollo." *Historia y Política* 34: 113–146.

——. 2015b. "Modernizing a Friendly Tyrant: US Public Diplomacy and Sociopolitical Change in Francoist Spain." In *US Public Diplomacy and Democratization in Spain: Selling Democracy?* ed. Francisco J. Rodríguez, Lorenzo Delgado Gómez-Escalonilla, and Nicholas Cull, 63–92. New York: Palgrave McMillan.

Del Pero, Mario, 2011. "The United States and the Crises in Southern Europe." In *Europe in the International Arena during the 1970s: Entering a Different World*, ed. Antonio Varsori and Guia Migani, 301–317. Brussels: Peter Lang.

De Pueyes, Manuel. 1992. "Tecnocracia y política en la reforma educativa de 1970." *Revista de Educación* S1: 13–29.

Díez Hochleitner, Ricardo. 1992. "La reforma educativa de la LGE de 1970: Datos para una crónica." *Revista de Educación* S1: 261–278.

Dizard, Wilson. 2004. *Inventing Public Diplomacy: The Story of the US Information Agency*. London: Lynne Rienner Publishers.

Gienow-Hecht, Jessica. 2010. "Culture and the Cold War in Europe." In Westad and Leffler 2010: 398–420.

Gilman, Nils. 2003. *Mandarins of the Future: Modernization Theory in Cold War America*. Baltimore: Johns Hopkins University Press.

González, Eduardo. 2009. *Rebelión en las aulas: Movilización y protesta estudiantil en la España contemporánea, 1865–2008*. Madrid: Alianza Editorial.

González Delgado, Mariano, and Tamar R. Groves. 2017. "Programmed Learning, UNESCO and the Attempts to Change the Curriculum in the Development Spain (1962–1974)." *Espacio: Tiempo y Educación* 4 (2): 73–100.

Groves, Tamar. 2012. "Everyday Struggles against Franco's Authoritarian Legacy: Pedagogical Social Movements and Democracy in Spain." *Journal of Social History* 46 (2): 305–334.

Hernández, Elena, Miguel A. Ruiz, and Marc Baldó. 2007. *Estudiantes contra Franco (1939–1975): Oposición política y movilización juvenil*. Madrid: La Esfera de los Libros.

Honeck, Mischa, and Gabriel Rosenberg, 2014. "Transnational Generations: Organizing Youth in the Cold War." *Diplomatic History* 38 (2): 233–239.

Jian, Chen, Masha Kirasirova, Mary Nolan, Marilyn Young, and Joanna Waley-Cohen, eds. 2018. *The Routledge Handbook of the Global Sixties: Between Protest and Nation-Building*. New York: Routledge.

Jiménez, Marta. 2000. *La Ley General de Educación y el movimiento de enseñantes (1970–1976)*. La Laguna: Universidad de La Laguna.

Klimke, Martin. 2010. *The Other Alliance: Student Protest in West Germany and the United States in the Global Sixties*. Princeton, NJ: Princeton University Press.

Koda, Naoko. 2018. "The US Cold War and the Japanese Student Movement." In Jian et al. 2018: 399–411.

Koivunen, Pia. 2017. "Friends, 'Potential Friends,' and Enemies: Reimagining Soviet Relations to the First, Second, and Third Worlds at the Moscow 1957 Youth Festival." In *Socialist Internationalism in the Cold War: Exploring the Second World*, ed. Patryk Babiracki and Austin Jersild, 219–247. New York: Palgrave Macmillan.

Kotek, Joel. 1996. *Students and the Cold War*. New York: St. Martin's Press.

Krekola, Joni, and Simo Mikkonen. 2011. "Backlash of the Free World: The US presence at the World Youth Festival in Helsinki, 1962." *Scandinavian Journal of History* 36 (2): 230–255.

Landa, Robert, James Miller, David Patterson, and Charles Sampson, eds. 1993. *Foreign Relations of the United States: Western Europe, Volume II, Part 2*. Washington, DC: US Government Publishing Office.

León, Pablo. 2009. "Los canales de difusión del mensaje norteamericano en España, 1945–1960." *Ayer* 75:134–158.

Lindo-Fuentes, Héctor, and Erik Ching. 2012. *Diálogos: Modernizing Minds in El Salvador: Education Reform and the Cold War, 1960–1980*. Albuquerque: University of New Mexico.

Lora Tamayo, Manuel. 1993. *Lo que yo he conocido: Recuerdos de un viejo catedrático que fue ministro*. Cádiz: Federico Joly y Cía.

Martín García, Óscar J. 2011. "Walking on Eggs: La diplomacia pública de los Estados Unidos y la protesta estudiantil en España, 1963–1969." *Historia del Presente* 17: 27–40.

——. 2013. "A Complicated Mission: The United States and Spanish Students during the Johnson Administration." *Cold War History* 13 (3): 311–329.

——. 2018. "'The Most Developed of the Underdeveloped Nations': US Foreign Policy and Student Unrest in 1960s Spain." *International History Review*, published online 23 March. https://doi.org/10.1080/07075332.2018.1446999.

Milito Barone, Cristina C., and Tamar R. Groves. 2013. "¿Modernización o democratización? La construcción de un nuevo sistema educativo entre el tardofranquismo y la democracia." *Bordón* 65 (4): 135–148.

Niño, Antonio. 2003. "50 años de relaciones entre España y Estados Unidos." *Cuadernos de Historia Contemporánea* 25: 9–33.

Niño, Antonio, and José Antonio Montero, eds. 2012. *Guerra Fría y Propaganda: Estados Unidos y su cruzada cultural en Europa y América Latina*. Madrid: Biblioteca Nueva.

Ortega, Félix. 1992. "Las ideologías de la reforma educativa de 1970." *Revista de Educación* S1: 31–46.

Osgood, Kenneth. 2006. *Total Cold War: Eisenhower's Secret Propaganda Battle at Home and Abroad*. Lawrence: University Press of Kansas.

Paget, Karen. 2003. "From Stockholm to Leiden: The CIA's Role in the Formation of the International Student Conference." *Intelligence and National Security* 18 (2): 134–167.

Pardo, Rosa. 2003. "La política norteamericana." *Ayer* 49: 13–53.

Peacock, Margaret. 2012. "The Perils of Building Cold War Consensus at the 1957 Moscow World Festival of Youth and Students." *Cold War History* 12 (3): 515–535.

Rodríguez, Sergio. 2009. *Zonas de libertad: Dictadura franquista y movimiento estudiantil en la universidad de Valencia (1939–1965)*. Valencia: Publicacions de la Universitat de València.

——. 2015. "The Anti-Franco Student Movement's Contribution to the Return of Democracy in Spain." *Espacio: Tiempo y Educación* 2 (2): 77–106.

Rodríguez-Jiménez, Francisco J. 2010. *¿"Antídoto contra el antiamericanismo"? American Studies en España, 1945–1969*. Valencia: Publicacions de la Universitat de València.

Schmitz, David F. 2006. *The United States and Right-Wing Dictatorships, 1965–1989*. New York: Cambridge University Press.

Scott-Smith, Giles. 2011. "Psychological Warfare for the West: Interdoc, the West European Intelligence Services, and the International Student Movements of the 1960s." In *The Establishment Responds: Power and*

Protest during and after the Cold War, ed. Kathrin Fahlenbrach, Martin Klimke, Joachim Scharloth, and Laura Wong, 123–138. London: Palgrave Macmillan.
——. 2015. "US Public Diplomacy and Democracy: Promotion in the Cold War, 1950s–1980s." In *US Public Diplomacy and Democratization in Spain: Selling Democracy?* ed. Francisco J. Rodríguez-Jiménez, Lorenzo Delgado Gómez-Escalonilla, and Nicholas Cull, 15–35. New York: Palgrave Macmillan.
Slobodian, Quinn. 2011. "What Does Democracy Look Like? (and Why Would Anyone Want to Buy It?) Third World Demands and West German Responses at 1960s World Youth Festivals." In *Cold War Cultures: Perspectives on Eastern and Western European Societies*, ed. Thomas Lindenberger, Annette Vowinckel, and Bernd Stöver, 254–275. New York: Berghahn Books.
Suri, Jeremi. 2010. "Counter-Cultures: The Rebellions against the Cold War Order, 1965–1975." In Westad and Leffler 2010: 460–481.
Varsori, Antonio. 2009. "Crisis and Stabilization in Southern Europe during the 1970s: Western Strategies, European Instruments." *Journal of European Integration History* 15 (1): 5–15.
Westad, Odd Arne. 2010. "The Cold War and the International History of the Twentieth Century." In Westad and Leffler 2010: 1–19.
Westad, Odd Arne, and Melvyn P. Leffler, eds. 2010. *The Cambridge History of the Cold War*. Cambridge: Cambridge University Press.
Ysás, Pere. 2004. *Disidencia y subversión: La lucha del régimen franquista por su supervivencia, 1960–1975*. Barcelona: Crítica.

Chapter 7

How a Cold War Education Project Backfired

Modernization Theory, the Alliance for Progress, and the 1968 Education Reform in El Salvador

Héctor Lindo-Fuentes

At the end of the 1960s, numerous countries embarked in ambitious efforts to reform their educational systems inspired by new theories about the role of education in development policies and the availability of new technology that could be harnessed for educational purposes. A prominent European example is the previously discussed Spanish effort that crystalized in the Ley General de Educación of 1970. Such initiatives were not the exclusive domain of European countries. Poorer countries such as El Salvador used similar rationales to revamp their educational systems. In 1968, Salvadoran authorities began a massive education reform that had the use of educational television as its main feature. The reform was no minor upgrading of textbooks or a mere tinkering with curricula. It was a deep and comprehensive overhaul of the nation's public school system, particularly at middle and high school levels. It was ambitious and well funded, and policy makers conceived it as transforming El Salvador into a modern, urban, industrializing nation.

That is, it was a project with a general orientation that did not much differ from the Spanish project discussed in earlier chapters of this book. The most comprehensive account of the Salvadoran reform identified eleven main components: a reorganization of the Ministry of Education, extensive teacher training, curriculum revision, development of new teacher's guides and student workbooks, improvement of school supervision to provide "advice" instead of inspections, development of a wider diversity of technical training programs in grades 10–12, extensive building of new schoolrooms, elimination of tuition in grades 7–9, the use of double sessions and reduced contact hours to teach more pupils in existing facilities, a law regulating teachers' hours and pay scales, a new student evaluation system incorporating changes in promotion and grading policies, and the installation of a national instructional television system Televisión Educativa (Educational Television—TVE) for grades 7–9 (Mayo et al. 1976: 23). These components were not conceived together as part of a concerted planning effort. Rather, the reform was carried out in a rather hodgepodge manner with each step being conceptualized as the process went along. But television was there from the inception. In the words of one report:

> The present educational reform in El Salvador was first conceived as little more than the placing of a television receiver in each classroom. As plans developed, however, and as the full implications of the introduction of new technology became clear, it was seen that television was not only an innovation important in its own right, but also a catalyst of change that would affect every aspect of education in El Salvador. (Schramm 1970: 3)

This chapter will show the educational television reform project was the result of both: the domestic political needs of the military regime, and the influence of an international context where new ideas about modernization and human capital were put at the service of the Cold War. Just as in the case of the reform promoted by Francisco Franco's regime, it is impossible to ignore its political motivations. The educational reform in El Salvador represented a vehicle to legitimize a military regime that felt threatened by the recent Cuban revolution. For the United States, the challenge represented by Castro's triumph was the incentive to create the Alliance for Progress (AfP), the ambitious US program of international aid conceived and promoted by modernization theorists such as Walt Rostow (AfP funds financed the Salvadoran reform).[1] To these elements one must add the ability of an individual, Wilbur Schramm, to position educational television as a privileged tool for modernization and, therefore, to combat communism. The result of this combination of factors was a well-funded reform, implemented with military inflexibility, which created an enormous conflict with teachers to the degree that the most numerous group of civil servants ended up radicalized and became an important part of the Salvadoran revolutionary movement in the 1980s.

Antecedents of the Reform

The conditions for the reform began to fall into place in 1962 when a military government that had achieved power through a coup d'état organized presidential elections. Colonel Julio Rivera won the uncontested vote and was inaugurated on 1 July 1962. The legitimacy of the new presidency was in question from its inception. At the same time, the issue of school quality and past governments' poor record on improving education emerged as topics of public debate. In the months preceding Rivera's inauguration, newspapers published almost daily references to the problems of public education.[2] Even an unofficial government publication called *El Popular* printed frequent articles about the dire state of Salvadoran schools.

Most of the newspaper debate about education focused on flaws in the current system rather than possible solutions. One notable exception was a series of articles published in April 1961 about Japan's education system. The author of the articles was a young diplomat, Walter Béneke, then serving as the Salvadoran Consul General in Tokyo, who had become an enthusiast of the Japanese system. As a result, he worked tirelessly through public and private channels to encourage Salvadoran authorities to attempt to implement a version of it in El Salvador. Béneke believed the Japanese system illustrated how education could help industrialize an agricultural economy by creating an abundant skilled labor force.

It is no surprise that incoming President Rivera made education a focal point of his new government's platform. He and other governing officials may or may not have had an intrinsic interest in educational quality, but they realized the issue provided them with an opportunity to boost their legitimacy. Moreover, since the 1950s the local discussion around education shifted from an "education for citizenship" focus to the "human capital" discourse pioneered by economists like Theodore Schultz. Directly and indirectly, human capital ideas had influenced local policy makers. Bert F. Hoselitz, one of Schultz's colleagues at the University of Chicago, had advised previous Salvadoran governments on industrial policy stressing the need of an educated labor force.[3] In his inaugural address, Rivera (1962: 10) presented education as a way for El Salvador to both industrialize the economy and defeat communism, a winning combination in 1960's El Salvador. He labeled communism as the "greatest danger" facing the country and said one strategy his government would use to meet that threat was socioeconomic reform, including education reform, and well-planned development projects, all in the spirit of the AfP, which he embraced "without prejudice or reserve."

The charter of the Alliance for Progress encouraged governments to prepare planning documents and, in response, the Rivera administration issued a five-year plan for 1965–1969. The section on education provided a succinct expression of the Rivera administration's view of the relationship between education and industrialization. Hoselitz's advice had left a lasting impression: the plan highlighted the need for a better-educated workforce to promote industrialization. It also stressed the need for agricultural entrepreneurs who could command modern techniques (CONAPLAN 1964). As solutions to these problems, the five-year plan set out a series of lofty goals and called for aggressive policies to achieve them. Some of the goals included immediate universal enrollment for students at the primary level, and a similar degree of enrollment at the junior high school level in the near future. The five-year plan did not mention educational television, but the government had already considered the possibilities of this new technology. Béneke was a key player in bringing the prospects of educational television to the attention of Salvadoran policy makers. Predictably, he encouraged officials in the Rivera administration to imitate the Japanese model in which televisions were used in schools.

In 1964, Guillermo Borja Nathan, the Executive Secretary of the government's Planning Department, delineated the official rationale for educational television in a letter to the World Bank:

> Education, at the high school and university levels, is particularly important for accelerated economic growth. It is estimated that during the next five years it will be necessary to create at least 30,000 new jobs each year. Most of these jobs will be in the commercial, industrial and service sectors, and many of them will need training at the secondary or vocational school levels . . . Education by television could play an important role in all these levels. Particularly where school enrollments are small, the use of a monitor instead of a teacher could make it possible that high quality teaching would be available in places where it would not be otherwise available. Supervision would be left in the hands of moderately trained teachers. The advantages of this system could be significant for secondary and vocational education in the rural areas of the country.[4]

A United Nations Educational, Scientific and Cultural Organization (UNESCO) mission that went to El Salvador at the end of 1964 highlighted the firm belief among international development experts that the country's success depended on vigorous action by government leaders to transform the economy through educational reform. It submitted a report that recommended the creation of a system of educational television, bolstering Béneke's plan.[5]

The reformist agenda started by the Rivera administration between 1962 and 1967 accelerated after the inauguration of his chosen successor and fellow army man, Fidel Sánchez Hernández, in July 1967. Sánchez selected Béneke as his Minister of Education. He lost no time in taking the steps necessary to advance an ambitious agenda for reform that was predictably focused on educational television. Thus, by 1968, key authorities in the Salvadoran government had embraced the idea that a massive education reform needed to be undertaken linking economic development to the agenda to stop the advance of communism and that the use of educational television should be one of its main components. Early support from UNESCO helped turn the simple and original idea of using "a monitor instead of a teacher" into a concrete project that made television a key tool to promote economic development.

The Alliance for Progress, Modernization Theory, and the Cold War Agenda

The Salvadoran plan could not get started without significant investment. Before the Cuban Revolution, it would not have been possible to find foreign financing for such an ambitious project. But the situation had changed: the Cold War had entered a new stage, and the United States and its Alliance for Progress were eager to help. The idea of using foreign aid to finance development programs was relatively new for El Salvador (Park 1995). The overall amount of nonmilitary US funding to El Salvador throughout the 1950s had been very modest, less than $1 million per year. The preoccupations raised by the Cuban Revolution had ushered in a new attitude towards foreign aid. After 1960, mainly under the auspices of the AfP, the amount of annual aid to El Salvador increased between ten- and twenty-fold.

The anti-communist impulses behind the aid were clearly evident in discussions over the first aid package that was arranged in February 1961. A portion of that package was devoted to education and literacy programs. US officials made clear that anti-communism was their top priority, worrying that the proposed literacy program could aid communists' propaganda efforts. Literate rural peoples could read their printed propaganda, after all: "A literacy campaign could represent one of the target points for communist influences in the government. By the same token, it represents a point where US aid could be made effective: not only in supplying anti-communist literature and pamphlets, but also in supplying soundly conceived educational materials apart from political orientation." That same anti-communist impulse supported the idea of developing new school textbooks in hopes of filling the "intellectual and even emotional void in the urban and rural schools which now can only too easily be filled by literature supplied from leftist sources." When it came to buying books for libraries, US aid officials wanted to make sure the topics of the new books "get directly to the area of educational and spiritual response in which the communists can make their greatest inroads."[6]

Eventual US support for El Salvador's TV-centered education reform also had to do with the fact that President Lyndon B. Johnson took a keen interest in educational television. It was under his watch, in 1966 and 1967, that the Corporation for Public Broadcasting was created in the United States. Johnson believed that just as education television had the potential to promote learning at home, it could also promote economic development abroad. During a stopover at American Samoa in October 1966, he celebrated the island's cutting-edge use of television in classrooms. Upon his arrival at Pago Pago's airport, the president said the island had "become a showplace for progress" and that "the pilot program of education which you have started may point the way to learning breakthroughs throughout the Pacific islands and Southeast Asia. Samoan children are learning twice as fast as they once did."[7] A month after returning from Pago Pago, Johnson created a task force to "assess the value of educational television broadcasting for primary and secondary schools in less-developed countries."[8] It came to be called the White House Task Force on Educational Television in Less-Developed Countries.

In April 1967, Johnson attended a summit with the Latin American heads of state at Punta del Este, Uruguay, to discuss how to "work toward modernization of Latin life."[9] The White House Task Force on Educational Television had told the president in March that the Uruguay Conference provided an ideal opportunity to promote educational television and recommend a "pilot project" in El Salvador.[10] While at Punta del Este, Johnson met with the president-elect of El Salvador, Colonel Sánchez Hernández, to discuss "the potentialities of instructional television for speeding educational development." The project was of sufficient importance that Johnson mentioned it explicitly in his formal remarks at the opening session with the other heads of state. He promised US technical and monetary support to create "an inter-American training center for educational broadcasting" and to set up "a pilot educational television demonstration project in a Central American country that will teach the children by day and entertain and inform their families at night."[11]

By June 1968, US agencies were ready to support El Salvador with a detailed document outlining the details of the education reform and recommending the authorization of a $1,900,000 loan.[12] The following month, President Johnson traveled to El Salvador for a meeting with the five Central American presidents. During the trip, he visited a teacher training school, where he announced the loan and an additional donation of $700,000.[13] In his official remarks, Johnson mentioned he had been "greatly inspired" by the educational television experience in American Samoa and was delighted the Samoan accomplishments were "going to be done and improved" in El Salvador. Since the television initiative in El Salvador was a pilot project, the United States Agency for International Development (USAID, the agency managing AfP funds), planned to follow its progress with rigorous social science investigations. To design and carry out the research, USAID hired a team from the Institute for Communications Research at Stanford University, headed by Wilbur Schramm. Not coincidentally, Schramm had been the main author of the reports that persuaded Johnson that the experiment with educational television in American Samoa had been a rousing success. Johnson, who had a keen interest in the television medium, was well aware of Schramm's work; in 1964, he wrote a foreword for one of his books (Lerner and Schramm 1967).

The selection of Schramm to head the investigation team in El Salvador demonstrated the importance that the Johnson administration placed on the Salvadoran project. By then, Schramm was an expert in the field of communications and development and had contributed to transforming the idea of television from a technological innovation with educational potential into a development tool and a weapon in the Cold War. Schramm had been a highly prominent advocate of educational television in the United States in the 1950s, and in the following decade, he publicized it as a means to modernize traditional peoples in developing countries. The success of Schramm's efforts can largely be attributed to his ability to frame his advocacy in the language of modernization theory. He promoted the idea of using communications to modernize "traditional societies," a theme he developed in his book *Mass Media and National Development*, which was translated into many languages. He published his work at a critical time, when some theorists considered the modernization process to be inexorable and many Latin American nations to be in the "preconditions to take off" stage.[14] It was at a crucial stage since, according to modernization theory, it was the point where countries were vulnerable to the "disease of transition," communism, an alternative and undesirable route to modernity. Thus, they argued the United States needed to devote large amounts of money to foreign aid programs to help countries along the modernization process and to stop communism.

Wilbur Schramm was one of the most influential authors linking modernization to mass communications and eventually to educational television. To overcome politically dangerous backwardness, the citizens of poor countries had to change their traditional mores. "Unless they change," Schramm argued in *Mass Media and National Development*, "they will have to watch technological growth from the sidelines; social change will happen to them, rather than their playing an active part in bringing it about" (1964: 19). Schramm cited Max Millikan and Donald Blackmer (1961: 23), who had said, "The paramount requirement of change in any society is that the people themselves must change." To this comment, Schramm added, "This is the point where modern communication becomes so important to economic development" (1964: 26).

For Schramm, mass communications was the most effective instrument to turn traditional social structures into modern ones. Mass media would increase the flow of information from industrialized countries and create a climate of change by raising people's aspirations: "In the service of national development, the mass media are agents of social change. The specific kind of social change they are expected to help accomplish is the transition to new customs and practices and, in some cases, to different social relationships. Behind such changes in behavior must necessarily lie substantial changes in attitudes, beliefs, skills, and social norms" (114). Schramm believed the way to achieve these changes was through the educational system: "Public education is both a leading channel of information to the people and a chief support of the mass media. Schools build literacy. They instill the kinds of interests and needs that require mass media" (110). Such an argument about the link between education and mass media converged perfectly in the policy of instructional television. For him, television technology was an effective way to disseminate quality instruction at minimal cost:

> In Chicago, the entire curriculum of a junior college is offered by television and studied quite successfully by hundreds of students who have no other contact with the college except at examination time or when they send in written assignments or ask questions. It may well be that in the atmosphere of need in a developing country, the media can carry a much larger share of the teaching load

than they have been asked to carry in economically better developed countries. (144)

This is the optimism that led to the Salvadoran "pilot project." Schramm's work in El Salvador was the result first of his success in casting his ideas in the dominant paradigm of modernization theory, and second in skillfully placing them in the agenda of international development organizations. *Mass Media and National Development* was a decisive work in advancing those ideas. It also accounts for the depth of his collaboration with UNESCO in the mid-1960s. In fact, the book was commissioned by UNESCO and published on its behalf.

In 1951, the General Conference of UNESCO had authorized its Director-General "to bring to the attention of Member States information and suggestions to stimulate the more rapid development and application of television" for the purpose of furthering international understanding through education, science, and culture. This project could have taken many different directions, but in the end, it was guided by Schramm's ideas. During the 1960s, the organization's ideas on development came to be heavily influenced by modernization theory, a transformation that took place, by and large, during the tenure of René Maheu as Director-General (1962–1972). Maheu was in full synchronicity with the ethos and can-do spirit of the emerging development community. He perceived of the 1960 UNESCO General Conference as giving the institution a completely new direction when it decided "priority should be given to education for the implementation of national plans for social and economic development."[15] UNESCO's Executive Board explicitly endorsed the Alliance for Progress and directed the Director-General to ensure UNESCO's "closest possible participation" in the development of educational and social programs helping Latin American countries prepare projects to be presented as part of the AfP program.[16]

Schramm shaped UNESCO's approach toward instructional television so much that scholars referred to it as "the UNESCO-Schramm" strategy of communications. His writings became obligatory reference material for anyone interested in instructional television, and the outlines of his ideas reappeared in narrative form in countless reports by international aid missions. In the Spanish case, ideas advocating educational television and establishing a link between education and economic development reached educational leaders through document series like "Reports and Papers on Mass Communication," magazines like *The UNESCO Courier*, and international training seminars and conferences attended by Ministry of Education officials. The same international communications apparatus devoted to the dissemination and legitimization of the new approach to education policy influenced Salvadoran authorities. Schramm had been instrumental in framing the message in the language of modernization theory.

The fact that countries as different as Spain and El Salvador were receptive to educational television had to do with the fact that one of the basic premises of modernization theory was that its prescriptions were universally applicable. As Walt Rostow put it in *Stages of Economic Growth*, "there is emerging from the intensive work of social scientists on the development problem a recognition that there are common elements in the patterns of development of different countries which have implications for development policy elsewhere." Cultural differences received attention insofar as they could delay industrialization, but they were seen as "mere 'obstacles' destined to the dustbin of history" (Gilman 2003: 52). All countries, regardless of their history, could follow the same path to modernity and eventually resemble industrialized countries. And so, if educational television could help one country advance along the path to modernity, then it could help them all. The Japanese experience and Italy's *Telescuola* became models that were to be followed. According to one UNESCO report, "It may well be envisaged that classes in Asian countries will gather around the television screen and that the bulk of instruction will be provided over the air" (UNESCO 1967: 14).

Be it through his influence in US President Johnson's speeches, the Alliance for Progress advisers, or UNESCO reports, the influence of Schramm's version of modernization was present in the discourse and actions of Salvadoran leaders, even if they were not aware of it. By the time Colonel Sánchez Hernández became president of El Salvador, the leaders of the military regime had already established that education would be a privileged instrument to legitimize the political system and that they would introduce educational television. At the same time, UNESCO and the AfP were already working in tandem to promote educational television following Schramm's scheme.

Implementation of the Reform

As a five-year presidential term was a short time to accomplish all that Sánchez Hernández and his team wanted to do, the reform was executed implacably pushing aside any obstacles. Educational television determined most every other aspect of the reform; the reports produced by the Stanford University research team directed by Schramm called education television the "catalyst" for the entire reform. (It is worth noting the Stanford Reports were mandatory reading for Salvadoran policy makers and provided feedback and guided policy at every stage). The revision of teacher training in 1968 emerged directly from the need to retrain teachers to become "partners" with the teleteachers. The reorganization of the ministry's administration eased its ability to implement an ambitious project like TVE. The new teaching style that accompanied the use of television required more support for teachers, which in turn prompted the creation of a new system of school supervision in 1969. Television also addressed one of the main problems faced by the reform's designers: increasing the percentage of children in school without adding to the cost needed to educate each student. Television had high start-up costs, but once the system was operational, it was supposed to be a cheap way to reach large numbers of students. In late 1971 and early 1972, the curricula, textbooks, and teacher manuals were thoroughly revised for all levels, mainly at the middle school level, with the goal of facilitating teleclasses and introducing the modernizing agenda, particularly in subjects like social studies.

Televised classes had a relatively simple format: students watched a twenty-minute lesson on television, and then the classroom teacher elaborated and answered questions. Béneke said on one occasion that his idea was to find the best teachers and then "can" (as in canning tomatoes) their taped lessons so he could make the highest-quality product available to the largest number of consumers.[17] Education authorities defined the classroom teacher and the teleteacher as "partners." By 1970, the system covered 219 public seventh-grade classrooms, which meant more than half of all students at that level received some of their education through televisions. That same year, a trial run in the eighth grade covered thirty-two classes (Schramm 1971: 14). By 1972, most students in all three grades of public middle schools received their classes from teleteachers.

The international supporters of educational television (UNESCO, USAID, and the Stanford team under Schramm) celebrated the uniformity and centralization that television introduced into the system. UNESCO's consulting team saw virtue in having each classroom presided by only one specialized teleteacher "with the same curriculum and the same quality control, and experiences that require high-cost laboratories and aspects of modern scientific development." It also saw television as a way to solve the problem of poor-quality teaching, because even teachers with "short and general training" could teach effectively with TV with a modest amount of additional training (Mayo et al. 1975). The Stanford team concurred, saying, "television can present exactly the same instruction to all students at the same time. This makes possible a common evaluation of learning since a common curriculum was used and core instruction was identical" (McAnany et al. 1970: 5).

Middle school students received their English, Social Studies, and Spanish lessons in new ways, with a new curriculum and a retrained teacher working in partnership with a teacher that appeared at regularly scheduled times on the TV monitor. School supervisors were supposed to drop by at regular intervals to provide helpful advice. More and more students were being taught in airy new school buildings with wide corridors. It was not unusual for the "reformed classrooms" to receive visits from researchers and international visitors interested in the "pilot project." Each aspect of the education reform converged in a concrete way in the middle school classroom, where the first of many students' minds were supposed to be modernized. At least that was the plan, but daily reality in the school did not necessarily conform to the expectations of international development specialists and government policy makers in San Salvador, Washington, and Paris. How did teachers perceive the radical transformation of their daily experience? At first, many teachers seemed open to the innovation of televised teaching. The Stanford team surveyed a sample of teachers in 1969 (including users and nonusers of TVE) and reported that 73 percent believed "students learn more by television than by teaching without TV," and 76 percent felt "classroom teachers improve their teaching method by observing the television teacher" (Ingle 1973: 33).

Teaching with television altered radically the traditional class routine and the teachers' professional responsibilities. "It was no longer a matter of simple class planning . . . [There were] too many books," said one former teacher, commenting on the extra work required.[18] Various teachers stressed that television would have been good if it had been used in support of the classroom teacher, because "children preferred a [live] lecture class," and "the best thing is the teacher-student interaction."[19] With television, the children became "mere spectators; without participation, they did not learn."[20] Coincidentally, a former student said that, in the presence of the teleteacher, the classroom teacher became "a passive person." Many educators found the rigidity of the schedule imposed by the centrally broadcast teleclasses to be jarring. Some teachers remember the system as "impersonal and unidirectional."[21] A former teacher described how "teachers could not incorporate a new activity into the class, if you missed a class you lost it . . . Educational television enslaved you."[22] For another teacher, the problem was that the class instructor had only ten minutes to answer the questions raised by the teleclass and reinforce the key points: "The annoying thing is that teachers had no time . . . after one teleclass came another one, and another one." It was as if education was happening on an assembly line. The rigid schedule of the broadcasts put time constraints around every aspect of school. For the most responsible teachers (and for those who had time to spare), this situation forced them to spend time with students after school and help them catch up on the material covered by the teleclasses.[23]

Only 20 percent of instructors possessed training appropriate for the class level they were teaching. Not surprisingly, many of them found the experience of teaching new curriculum in tandem with the teleteacher to be demoralizing because it exposed their limitations before the students. The Stanford team's class observations provide ample accounts of this happening. In a Social Studies class, the teacher had an authoritarian style that the students contrasted unfavorably to the charming teleteacher (Mayo et al. 1973: 100–102). English teachers had an almost impossible task of matching up to the teleteacher, whose accent was almost flawless. The report from one class observation said, "Attitudes toward English benefited most from the introduction of ETV, since English was little liked by non-ETV students but well regarded by ETV students." A footnote to the report used that evidence to justify the use of educational television, saying English teachers in the country were ill prepared, and therefore TV was particularly effective in that subject (Wolff 1973).

Seemingly unaware of the implications of what it was revealing, a Stanford report said, "The classroom teacher's word is no longer the only word" (Hornik 1970: 156). Advocates of the system promoted the teleteacher as someone to imitate, as "a model of good teaching techniques that can be emulated by the classroom teacher." The Stanford reports saw the interaction not as a threat to the self-esteem of the local instructor but rather as an incentive to improve: "In some instances, the classroom teacher develops a feeling of competition with the teleteacher, and he works very hard to show his students the he is as competent and creative as the teleteacher" (158). Interviewers with TVE alums revealed more about how the competition played out in real life. One former student from a rural area reported that a teacher in his school went to great lengths to imitate the teleteacher, such that he and his classmates gossiped about it during recess. The classroom teacher began dressing like his urban, televised counterpart, including wearing cufflinks, an unusual affectation for a small rural town.[24] A female teacher remembers that children were "more motivated" looking at a well-dressed teleteacher "with resources." In contrast, "the village instructor, with her presentation, would not be equally motivating . . . It affected the self-esteem of the rural teacher; the teleteacher left her lacking in every aspect."[25]

Some teachers believed TVE was part of a grand plan to replace the classroom teacher by "trying to tell the teacher that she or he didn't know anything." Some reasoned that the teachers chosen to appear on TV were selected less because of their proficiency and more because of their political reliability; "the government was always interested in the sycophantic ones" at the expense of independent teachers.[26] In the power conflict between flesh-and-bones teachers and the image on television, the latter invariably won. During the height of the reform, teachers came to feel their sense of professionalism threatened by television. One of them, a union activist, felt he had been "trained with great humanism" in the normal school and that no television could replace him.[27] Older teachers lamented the end of the old system of normal schools, feeling their time in school had built a *sprit de corps* and a sense of collective mission.

As in the Spanish case discussed in earlier chapters, the swift introduction of changes in educational policy was done in a fashion that reflected a political system accustomed to imposing its will from above expecting unquestioning acquiescence. This attitude had the effect of alienating teachers. Some teachers describe both TVE and the entire 1968 reform with blanket condemnation. One union activist remembers it as an example of the "vertical attitude of the government that demonstrated contempt for teachers."[28] A veteran teacher said, "Walter Béneke's reform destroyed education in order to deliver classes by television."[29] Another teacher suggested Béneke's motive for pushing TVE was personal greed: "The rumor was that he has done great business with Japan in the television deal."[30] That charge is inaccurate, since the monitors were purchased in the United States, but it reveals a level of anger and suspicion that has survived decades.

Apart from the philosophical and political qualms they may have had about the reform, teachers felt it had negatively impacted their daily life. Early in 1971, the ministry had begun the policy of expanding enrollments by eliminating middle school tuition. The policy was successful in bringing more students to the TVE classrooms, which, given the limited number of schools, created a space crisis. The solution to the rapid increase in the number of students was a policy of "double shifts" that forced teachers to work extra hours. "Part of the reform that was highly criticized was the schedule change," said one teacher.[31] In addition, many teachers were required to take additional training classes on Saturdays, ironically via television, as an early form of distance learning. One teacher recalls the additional classes "were not well received; many left the classroom; we were already working Monday through Friday."[32]

Even if teachers were initially open to the idea of experimenting with educational television, they grew disenchanted with it. The quotidian experiences of teachers were far more complex. The system put new demands on them. They had to go through retraining. Students inevitably compared them to the teleteachers, rarely to their advantage. As the system progressed, many had to teach two shifts and longer hours without commensurate compensation. Moreover, the reform, with all its alienating features, came at a time when they were already unhappy with their working conditions and the benefits they were receiving. Government authorities were so enamored of their project and so eager to put it in place that they were oblivious to how teachers perceived it. The Sánchez Hernández administration, true to the authoritarian nature of the military regime, steamrolled every obstacle to impose its vision of modernity, while teachers felt estranged, powerless, and ignored by the authorities.

Political Consequences

As the implementation of the reform progressed without respite, the relation between the state, the teachers, and the teachers' union (Asociación Nacional de Educadores Salvadoreños—ANDES) became confrontational.[33] From the political point of view, the gradual alienation of teachers was part of a wider picture. Teacher grievances can be better understood in the larger context of the political polarization and activism occurring in the late 1960s and early 1970s, not only in El Salvador but also the rest of the world. The type of student activism discussed by Oscar J. Martín García (chapter 6) had its equivalent in the streets of San Salvador. The recent literature on the "global sixties" (e.g., Jian et al. 2018) reminds us of the particular vigor of social mobilization during those years, from Paris in 1968 to Tlatelolco in 1969, passing through the protests against the Franco regime and activism in Africa and Asia. The fact that the education reform was taking place in a political environment that was becoming increasingly unsettled and polarized gave a particularly defiant stance to the groups that opposed it.

The relationship between the educational reform and the teachers' struggles was complex. When the reform was enacted, it fueled a fight that was already in its initial stages. In an interview, Arnoldo Vaquerano, a union leader, mentioned that teachers resented the fact that they had not been consulted in the design of innovations that were going to have a profound impact on their profession. Educational television was a classic example. Even if it was affecting only a small number of teachers at the middle school level at first, teachers saw it as an indication of their endangered future. Vaquerano explained he believed the government intended to replace teachers with television monitors: "One of their [government officials'] objectives was to stop producing new instructors, that is, with a TV monitor in the classroom and a team of educators teaching classes from the headquarters of educational TV . . . They needed no more than two or three teachers for several grades." The reform also implied a sense of direction for the economic development of the country that union leaders did not agree with: "The development of the country had to be based on an education reform; the mistake was the way they tried to develop [the country]."[34]

Numerous and diverse factors increased the state of conflict between teachers and the military regime. In 1968, the union organized its first strike to demand better retirement benefits, and in 1971, it asked for salary improvements. By 1971, teachers had come to believe they were woefully underpaid. They had not received a raise since 1962, and the government was using a 1941 formula to set base pay and determine raises (Anaya Montes 1972: 11). Furthermore, as a consequence of the education reform, teachers were required to work longer hours each day and teach many more students with only a modest raise in the offering as compensation. The breaking point for ANDES came when the legislature approved the Ley General de Educación (General Education Law) on 8 July 1971 after a three-week debate. The law was the comprehensive legislation for the education innovations. Its contents addressed most every aspect of the reform, including a 10 percent raise for teachers and an amended formula for raises, one less generous than ANDES had requested.

After the vote, ANDES spokespersons declared the union to be on indefinite strike. In explaining their reasons for doing so, they mentioned teacher pay but situated their decision in broader terms. ANDES accused the government of "continually and profoundly marginalizing education" by "favoring and accentuating the education of elites" at the expense of the rural poor. The union also expressed opposition to the changes introduced by the reform in secondary education, to TVE, and to the conditions imposed by the United States in the loans that financed the various components of the education reform.[35] To deal with a strike that was perceived as an extraordinary challenge, the state turned to coercion quickly. The government immediately declared all striking teachers would have their salaries deducted for every day of missed work, and it occasionally dangled the carrot of receiving back pay if they returned to work the following day.[36] In addition, a virulent press campaign accused the teachers of being puppets of a communist conspiracy with nefarious purposes. When those tactics failed to end the strike, the state turned to threats, intimidations, violence, and outright murder, not unlike the tactics used by Franco's regime against similar protests in Spain.

ANDES leaders said they were receiving death threats and saw unmarked cars driving by their homes. They began sleeping in different houses every few nights for security reasons.[37] Meanwhile, out in the streets, the army cracked down on demonstrators with tear gas, violence, and mass arrests. At least two teachers and three or more university students were killed. Not surprisingly, the murdered teachers were ANDES leaders, and they disappeared under mysterious, death-squad-like circumstances (Anaya Montes 1972: 48–49). So fierce was the violence that ANDES spokespersons said, "It seems the government wants the strike to continue so that it can break the teachers' resistance physically."[38] Throughout the strike, TVE classes were transmitted regularly, as if to show the system could function without teachers.

Accompanying the heightened activities in the streets was a more radicalized rhetoric in which teachers identified themselves with workers and peasants. ANDES Secretary General José Mario López said teachers would fight for a labor code that "represents the true interests of the working class in which not only is labor valued, but the laborer is valued as a human being, and peasants have the right to unionize."[39] ANDES received a strong support from an already growing opposition movement. Paul Almeida, in a careful study of social movements in El Salvador, describes how the strike "tapped into the organizational infrastructure support" of the entire labor movement as well as "high school and public university student associations, the newly formed Jesuit university, oppositional political parties, and even the incipient peasant movement" (2008: 93). The strikes mobilized up to fifty thousand people, including teachers and their supporters. To put this figure in context, the total labor force involved in manufacturing in 1970 was about 108,000 workers (USAID 1973).

The strike ended after fifty-three days. The striking teachers had none of their main demands met, and the government's only concession was to foreswear reprisals against striking teachers. But the impact of the strikes cannot be measured in terms of the concessions obtained by the union. In the key decade of 1962 and 1972, the period when most of the civil society infrastructure that would play a major role in mass mobilization in the late 1970s and early 1980s was created, the teachers' strikes were pivotal moments. ANDES, pushed by governmental repression and arrogance, positioned itself "in the vanguard of the class struggle," according to an observer (Lungo 1987: 62). A conservative editorialist, Juan Ulloa, offered his assessment of the 1971 strike and of ANDES's emergent radicalism. He described the strike as a "failed communist plan" and said the striking teachers proved the "communist plague is amongst us." He went on to say that the way to handle communists had been demonstrated by General Martínez in 1932: "[He] shot them" (1971: 7). He was referring to an infamous event in Salvadoran history when the government repressed a peasant uprising with indiscriminate massacres that claimed at least ten thousand victims. The political polarization of the 1970s had begun in earnest.

The story of the education reform and of the conflict between teachers and the state ended tragically. El Salvador's Ministry of Education slowly abandoned educational television in the late 1970s and early 1980s. No one thought of replacing the TV monitors when they fell into disrepair. Guerrillas bombed the transmission towers. The government's political communication officers who took over the broadcasting station during the war destroyed the taped lessons.[40] The teachers' union joined one of the mass revolutionary movements that supported the guerrillas. Death squads announced in 1975 they would eliminate union leaders and identified teachers as one of their main targets (Dunkerley 1982: 69). Former education minister Béneke was assassinated by a guerrilla group a few months before the civil war started in earnest. Former ANDES leader Mélida Anaya Montes was murdered in April 1983, stabbed dozens of times by a rival guerrilla as part of an internal power dispute within the guerrilla front she had joined (Dickey 1983). Other leaders of the teachers' union became guerrilla commanders, including Salvador Sánchez Cerén, who was elected president of El Salvador more than a decade after the end of the civil war. Perhaps the most telling metaphor for the fate of the TVE-led educational reform was the closing down of the teacher training school to turn it into a garrison for the infamous US-trained Atlacatl Battalion, a military unit responsible for some of the worst human rights violations during the civil war.

It must also be recognized that US foreign aid funds were not the only ones at the disposal of Salvadoran authorities. The Alliance for Progress was rarely a solo act, neither in conception, financing, nor execution. Various other development agencies, in particular UNESCO, made explicit efforts to act in concert with the AfP. For their part, Salvadoran government authorities took full advantage of the common goals of international aid agencies. They brought in Spanish art teachers, Japanese gym teachers, Japanese funds for the industrial high school, British money for a technology institute, and Italian support for television programs. In fact, studies of the impact of the AfP fail to mention the extent to which US foreign aid activities in the 1960s and 1970s were coordinated with resources from other countries and other development organizations. What made the TVE project attractive to Alliance for Progress officers was its core proposition that mass communication could promote development in poor countries. That belief was rooted in modernization theory and was seen as an inspired tool to stop the advance of communism. With the 1968 educational reform, Schramm's grand Cold War scheme found its way into Salvadoran classrooms, thereby altering the quotidian experience of thousands of teachers and students.

Students experienced the conflict that emerged from the reform, such as their teachers going on strike, sometimes returning angry and politicized, sometimes disappearing or returned after a stint in jail. During the teachers' strikes, tensions arose between parents and teachers. After seeing what happened to their teachers, some students concluded that the nation's power relations were out of balance, and many of them joined student organizations that quickly became radicalized. Teachers felt threatened by the possibility of being replaced by a machine; the daily routine of many of them was one of competition with an imperturbable electronic box that presided over their classrooms and commanded the attention of students. They saw the government giving great attention to education while simultaneously downplaying the importance of teachers; the expenditures on educational technology went up while teachers' workloads increased without a proportional change in salary. The modernization project that was meant as an enlightened approach to avoid a communist-inspired revolution backfired. It alienated educators to such an extent that the teacher's union became a key element of the Salvadoran insurgency of the 1980s.

Héctor Lindo-Fuentes received his History PhD from the University of Chicago. He is currently Professor of History and Latin American Studies at Fordham University in New York City. His publications include books on the economic history of Central America, the history of education, and the politics of memory in El Salvador. His most recent book, written in collaboration with Erik Ching, is *Modernizing Minds in El Salvador: Education Reform and the Cold War, 1960–1980* (2012), which received the Alfred B. Thomas Award for Best Book on a Latin American theme published by a member of the Southeastern Council of Latin American Studies. He served as director and is currently a member of Fordham University's interdisciplinary Latin American and Latin American Studies program. He has taught courses at the University of Illinois at Urbana Champaign; the University of California, Santa Barbara; the University of California, Los Angeles; Columbia University, and universities in El Salvador, Costa Rica, and Nicaragua.

Notes

1. The literature on the Alliance for Progress and modernization theory is vast and constantly growing. For the AfP, a good early reference is Levinson and Onís (1970). See also Rabe (1999); Smith (1991). For the specifics of the AfP in Central America, see Coatsworth (1994); Grandin (2006). For modernization theory, see Engerman et al. (2003); Latham (2000).
2. See *La Prensa Gráfica*, 19 March 1962, 3.
3. The influence of Hoselitz and human capital ideas in El Salvador is discussed in some detail in Lindo-Fuentes and Ching (2012: chap. 1).
4. "Letter to Orvis Schmidt, Director of Operations, World Bank," 25 June 1964, Reg. X07.21(728.4) Relations with El Salvador—Official, Paris, UNESCO Archives (UA).
5. L. H. S. Emerson, Guilhermo Dutra da Fonseca, J. A. Laing, and Maya J. Paez, "Educational Priority Projects for Development: El Salvador—Mission Foreword by Director General R. Maheu," 1965, UNESCO.
6. "Action Program for El Salvador: Act of Bogotá Main Points," 11 February 1961, Joint Embassy USOM USIS, 1961 *DOS-IAES 1960–1963*.
7. "Memorandum on Appointing a Task Force to Study the Role of Educational Television in the Less-Developed Countries," 26 November 1966, The American Presidency Project, University of California, Santa Barbara (APP), http://www.presidency.ucsb.edu/ws/?pid=28048 (accessed 5 July 2008).
8. "Remarks Upon Arrival at Tafuna International Airport, Pago Pago, American Samoa," 18 October 1966, APP, http://www.presidency.ucsb.edu/ws/?pid=27945 (accessed 5 July 2008).
9. "Remarks in Punta del Este at the Public Session of the Meeting of American Chiefs of State," April 1967, APP, http://www.presidency.ucsb.edu/ws/?pid=28201 (accessed 7 July 2008).

10. "White House Task Force on Educational Television in Less-Developed Countries: summary and recommendations," 27 June 1967, USAID Development Information Center.
11. *White House Diary*, 14 April 1967, Lyndon B. Johnson Presidential Library. http://www.lbjlib.utexas.edu/johnson/archives.hom/Diary/1967/670414-05.asp (accessed 15 November 2008).
12. "El Salvador: Educational Reform Program Including ITV, AID-DLC/P-738, June 1968." Agency for International Development, Department of State, 1968.
13. "Remarks at the Alberto Masferrer Normal School, San Andres, El Salvador." July 1968, APP, http://www.presidency.ucsb.edu/ws/?pid=28994 (accessed 5 July 2008).
14. Rostow (1960) in his classic work on modernization theory identified five stages of economic growth: traditional society, preconditions for takeoff, takeoff, drive to maturity, and age of high mass consumption.
15. "Memorandum to Resident Representatives," 17 December 1963, Reg. X07.21(728.4) TA "65/66" El Salvador-TA Programme for 1965–1966, UA.
16. "UNESCO, Executive Board, 60th session, 60 EX/Decisions," 22 December 1961, Executive Board, Paris, UA.
17. The "canning" metaphor was attributed to Béneke by one of his main aides, Gilberto Aguilar Avilés. Interview with Gilberto Aguilar Avilés, San Salvador, 22 August 2002.
18. Interview with anonymous Co-ANDES activist, 8 June 2005.
19. Interview with Susana Contreras de Santamaría, 8 June 2005.
20. Interview with anonymous Co-ANDES activist, 8 June 2005.
21. Interview with Julio César Najarro, San Salvador, 16 June 2009.
22. Interview with Susana Contreras de Santamaría, 8 June 2005.
23. Interview with Julio César Najarro, San Salvador, 16 June 2009.
24 24. Interview with Osmín Ortiz, 16 June 2009.
25. Interview with Susana Contreras de Santamaría, 8 June 2005.
26. Interview with Margarita López de García, San Salvador, 28 June 2005.
27. Interview with Julio César Najarro, San Salvador, 16 June 2009.
28. Interview with Julio César Portillo, San Salvador, 28 June 2005.
29. Interview with Julio Alberto Gómez, San Salvador, 25 June 2005.
30. Interview with Susana Contreras de Santamaría, 8 June 2005.
31. Ibid.
32. Interview with Margarita López de García, San Salvador, 28 June 2005.
33. The full name of the union is Asociación Nacional de Educadores Salvadoreños (ANDES) 21 de Junio (National Association of Salvadoran Educators June 21).
34. Interview with Arnoldo Vaquerano, San Salvador, 18 July 2007.
35. *La Prensa Gráfica*, 8 July 1971, 36.
36. Ibid., 3.
37. Interview with Arnoldo Vaquerano, San Salvador, 18 July 2007.

38. *La Prensa Gráfica*, 29 July 1971, 11.
39. *La Prensa Gráfica*, 3 August 1971, 4.
40. Interview with Eduardo Suvillaga, Santa Tecla, 23 November 2004.

References

Almeida, Paul. 2008. *Waves of Protest: Popular Struggle in El Salvador, 1925–2005*. Minneapolis: University of Minnesota Press.

Anaya Montes, Mélida. 1972. *La segunda gran batalla de ANDES*. San Salvador: Editorial Universitaria.

Coatsworth, John, H. 1994. *Central America and the United States: The Clients and the Colossus*. New York: Twayne.

CONAPLAN (Consejo Nacional de Planificación y Coordinación Económica). 1964. *Primer Plan de Desarrollo Económico y Social, 1965–1969*. San Salvador: CONAPLAN.

Dickey, Christopher. 1983. "Salvadoran Rebel Intrigue: Dispute Leads to Deaths of Two Guerrilla Leaders." *Washington Post*, 27 June.

Dunkerley, James. 1982. *The Long War: Dictatorship and Revolution in El Salvador*. London: Verso.

Engerman, David, Nils Gilman, Mark H. Haefele, and Michael E. Latham, eds. 2003. *Staging Growth: Modernization, Development, and the Cold War*. Amherst: University of Massachusetts Press.

Gilman, Nils. 2003. "Modernization Theory: The Highest Stage of American Intellectual History." In Engerman et al. 2003: 47–80.

Grandin, Greg. 2006. *Empire's Workshop: Latin America, the United States, and the Rise of the New Imperialism*. New York: Metropolitan Books.

Hornik, Robert C. 1970. "Television and Educational Reform in El Salvador: Summary Report of the First Year of Research (02/01/69–11/01/69)." Stanford University Institute for Communications Research.

Ingle, Henry T. 1973. "Television and Educational Reform in El Salvador: Report on the Fourth Year of Research." Academy for Educational Development.

Jian, Chen, Masha Kirasirova, Mary Nolan, Marilyn Young, and Joanna Waley-Cohen, eds. 2018. *The Routledge Handbook of the Global Sixties: Between Protest and Nation-Building*. London: Routledge.

Latham, Michael. 2000. *Modernization as Ideology: American Social Science and "Nation Building" in the Kennedy Era*. Chapel Hill: University of North Carolina Press.

Lerner, Daniel, and Wilbur Schramm. 1967. *Communication and Change in Developing Countries*. Honolulu, HI: East-West Center Press.

Levinson, Jerome, and Juan de Onís. 1970. *The Alliance That Lost Its Way: A Critical Report on the Alliance for Progress*. Chicago: Quadrangle Books.

Lungo, Mario. 1987. *La lucha de las masas en El Salvador*. San Salvador: UCA Editores.

Mayo, John K., Robert C. Hornik, and Emile G. McAnany. 1973. "Television and Educational Reform in El Salvador: Report on the Fourth Year of Research." Stanford University, Institute for Communication Research.

——. 1975. "Instructional Television in El Salvador's Educational Reform." *Prospects: Quarterly Review of Education* 5 (1): 120–126

——. 1976. *Educational Reform with Television: The El Salvador Experience*. Stanford, CA: Stanford University Press.

McAnany, Emile G., John K. Mayo, and Robert C. Hornik. 1970. "Television and Educational Reform in El Salvador: Complete Report on the First Year of Research." Academy for Educational Development.

Millikan, Max F., and Donald L. M. Blackmer. 1961. *The Emerging Nations: Their Growth and United States Policy*. Boston: Little Brown.

Park, James William. 1995. *Latin American Underdevelopment: A History of Perspectives in the United States, 1870–1965*. Baton Rouge: Louisiana State University Press.

Rabe, Stephen. 1999. *The Most Dangerous Area in the World: John F. Kennedy Confronts Communist Revolution in Latin America*. Chapel Hill: University of North Carolina Press.

Rivera, Julio. 1962. *Mensaje del Teniente Coronel Julio A. Rivera al pueblo salvadoreño al tomar posesión de la presidencia de la república*. San Salvador: Secretaría de Información.

Rostow, Walt Whitman. 1960. *The Stages of Economic Growth: A Non-Communist Manifesto*. Cambridge: Cambridge University Press.

Schramm, Wilbur. 1964. *Mass Media and National Development: The Role of Information in Developing Countries*. Stanford, CA: Stanford University Press.

——. 1970. "Television and educational reform in El Salvador, Summary Report of the First Year of Research." Project Report Series, no. 10. USAID Supported Study/Document, Academy for Educational Development.

——. 1971. "Television and Educational Reform in El Salvador, Report on the Second Year of Research." Academy for Educational Development.

Smith, Tony. 1991. "The Alliance for Progress: The 1960s." In *Exporting Democracy: The United States and Latin America, Themes and Issues*, ed. Abraham F. Lowenthal, 71–89. Baltimore: Johns Hopkins University Press.

Ulloa, Juan. 1971. "Plan comunista que fracasó en El Salvador." *La Prensa Gráfica*, 13 September.

UNESCO (United Nations Educational, Scientific and Cultural Organization). 1967. "Radio and Television in the Service of Education and Development in Asia."

Reports and Papers on Mass Communication, no. 49. Paris: UNESCO.

USAID (US Agency for International Development). 1973. *Statistics for the Analysis of the Education Sector: El Salvador*. Washington, DC: USAID.

Wolff, Laurence. 1973. "Educational Reform and Instructional Television in El Salvador: A Summary of Research Findings." Academy for Educational Development.

Chapter 8

"Passing through a Critical Moment"

The United States and Brazilian University Reform in the 1960s

Colin M. Snider

At the end of 1968, Brazil's military dictatorship (1964–1985) issued its Reforma Universitária (University Reform), the country's first major higher educational policy in more than thirty years. The reform promoted the rapid expansion of Brazil's higher education system, restructured higher education by replacing isolated faculties with departments, gave rectors greater administrative control over universities, strengthened the federal government's role in public education, and emphasized science and technology over other academic fields in the name of national development.[1] The product of more than three years of studies by actors both domestic and foreign into the question of higher education, the Reforma marked a transformational moment that dramatically changed the development of higher education in Brazil in complex ways. Frank M. Tiller was one of those foreign actors involved in that process. Tiller, an engineering professor and Director of the Center for Study of Higher Education from the University of Houston, delivered a report on university reform to the Pontifícia Universidade Católica do Rio de Janeiro (Pontifical Catholic University of Rio de Janeiro—PUC-RJ) just a few weeks after the Reforma was issued. In his report, Tiller recommended that reforms to the university focus on administrative and fiscal matters, with power being more centralized in the rector's office, while addressing none of the issues of expansion, exams, or other academic matters the Reforma had addressed.

The juxtaposition of these two reports illustrates the complexity of university reform in Brazil. Throughout the 1960s, the United States, drawing on modernization theory, sought to wield the promise of educational assistance and reform as a means to maintain allies in

Latin America and Spain as part of the geopolitical cultural struggles of the Cold War. Like Spain and El Salvador, Brazil marked another country where US agents—governmental and nongovernmental alike—played a role in broader debates over what university reform in Brazil should look like, whom it should benefit, and what ends it should serve. Certainly, as other chapters in this volume demonstrate, US government officials were not the only ones to attempt to shape educational policies in other countries, as international organizations like UNESCO and the World Bank played a role in Spain and Latin America. Yet, not all agents of the United States' efforts operated at the level of a federal government or international organization. Institutions like the University of Houston and individuals like Frank Tiller also served as important interlocutors of the United States' visions of modernity and development in the Cold War. These institutions and actors, alongside institutions like the United States Agency for International Development (USAID) were neither homogeneous nor all-powerful in their participation, as Brazil's Reforma, which adopted some of the United States' recommendations while outright rejecting others, makes clear.

This chapter focuses on the presence of three actors in the United States' interaction with Brazil's military dictatorship regarding the question of university reform: USAID, Rudolph Atcon, and the University of Houston, represented by Frank Tiller. The former two have been subjects of a fair amount of historiographic attention, particularly in their symbolic importance to national politics in Brazil during the 1960s (Boschetti 2007; Cunha 2007; Fávero 1991; Ribeiro 2002; Taffet 2007; Vieira 1982). However, this focus has led to a somewhat simplified narrative that treats the United States as a homogeneous, culturally imperial power without exploring the heterogeneity of US visions of reform. Likewise, this scholarship has ignored the agency of Brazilians—both in support of and in opposition to the military regime—as they engaged in the debates around university reform in Brazil in the 1960s. Drawing on underused archival sources in both Brazil and the United States, this chapter situates educational reform in a broader global process of Cold War educational politics in Latin America and Spain. The chapter complicates and deepens understandings of the United States' role in Brazil's university reform process by focusing on the specific discourses about the social and economic functions of universities, and of the various types of reforms US actors from both governmental and educational institutions recommended. This focus simultaneously allows us to situate Brazil in the global field of the cultural Cold War, even as it illuminates the particular ways the United States sought to transfer its own vision of education and reform to Brazil yet recognizing the limitations of US policy and Brazilian actors' own agency in determining their path toward university reform without parroting or blindly accepting US recommendations. Ultimately, US efforts to shape reform reinforced extant discourses of modernity, development, and higher education in Brazil even while encountering obstacles in their own heterogeneous and not-always-unified vision of reform and Brazilians' own efforts to diagnose the role of higher education in the country.

Modernity, Development, and University Reform in Brazil's Long 1960s

Shortly after Brazil's military dictatorship took power via a coup on 1 April 1964, it turned its attentions to the role of universities in society and national development. However, rather than marking a sudden transformation in educational emphases, the military regime was just the latest in a series of regimes to examine and situate higher education in a privileged position in national developmentalist plans. Since the presidency of Juscelino Kubitschek (1956–1961), which viewed university reform and modernization as a key to Brazil's economic "autonomy" (Snider 2016), Brazilian governments across both democratic and authoritarian regimes sought to insert universities into state-led development projects that would rapidly industrialize and create an independent national economy (Almeida 2006; Dinius 2010; Ioris 2014; Skidmore 1988). After the brief, erratic presidency of Jânio Quadros, who resigned after just seven months, João Goulart (1961–1964) continued this emphasis on higher education and its role in national development.

Although their political and ideological backgrounds differed from Francisco Franco's dictatorship in Spain in fundamental ways, Kubitschek and Goulart, like Franco, viewed university education as essential to national development, although in very different national contexts. Goulart's government envisioned a dual role for universities in which they would not only help advance the nation's scientific and technological capacities but also help foment cultural development among the popular classes.[2] This emphasis on industrialization and technological advancement merged with mid-century attitudes of modernity and (under)development even as they reinforced narratives of Brazil's unfulfilled potential. Nor did these administrations exercise a monopoly on debates regarding development and education's contributions to it; as in Spain and elsewhere in Europe, Latin America, and other parts of the world in the "global sixties," groups including Brazilian students and academics increasingly defined development differently, viewing it in terms of greater social equality and justice domestically while eschewing models and definitions of development oriented toward expansion of capitalist production and consumerist ideologies (Langland 2013: 67–81; Vieira Pinto 1994).

Like their Spanish counterparts in the higher echelons of the authoritarian Francoist state, the visions of development and modernity of Brazilian officials as fueled by university-trained white-collar professionals in both democratic and authoritarian regimes in many ways overlapped with and echoed modernization theorists from the United States and elsewhere in the Global North. The most (in)famous of articulators of modernization theory was the economist Walt W. Rostow (1960), whose *The Stages of Economic Growth: A Non-Communist Manifesto* argued that societies went through five stages of "development," from "traditional" agricultural societies to "modern" consumerist capitalism based on industrialization (Kirkendall 2010: 7, 25; Lindo-Fuentes and Ching 2012: 79–80). Rostow argued the United States was one of the few "developed" nations in the world that could halt the spread of communism by providing funds and technical expertise to "underdeveloped" nations, advancing "Democracy, Development, and Stability" through "social programs," as one US government document at the end of the 1960s succinctly put it.[3] It was in this intellectual current and the framework of the Cold War that USAID came into being. Established in 1962 as a means to help implement President John F. Kennedy's Alliance for Progress (AfP), USAID covered a wide range of projects, including "agricultural improvement, technology infusion, postharvest production transportation plans, irrigation improvement, rural education, rural electrification, and road improvements to democracy reform operations or police training programs" (Price 2016: 122).

Just as Brazilian politicians' concerns turned toward higher education and its place in Brazilian development in the late 1950s, so too did officials begin to turn to the United States. Kubitschek warned of the threat of revolution should the United States not do more to work with Latin American nations to help them develop—warnings that fell on deaf ears, illustrating the "asymmetry and influence" that would define US-Brazil relations in a very different fashion in the 1960s (Long 2015: 25–73). In the aftermath of the Cuban Revolution and the United States' belated desire to implement the types of programs Kubitschek warned were needed, the Kennedy administration created the Alliance for Progress, building on the theories advanced in the works of Rostow (who would serve as an adviser in the Kennedy and Johnson administrations) and his acolytes. Upon taking office, Goulart attempted to take advantage of the AfP in order to stabilize and advance Brazil's economic production, though he met with recalcitrance from the Kennedy administration, whose officials viewed Goulart as susceptible to communism (Taffet 2007). Nonetheless, Goulart successfully entered into an agreement with the Inter-American Bank of Development (IDB), which secured foreign loans to help Brazil improve the educational system. Despite some institutional opposition from within the Brazilian government, which did not believe education was a "basic investment for national economic development,"[4] Goulart managed to succeed in acquiring the funding despite mounting US suspicions of his presidency.

After the military coup of 1964, aid from the IDB continued to flow into Brazil, which received more than $172 million to investigate and attempt to address educational reform (Castelo Branco 1966: 2:90; Skidmore 1988: 38). Likewise, shortly after the 1964 coup, the military regime sought aid from the International Bank for Reconstruction and Development (IBRD) to fund "projects for secondary and higher education, associated with the economic development of the country," with particular emphasis in two areas: creating a labor service to address the need for "human resources" and completing a new building at the National Engineering School (a part of the University of Brazil), allowing for better training for engineers[5]—a project the University of Houston would also be connected to.

This funding from the IDB and IBRD reveals Brazilian officials' willingness to turn to international and US-led agencies and the United States' financial presence in Brazil's efforts to address the issues of educational reform, and especially university reform, before the right-wing military regime of 1964–1985. However, the most infamous instance of US collaboration with Brazil's military dictatorship would not be via the IDB or IBRD but through USAID's agreements with the Ministry of Education and Culture (MEC). For the military regime, as with its predecessors, universities were a key locus and actor in facilitating national development. While the armed coup that overthrew Goulart was a rupture in terms of human rights, political ideology, labor relations, foreign relations, and other arenas, there were also continuities in the educational field. Shortly after taking office in April 1964, Humberto Castelo Branco (1964–1967), the first of five military presidents during the military regime, echoed Goulart's emphasis on universities as sites where the scientific and technological know-how needed to "defeat the barrier underdevelopment" resided (see, e.g., Castelo Branco 1966: 1:141, 149, 152; 2:172; 3:149, 152–153, 158). Indeed, Castelo Branco (1966: 1:134; 3:158–159, 170–171) further extended Goulart's faith in higher education, proclaiming the new military regime understood that improving and modernizing higher education would allow the government to resolve almost all of Brazil's economic and social problems while allowing Brazil to survive in the modern world. Much like its fellow right-wing counterpart in Spain, Brazil's military maintained this vision of educational reform serving as a fulcrum for national development (see chapter 2).

Shortly after taking power, the military regime turned to USAID to investigate the question of educational reform, and USAID funding to Brazil intensified, as the United States found in the military dictatorship a new anti-communist ally after the removal of the left-leaning Goulart, who had raised the suspicions of the United States since 1962 (Taffet 2007: 104–116). This increased spending included projects in agriculture, health, public administration, labor, and public safety, among other fields. To aid in its own studies and outreach, USAID relied on US academics in the social and practical sciences (Latham 2000; O'Brien 2007: 235; Rohde 2013; Simpson 1998)—some of whom were unaware the agency relied on their studies in making its own policy decisions for individual countries (Price 2016). Yet, such professorial alliances were not limited to the social sciences; in Brazil's case, the emphasis on science for national development led several US academics in applied sciences to become involved in the question of university reform in Brazil.

In Brazil, USAID funding went to projects as diverse as "agrarian reform, fish production, malaria eradication, textbook production, training of labor union leaders, and expansion of capital markets" (Skidmore 1988: 39), among others. Higher education was particularly valuable to USAID, however. Both the AfP and USAID valued universities for their ability to create white-collar professionals in technical fields who the United States expected would "help ensure long-term growth" in Latin America (Taffet 2007: 49). Thus, higher education support in Brazil typically ranked behind agricultural programs only in terms of spending and reform efforts; in 1967–1969 alone, the program allotted nearly 20 percent ($183.4 million) of its spending for education.[6] Yet, if education was the second in actual USAID funding in Brazil, it was first in public visibility in that country, due in no small part to the military's policy and student opposition.

The MEC-USAID accords set out to analyze higher education in Brazil and diagnose areas for reform, including curricula, entrance exams, and expansion—similar issues that UNESCO and the OECD attempted to transform in Spain. The ultimate cost of the accords themselves is debatable. While the agreements included financial aid for education, Castelo Branco used that money to pay off foreign debts, and USAID's impact seemed to fall further on the side of "analysis" than on funding (Ribeiro 2002: 22–23; Skidmore 1988: 60). Though the US government had expressed concern over Castelo Branco's use of USAID funds to reduce foreign debt, USAID still renewed the accords in 1967. Ultimately, drawing on the US university system as a model, the MEC-USAID accords advocated streamlining Brazil's university system so that it might better serve national development by emphasizing science, technology, and professional training for white-collar workers.[7]

MEC-USAID stood out for two reasons. First, unlike subsequent reform recommendations from US agents collaborating with Brazilian authorities, the MEC-USAID accords addressed issues that students themselves had been raising since the 1950s, including the structure of entrance exams and the lack of openings for a growing university population. Second, and perhaps most importantly, the MEC-USAID accords were the first comprehensive attempt of the military regime to systematically explore the question of university reform, and the fact that it turned to the United States to aid in the study carried incredible symbolic heft. This turn made sense, as the Brazilian military's view of education and development, especially the need to focus on "human resources" to further national development (see, e.g., Castelo Branco 1966: 2:170–172; 3:148–162),[8] overlapped considerably with modernization theory originating in the United States. Such language fit within ideological visions of modernization in the Western World that prioritized notions of educated individuals as "human capital" that educational reformers and bureaucrats deployed in Spain and elsewhere (see chapters 1 and 2).

Governmental officials were not the only actors to read symbolic value into Brazil's turn to the United States. As in much of Europe, including Spain, and Latin America, Brazilian students were situated within a transnational context in which education served as a major arena through which students criticized the United States' cultural imperialism and students' own countries' complicity with the United States (for the Spanish case, see chapter 6). Yet, whereas students in West Berlin, Italy, or the United States mobilized in democratic regimes, in Brazil, as in Spain, the authoritarian regime had attempted to curb student mobilization by cracking down on student movements. However, the MEC-USAID agreements played an important part in the reconstitution of student mobilization and protest after the military's initial crackdown on student groups in 1964. From late 1965, when the accords were first signed, through 1968 and the height of student mobilization in Brazil in the 1960s, the MEC-USAID accords regularly featured in student demonstrations, as left-leaning student leaders and anti-dictatorship demonstrators alike saw in the agreements the clear hand of the United States' perceived Cold War imperialism that "aimed at destroying the revolutionary potential of the world's population" (Iber 2017: 97).

Students particularly feared MEC-USAID would sacrifice Brazilian political and social autonomy by serving as a vehicle to transform public education into private education "controlled . . . by foreign countries."[9] As a result, numerous protests placed MEC-USAID as a centerpiece of student mobilization, criticizing the accords for opening the door to the attempted "ideological domination" of students, for accelerating the "elitization" of universities, and for marking a turn toward "neocolonialism" and education's "subordination" to capital.[10] Indeed, when the government sought student participation in the committee overseeing educational reform in 1967 debates, university students turned down in protest of the agreements.[11] By 1968, opposition politicians joined students, saying MEC-USAID rendered "the entire Brazilian university system dependent on the direct and immediate interests of North American economic power in Brazil" (Moreira Alves 1968: 24). The MEC-USAID accords were just one element of USAID's connections to the question of university reform in Brazil. Even as Castelo Branco's Minister of Education and Culture Flávio Suplicy de Lacerda was entering into the MEC-USAID agreements in 1965, the Departamento de Ensino Superior (Department of Higher Education—DESu) was seeking its own counsel on educational reform. That year, DESu contracted Rudolph Atcon to begin exploring the obstacles, challenges, and possible reform paths for Brazil's university system. Thus, in the first two attempts that the military regime made to analyze university reform, it turned toward the United States rather than to internal studies.

Atcon's connections to Brazilian higher education preceded the military dictatorship by several years. As early as 1957, working with UNESCO, he had begun studying higher education in Latin America, including Brazil (Atcon 1957), and in 1958, Brazilian pedagogical expert Anísio Teixeira invited Atcon to work with the Coordenação de Aperfeiçoamento de Pessoal de Nível Superior (Coordination for the Improvement of Higher Education Personnel).[12] That same year, Atcon published his "Outline of a Proposal for US Policy Concentration in

Latin America on University Organization and Economic Integration," followed by *The Latin American University* in 1963, which USAID published and was republished in both English and Spanish in 1966 (Atcon 1966a). From June to September 1965, he traveled Brazil, visiting twelve universities in the Northeast, Southeast, and South (Atcon 1966b)—the geographic regions where most of Brazil's public universities were located, at the same moment that US agents working with UNESCO and OECD were studying and composing policy recommendations for higher education in Spain. Although not a part of the MEC-USAID accords specifically, Atcon nonetheless was connected to USAID, with the agency providing his salary via his home institution of the University of Houston—a fact the university kept quiet well into the 1970s, fearing that making the university's ties to Atcon public knowledge would be "impolitic."[13] The following year, DESu published Atcon's findings in *Rumo a Reformulação Estrutural da Universidade Brasileira* (Path toward the structural reformulation of the Brazilian University) better known as the Plano Atcon, or Atcon Plan.

The Plano Atcon differed considerably from both the focus and recommendations of MEC-USAID, and from his *The Latin American University*. The latter offered general observations on privatizing education, expanding enrollment, and advocating the creation of Centers of General Studies rather than specific professional schools in order to create white-collar professionals who also had a well-rounded, humanist education. By contrast, the Plano Atcon focused far more on the advancement of sciences and the bureaucratic structuring of universities in Brazil. *The Plano Atcon* also toned down the vitriol toward students that Atcon did not conceal in *The Latin American University*, where he referred to Latin American students as consumed by "barricade manners and mentality," as lacking any "real policy of their own," as a threat to "the very foundations of social order," as "infantile, immature, and intolerant," as "the most reactionary element in the Latin American society today," and as "children" (Atcon 1966a: 82–92). Akin to US diplomatic officials' approach in Spain, Atcon's Plano was content to implicitly treat students as mere vessels through whom national development would occur, rather than openly antagonizing them as political agents. This marginalization and erasure of students' voices and political agency would be a shared characteristic with other University of Houston officials in the years to come.

Yet, there were just as many, if not more, parallels between the two reports, parallels that allow us to better understand his vision of the function of higher education. Both strenuously recommended increasing professorial pay and implementing administrative reform to help Brazil modernize its education. Likewise, despite his and MEC's protestations to Brazilian media that Atcon's report did not advocate privatizing higher education,[14] his studies insisted that the only ways universities could be truly autonomous is if they severed their alleged dependency from the state; while he was more vague about how universities would fund themselves in the Plano Atcon, *The Latin American University* made clear that the only answer was fees, tuition, and donations from private enterprise. Fitting within a broader matrix of US educational recommendations in Spain and other parts of the world, in Brazil, both reform plans also argued the executive branch needed to centralize its authority over education to more effectively and rapidly implement reform. Finally, professors needed to be better trained, especially in science, technology, and industry, to further the nation's consumer and intellectual productivity and lead its development. The end game here was quite clear: higher education had to produce the "human resources" the military regime itself sought in order to further the regime's nationalist economic developmental programs.

Atcon's focus on these issues completely disregarded the infrastructural issues, overcrowded institutions, and supply inadequate to the growing demand for higher education. This is not to say Atcon's recommendations and student demands were completely isolated—like students, Atcon viewed the *professor catedrático* as archaic and inhibiting Brazilian higher education. Even here, however, his reasons for critique diverged from students. Atcon believed the isolated position of *professor catedrático* retarded the production of scientific know-how, without any regard for how it affected student-professor relations.[15] By contrast, students criticized the position for its inflexibility and authoritarian tendencies that left students unable to ask questions or even have contact with their professors—critiques Spanish students themselves would raise at the beginning of the 1970s as educational reforms went into effect on the Iberian Peninsula (see chapter 6).

Given these visions of reform, and the failure to address—in substance or ideologically—the demands of students, it is clear why Atcon was a target of student demonstrations almost as regularly as MEC-USAID was.[16] By 1968, even professors and rectors began to distance themselves from Atcon's positions in the face of mounting student opposition,[17] illustrating just how student protests against US involvement in educational reform in Brazil shaped the responses of academic elites. For students, Atcon represented "the theory of domination" of the United States in the Cold War, while MEC-USAID represented "the imposition of domination," and any subsequent reforms from the two studies would be "the application of domination."[18] By 1968, Brazil's military regime had moved away from relying solely on advisers and experts from the United States to study the problem of university reform. In January, Colonel Carlos de Meira Mattos, a fierce anti-communist whom the regime had commissioned to study "the student question," echoed many of the findings of the Plano Atcon, including the perceived need to improve salaries and centralize authority within and over universities, even while visibly diverging from Atcon and MEC-USAID in its advocacy for the expansion of the university system and its willingness to have a greater police presence on campus to crack down on student movements (Vieira 1982: 136–137).

Building on the Meira Mattos Report, by mid-1968, the regime had formally established a Grupo de Trabalho (Work Group—GT) to investigate the question of university reform. The GT's report, like modernization theorists and agents like Atcon, emphasized science and technology in higher education, including the postgraduate level, even while the report, unlike Atcon, suggested federalizing more schools and rapidly expanding the public university system.[19] As Atcon stepped away from his positions with Brazil's rectors and the MEC-USAID accords wound down in 1968, it publicly appeared that the United States' role in higher educational reform had diminished as Brazilian officials and experts took the lead on the question of university reform in the months leading up to the regime's Reforma Universitária of November 1968.

As important as both Atcon and MEC-USAID were, symbolically and policy-wise, focusing solely on them obscures other voices and ways the US involvement in Brazil's educational reform attempts transcended mere symbolic importance or the role of one man, masking the more complex and multifarious expressions of consultation and interaction between the military regime and the US government in the educational arena in the late 1960s. As previously overlooked documents reveal, the United States' presence in higher educational reform in Brazil was not limited to just the MEC-USAID accords or Rudolph Atcon. Rather, officials from the University of Houston maintained direct contact with Brazilian rectors and universities, continuing to quietly push US-led visions of reform that simultaneously revealed the ways the United States attempted to impose a technocratic vision of modernity that situated higher education as a means to produce white-collar workers who would aid in national development, even while revealing that United States reformists' messages and emphases were anything but homogeneous and unitary.

Administrators as Reformers and Education as Enterprise: The University of Houston and the Question of Brazilian University Reform (1967–1969)

The University of Houston first began exploring institutional connections to Brazil in 1961, receiving assistance from the Organization of American States (OAS) in what was possibly an early effort for the United States to build bridges with Latin American countries in several areas to forestall the spread of communism in the aftermath of the Cuban Revolution. The following year, professors Abraham E. Duckler, Elliott I. Organick, and Frank M. Tiller all traveled to Brazil to offer short courses in the physical and computer sciences and in engineering, respectively. The courses were part of what was then the Universidade do Brasil's chemistry extension courses (in 1965, the regime would rename the university the Universidade Federal do Rio de Janeiro, UFRJ). The need and demand for these additional courses, offered not by Brazilians but by US professors, implicated the shortcomings of Brazilian higher education and the lack of graduate education in the sciences in Brazil at one of the country's more prestigious and historical universities.[20]

From the Brazilian perspective, the courses drew some attention, with national media reporting on the professors' visits and highlighting the university's efforts to "incentivize research and initiate regular graduate courses"[21] at the Instituto de Química in what was a glimpse of the path individual universities would take in an attempt to implement their own structural reforms in the 1960s and 1970s. Alberto Luiz Coimbra, later the first director of UFRJ's graduate program in engineering, reified discourses that equated the United States with modernity and development, celebrating the fact the professors would provide Brazil with "modern and advanced techniques" in engineering that were lacking. These courses—and the attention the media gave to them—illustrated the ways the United States sought to insert itself into higher education in Brazil early in the Alliance for Progress era while Brazilians also publicly expressed and reinforced their own subalternity via a self-critical modernization discourse that situated Brazil as underdeveloped. The inability of one of the country's most prestigious universities to provide the education and scientific know-how of its own without turning to professors from the United States made clear where Brazil fit in hierarchies of development. Such rhetoric indicated the willingness among some Brazilians to turn to the United States for guidance in shaping higher education, even as students increasingly spoke out against the United States' role in the hemisphere in the context of Cold War geopolitics (Langland 2013: 64–75). Both trends would continue throughout the 1960s.

From the US perspective, the courses provided first glimpse of early efforts—from the University of Houston and from the United States during the AfP more generally—to extend US educational models and knowledge as the symbols of "development" in the Cold War setting in what effectively marked an attempt to establish US scientific know-how as the metric for defining development as a model to emulate. While Duckler and Organick appear to have simply offered their courses before returning to the United States, Tiller, then the Dean of the College of Engineering at the University of Houston, took a more proactive role. Together with then-university President Philip G. Hoffman, Tiller met with Raymundo Moniz de Aragão,[22] Director of the Faculty of Biological Sciences at the University of Brazil and future Minister of Education and Culture. In the process, they established the connections that would come to play a role in national debates on higher education reform in Brazil in 1967 and 1968, marking an inconspicuous beginning of the University of Houston's much greater role in the question of higher education in Brazil in the 1960s.

Even before and immediately after the 1964 coup that overthrew Goulart, the University of Houston continued to work with Brazilian universities, especially UFRJ, with Tiller as the point man for contact as the new Director for the Office of International Affairs at the University of Houston beginning in 1963. By 1968, he was also the Director of the Center for Study of Higher Education in Latin America at the University of Houston.[23] Building on the connections established in his 1962 visit, Tiller, now the Director for the Office of International Affairs at the University of Houston, in 1963 helped UFRJ develop the degree-granting Coordenação dos Programas de Pós-Graduação e Pesquisa de Engenharia (Coordination of Graduate Programs and Engineering Research) with aid coming from the OAS, the Fulbright Program, and the Rockefeller Foundation money.[24] Additionally, the University of Houston sent twenty-five to thirty professors to Brazil to offer courses between 1962 and 1970,[25] with Tiller as a key figure in coordinating these programs, giving him a much greater international presence and a historiographically unacknowledged role in the United States' cultural imperialism in the Cold War, bringing US ideologies of modernization, educational reform, and development to Brazil.

When Tiller returned to Brazil in 1967, he did so to discuss matters quite different from the talks on filtration he gave in 1962. If Tiller's visit in 1962 implicitly sought to import US scientific knowledge to Brazil, by 1967–1968, his attempts to transform Brazilian higher education expressed US visions of higher education and managerial authority akin to capitalist modes of production was far clearer. Yet, the degree to which Brazilian authorities followed his and the University of Houston's recommendations would be mixed, revealing the limitations of importing US models of development and modernity into Brazil's higher educational system. Perhaps the clearest articulation of Tiller's vision of university reform is evident in materials from the Conference on Administrative Renovation, presented to the Conselho dos Reitores Universitários Brasileiros (Council of Brazilian University Rectors—CRUB). CRUB had been one of Atcon's (1966b) key proposals in 1966, and it was among the first recommendations Brazil's military regime accepted and implemented. Atcon himself served as CRUB's first Executive Secretary until 1968. The implications of Atcon's leadership were clear, suggesting that only a professor from the United States, and not any of the Brazilian rectors, could coordinate and lead the question of reforms facing Brazil. Atcon ultimately stepped down in June 1968, when pushback and mounting opposition from students led the rectors to elect Oscar de Oliveira, a professor and sub-rector at UFRJ.[26]

Yet, Atcon was not the sole representative from the United States trying to instruct Brazil's rectors on the best paths toward university reform via CRUB. At the conference in the northern city of Belém in August 1967, Tiller was the foremost among a handful of University of Houston professors and staff participating in the CRUB workshop on university reform in Brazil. The focus fell especially on administrative reform—a part of Atcon's own vision of reform in Brazil—but in ways that diverged from Atcon's own studies of higher education in subtle but substantial ways that revealed the unfolding "corporatization" of higher education just getting underway in the United States (Ginsberg 2013; Newfield 2011; Schrecker 2010). Collectively, the presentations of Tiller and his University of Houston colleagues consisted of a vision of higher educational reform that imposed the US vision of education in the service of industry and focused on producing jobs rather than educated citizens. Thus, even more so than Atcon, Tiller advocated a very top-down and mechanistic vision of reform that completely ignored the very real social and structural issues confronting Brazilian universities, viewing reform as a mere matter of administrative restructuring with no room for students or professors as agents.

Like many individuals involved with USAID and the AfP in Latin America and UNESCO and OECD in Spain, Tiller drew on and rearticulated broader notions of modernization theory and development during the Cold War. He viewed higher education as the fulcrum on which all subsequent transformations would occur. Universities would be "the key to open the door" to develop the nation economically, socially, and politically. Whether it was illiteracy, technological development, agricultural growth, or reducing poverty, Tiller insisted "a vibrant and alert university that functions efficiently and with modern techniques" was "the heart that pumps vitality into the country's veins." That vision of development was far more nakedly economic than anything in the Plano Atcon or MEC-USAID, however. While the Plano Atcon emphasized scientific development and the formation of well-rounded, educated members of society (Atcon 1966b), such visions of an educated citizenry for its own sake were absent from the University of Houston documents. Instead, universities were little more than economic instruments; a "strong" and "modern" university would, among other things, "manage and control finances" as it sought to "respond to the needs of the country."[27]

It was not by chance that Tiller framed the value of university reform in terms of "the short- and long-term profits" it could produce for the nation, turning the production of knowledge and of college graduates into little more than a commodity to improve the value and productivity of the nation. The business professor Herbert J. Johnson's report claimed the university's function was simply "to better serve the economy," explicitly insisting "the educational system should be structured to satisfy the economic needs of the country it serves."[28] Such a vision of higher education stripped universities of their projects of erudition or humanism that would produce informed citizens—something students themselves demanded[29]—instead framing universities as an intellectual assembly line to produce graduates whose technical knowledge would be applied to the management and production associated with consumerism and development. Addressing Latin America writ large, Tiller warned, "The future of underdeveloped countries is adversely held back by the inability of its higher education institutions to respond to the needs of the country and to provide graduates with adequate educations." Who defined those needs and what constituted adequacy was implicit when Tiller observed that the ones who most suffered the effects of underdevelopment in Latin America were not the poor or the marginalized but instead "the commercial establishments and governmental offices" that relied on the creation of white-collar employees to work for them.[30]

This vision of higher education was also unapologetically elitist. In his report, Tiller accurately acknowledged that, in Brazil specifically and in Latin America more generally, "the educational class is small compared to the total population."[31] This was especially an understatement in the Brazilian case; at the time of his report to CRUB in 1967, 212,882 students had enrolled in all universities and colleges in a country of 86.5 million people, just 0.25 percent of the population.[32] This inequality was not an issue Tiller addressed, however, and none of his reform recommendations included expanding higher education to make it more accessible in order to improve the overall quality of life of Brazilians and address social inequalities—another pair of recurring demands among student movements of the time (Langland 2013: 117–118). Instead, he accepted the fact that "a small number of academic groups exercise substantial influence in national issues." According to Tiller, there was nothing wrong with the fact that there were so few gaining an education; the problem was that a poorly educated minority would perpetuate Brazil's underdevelopment.[33]

This acceptance of the inherently elite nature of higher education, which Atcon (1966b) himself spoke out against, fit naturally with Tiller's and other University of Houston representatives' treatment of higher education as just another manufacturing enterprise, one that created white-collar workers instead of consumer goods. Indeed, the most frequent analogy Tiller and others at the CRUB meeting with University of Houston representatives turned to was that of university-as-a-business. In running a university, Tiller observed, "a financial and commercial manager . . . and a director of development and public relations" were among "the most necessary figures" to university reform. Tiller also submitted an article from *U.S. News & World Report* that juxtaposed Japan's and Great Britain's economies, finding the former booming because of the high number of university-trained managers whose education "is better oriented toward the training of personnel for industry and commerce," in contrast with British higher education's "emphasis on classical erudition" at the expense of managerial instruction.[34] The message was clear: Brazil could emphasize technical education that trained white-collar professionals, and flourish, as Japan had done, or, it could continue its erudite educational models that, like Atcon's own calls for general education, would create an educated and cultured society amidst a flagging economy.

For the University of Houston officials, this business-university encounter could also be a two-way street. University of Houston Vice President Patrick Nicholson's study (in Spanish) on public relations and universities directly linked industry and education, making the latter dependent on the former for financial support via donations. Frank Sparks, University Counsel at the University of Houston, pointed to the United States as a model, where "business has not only the right but also the obligation to help maintain higher education."[35] It did not take a great deal of imagination to see that these arguments unintentionally would have given great weight to students' own insistence that universities were being opened up to the possibility of sacrificing education to the "subordination" of universities to the interests of capital.

Collectively, the presentations before the conference in Belém illustrated a vision of higher education as vital to national development and thus needing reform. Yet, the reforms were extremely limited, top-down, and centralized only in the figures of administrators who, according to Tiller and the University of Houston contingent, had to exercise greater control over campuses. Professors were little more than the expression of financial inefficiencies on campuses, evident in low salaries that led the best minds to train future white-collar workers to find work outside of academia for greater pay and depriving universities of faculty "favorable to modernization" who could teach the next generation of white-collar professionals.[36]

As for the students themselves, they existed primarily as abstract "products" of reform who would enter the workforce to address the country's developmental needs. The report doubly silenced students, disregarding notions of reform that would address student demands for greater state funding for higher education, expanded enrollment, and a focus on social and humanist education, even as it also refused to include students as subjects and agents of change whose voices could contribute to the university reform question. Indeed, Tiller himself, while not as openly hostile toward students as Atcon, nonetheless found a silver lining in the military regime's crackdown on student movements, as Brazil had avoided "student domination" on university councils, something that other Latin American universities were not as "fortunate" to have experienced. This silencing of students in the Houston contingent's reports was as much institutional as it was political; students were often rendered invisible, such as when Tiller listed six areas (management and administration; finances; patrimony; academic structure; faculty; and public relations and fundraising) for reform in Brazil's university system. While administrators, "managers," and professors all received attention, students were not mentioned in a single one.[37]

The Belém conference may seem a limited arena of study, particularly given its self-proclaimed focus on administrative reforms. Yet, Tiller's efforts in particular were not limited to just the CRUB meeting in the Northeast, and a look at his other encounters with Brazilian universities reveals an equally limited vision of reform even in more open-ended contexts. Indeed, Brazilian officials themselves often invited Tiller to offer reports and studies of their own universities and systems, much as Spanish officials also invited US involvement in its reform process (see chapter 2). In November 1967, Tiller visited the Universidade Federal de Santa Catarina (UFSC) in southern Brazil, submitting a report to Rector João David Ferreira Lima in January 1968. In that report, Tiller's priorities echoed those in his lengthier presentation to CRUB earlier that year. The only areas the report said needed addressing were "financial administration, centralized student records, adoption of a more flexible academic system, professorial salaries, campus planning, and maintenance." Absent from any of those objectives were educational matters, academic affairs, or students themselves. Tiller's report even delved into minutiae like setting the date for matriculation and making recommendations on issues like traffic control, the location of buildings, and even water treatment and noise pollution; larger issues that actually confronted UFSM and the federal university system more generally, such as expansion of the system or funding for education, were completely absent. Indeed, in a passage that echoed Atcon's (1966a) own push toward privatizing education, Tiller even went so far as to recommend "establishing autonomy" in the fiscal arena by severing dependency on the government for funding in ways that, in Tiller's view, just led to "inefficiencies." Once again, students barely appeared in any of the university's operations; the only two items that dealt directly with students suggested creating "a system of advisers and student orientation" for students, and more clearly delineating the "academic statutes governing student suspension, withdrawal from courses, transfers of credit, and graduation requirements," without even nominally acknowledging issues like funding for education, expanding the higher education system and increasing enrollment, or of providing a social education.[38]

Even as the GT finished the report and the Brazilian government began work on the Reforma Universitária behind closed doors, in September 1968 Tiller submitted a report to UFRJ regarding the visit of Robert B. Howsam, Director of the Education College at the University of Houston, to UFRJ. In his cover letter, Tiller commented on how "Brazil is passing through a critical moment" in its educational system at all levels and that universities would now play the "utmost importance in the determination of the future." Tiller emphasized the need for graduate programs—this time in education—to lead Brazil into the future by producing better-trained professionals in a vision that focused on humans as "resources" rather than as subjects, citizens, or learned individuals. And in his report to the PUC-RJ in December 1968, Tiller once again highlighted "Organization and Administration," and "Budgeting and Financial Administration," with a centralized vision that coordinated and concentrated greater power in the hands of the rector and vice rectors while opening the university to private enterprise by means of outside consultant agencies.[39]

It is tempting to see these reports as an example of experts from the United States imposing their vision of higher education on other countries, and in some ways, such a view is not unfair. Yet, the views of Atcon, Tiller, and others matter in part because they had an audience willing to listen to them. The Brazilian authoritarian regime's technocratic acceptance of a vision of higher education framed by modernization and human resources theories showed receptivity to the United States' ideological model of higher education and paralleled similar views and attitudes among the technocrats of Francoist Spain. While the ideologies and visions of higher education that Tiller and Atcon espoused were anathema to students, many of Brazil's own educational elites and officials in the military government shared in their United States counterparts' vision of universities' function as creating "human resources" who would work "in service of progress and development."[40] Paulo Novaes, from the Institute of Administration and Management at the PUC-RJ, opened the proceedings at the August 1967 CRUB conference by observing that administrative reforms were important to universities for the same reasons "the ongoing training of managers and upper-level administrators is essential for the progress of a Business." Novaes prioritized administrative reform to include "knowledge of the human, material, and technological elements contained in their area of management" and outright referred to the university as an *empresa* (company).[41] By placing "human" resources alongside the material and technological aspects of the university system, Novaes reified the notion of the university not as creating educated humans or citizens but rather as treating people as another resource that factored into national development. Novaes's comments at the beginning of the workshop serve as an important reminder that, while the MEC-USAID accords and the messages they carried might have been counter to students' own visions of education, there were those within the bureaucratic structures of universities and the Ministry of Education that shared a broader discursive vision that envisioned universities operating as businesses in ways that also likely raised the specter of students having to pay tuition for public education.

Collectively, then, the vision that emerges from Tiller's and University of Houston officials' vision of educational reform carries subtle, but important, distinctions from those of MEC-USAID and the Plano Atcon, even as they tap into broader attitudes on the function of higher education in modernization theory and "developed" societies. To Tiller and the University of Houston representatives in Brazil, universities' function in society was simply to train white-collar workers through whom national development and "modernity" would occur. The function of education, once again, was to create jobs that would improve Brazil's developmental abilities. Treating universities' function as economic, these documents emphasized administrative reform in a way that made administrators and "managers" the sole agents necessary for reform, leaving professors' and students' voices silenced, their very real structural and social concerns unaddressed. If Tiller's vision of education was not already elitist enough in its failure to address the lack of access to universities for millions of Brazilians, then his vision on campuses was even more limited, for it would be administrators, and *not* professors or students, who would be the agents of reform. Thus, Tiller maintained, "a group of alert and responsible administrators is essential if education is going to attempt to play an important role in regional and national issues,"[42] thereby reinforcing a vision of transformation in which all improvements to the country would emerge from the university—already an elite institution—and all transformations within those universities would come from administrators alone.

Ironically, without realizing it at the time—Tiller's name never appeared in any of the broadly reported student demonstrations of 1967–1968—student critiques of Atcon and of USAID for treating universities as businesses that would only further entrench elites and socioeconomic inequalities in Brazil in fact rang true. While the University of Houston's presentation to CRUB was behind closed doors, its analogizing of universities to industries and of administrators to managers, its treatment of universities as economic instruments, and its focus solely on administration and top-down reforms in fact reflected a broader *mentalité* in which the function of higher education was to produce white-collar professionals to help further a nation's economy.

Yet, the Brazilian government did not blindly follow the United States' recommendations—be it via MEC-USAID, the Plano Atcon, or Tiller's various reports to rectors and universities. The Reforma Universitária of November 1968 did touch upon several areas that US officials raised, most notably in the emphasis on universities' roles in creating white-collar professionals to aid national development. Yet, this idea was not one that US officials introduced; since the 1950s, Brazilian presidents had emphasized higher education as a major agent in economic and industrial development. And the decision to dramatically expand the higher educational system, including public schools, ran directly counter to Atcon's and Tiller's recommendations of "autonomy" via the turn to private capital and fees to fund higher education. Admittedly, private higher education would expand dramatically in the following decade, but that would develop only as the dictatorship attempted to implement its reform in the 1970s.

Ultimately, what the 1968 Reforma did was embrace those elements of the United States' recommendations that already fit with the regime's own understandings of development and education and of its effort to centralize authority over higher education, even while rejecting some of the more classically liberal and narrow visions of reform as merely an administrative matter that Tiller, Atcon, and others advocated. Brazil's experience was just one part of the broader global matrix of Cold War politics and education, and whether it was in Brazil or Spain, these countries listened to, and even invited, the United States' heavy hand but ultimately shaped policy in ways that their own governments found to be in their nation's best interests. In Brazil, the result was that the United States was an active voice in debates on higher education, but ultimately, it was the military regime that had the final say.

Colin M. Snider is Associate Professor of Latin American History at the University of Texas at Tyler. He specializes in social movements, military regimes, higher education, state-society relations, and human rights and memory in Latin America. He has published articles on Brazilian student mobilization in *The Americas* and on education and student activism in the 2013 Brazilian protests in the *Latin American Research Review*. He has also published articles on university autonomy and social mobilization in Brazil and on transitional politics in the twenty-first century in *The Latin Americanist*. He has contributed chapters on educational demands and student movements in Brazil's long 1960s appears in *The Third World in the Global 1960s* (2013) and on the dynamics between student activism, religious movements, and political transformation in twentieth century Brazil in *Local Church, Global Church: Catholic Activism in Latin America from* Rerum Novarum *to Vatican II* (2016).

Notes

1. Lei 5.540, 28 November 1968. For a copy of the law, see Caixa 07-4674, Coleção DSI, Arquivo Nacional in Rio de Janeiro (AN).
2. See, e.g., "Texto sobre a função social da universidade na sociedade," AT pi Teixeira, A. 1952/1964.00.00/7, Centro de Pesquisa e Documentação da História Contemporânea at the Fundação Getúlio Vargas in Rio de Janeiro (CPDOC); "Texto de entrevista dada a 'O Cruzeiro' sobre o Plano Nacional de Educação," AT pi Teixeira, A. 1962.11.00,CPDOC; Darcy Ribeiro, *Universidade de Brasília*, Caixa 46, Coleção Paulo de Assis Ribeiro, AN.
3. "General Comments on NSSM-67, 3/13/1970, IPS-8/Cables In and Out/ Brazil 1967–1971," United States National Archives (USNA).
4. Letter to the President of BNDE from Susana Gonçalves, Caixa 68, Coleção Paulo de Assis Ribeiro, AN.
5. "Reunião para Exame da Possibilidade de Ajudo do BIRD para Educação," Caixa 317, Coleção Paulo de Assis Ribeiro, AN.
6. "Program Memorandum FY 1969 Brazil," Records of the Agency for International Development, IPS-1/ProjBudget/Brazil 1966–1969, USNA. My thanks to James Woodard for pointing me to this document.
7. See, e.g., letter from Juracy Magalhães to Jutay Magalhães, item IV-11, Pasta IV, Coleção Juracy Magalhães, CPDOC; AAP rev64 1967.05.09, CPDOC.
8. For Costa e Silva, "Plano de Metas da Educaçào Nacional—Plano Nacional de Cultura," 27 July 1967, and Ministério do Planejamento e Coordenação Geral—Programa Estratégico de Desenvolvimento, 1968–1970—Cap. XV—"Fortalecimento da Infra-estrutura Social: Educação," Caixa 299, Coleção Paulo de Assis Ribeiro, AN.
9. "Universidade Católica de Minas faz análise da crise," *Jornal do Brasil*, 11 May 1968.
10. See "Análise do Movimento Estudantil a partir de 1964," Dossie 6, Coleção Jean Marc von der Weid, Arquivo Público do Estado do Rio de Janeiro (APERJ); *Guerra Popular* (Órgão Nacional do Setor Estudantil do P.C. do Brasil—Ala Vermelha), No. 1, Ano 1 (October 1968) and Ano 2 (January 1969), Dossie 9, Caixa 5, Coleção Daniel Aarão Reis, APERJ; *O Metropolitano* (19 November 1966), Pasta 5, Setor Estudantil, Coleção DOPS, APERJ. Evidence of MEC-USAID's students crosses numerous archival sources. For just a handful of illustrations, see, e.g., "DOPS paulista entrega à Polícia Federal estudantes presos no Largo de S. Bento,"*Jornal do Brasil*, 21 July 1967; "A revolta dos estudantes," *Jornal do Brasil*, 7–8 April 1968; Soares (1968); individual interviews with Adriano Diogo, Cesar Maia, Jean Marc von der Weid, José Genoíno, José Luís Guedes, and Maria Augusta Carneiro Ribeiro, Arquivo Projeto Memória Movimento Estudantil (PMME).
11. See Ministério do Planejamento e Coordenação Geral, Ministério da Fazenda, and Ministério da Educação e Cultura, *Reforma Unviersitária: Expansão do ensino superior e aumento de recursos para*

a educação—Relatório da Subcomissão Especial do Grupo de Trabalho da Reforma Universitária, Coordenada por João Paulo dos Reis Velloso e Fernando Ribeiro do Val, Caixa 21, Encadernado 8, Coleção DAU-SESU, Coordenadora Regional do Arquivo Nacional in Brasília (COREG).

12. "Moniz lutará por percentual para Educação na nova Carta," *Jornal do Brasil,* 9 December 1966.
13. "University of Houston in Brazil," Box 60, President's Office Records, University Archives of the University of Houston (UAUH).
14. See, e.g., "MEC diz que a Universidade não passará a fundação só com recurso particular" and "Atcon pede algo mais do que crítica destrutiva," *Jornal do Brasil,* 2 June 1968; "Reitores desistem de nota violenta contra o Governo," *Jornal do Brasil,* 5 June 1968.
15. See *Luta Atual pela Reforma Universitária,* Livros Apprendidos pelas Polícias Políticas, APERJ; see also interview with Roberto Amaral, PMME.
16. See, e.g., interview with José Luís Guedes, PMME; "Atcon cuida por sua conta da reforma universitária," *Jornal do Brasil,* 5 January 1967; "Professor diz que acordo MEC-USAID interessa ao Brasil," *Jornal do Brasil,* 30 April 1967; "DOPS paulista entrega à Polícia Federal estudantes presos no Largo de S. Bento"; "A revolta dos estudantes"; "Reformulação dos estatutos da UnB será denunciado por Diretorios Academicos," *Jornal do Brasil,* 3 May 1968; "Paulistas invadem Reitoria," *Jornal do Brasil,* 13 June 1968.
17. See, e.g., "Professor mineiro vê universidade em falência," *Jornal do Brasil,* 12 November 1967; "Reitor da UFRJ é contra fundação," *Jornal do Brasil,* 8 June 1968; "Professores afirmam que ouviram tarde as denúncias de alunos," *Jornal do Brasil,* 16 June 1968; "UEG foi tratar de si e se integrou no resto," *Jornal do Brasil,* 29 June 1968; "Suplici nega inspiração estrangeiro à reforma," *Jornal do Brasil,* 21 September 1968.
18. "Reformulação dos estatutos da UnB sera denunciada por Diretórios Academicos."
19. Ministério do Planejamento e Coordenação Geral et al., *Reforma Unviersitária.*
20. "Encontro Universitário," *Jornal do Brasil,* 29 June 1962, Caderno B., p. 2.
21. For more on the courses offered, see ibid.; "Mestres em Ciencia já virão do Instituto de Química da UB," *Jornal do Brasil,* 21 September 1962.
22. "University of Houston in Brazil."
23. Frank M. Tiller Curriculum Vitae, Box 22, University of Houston Faculty Vita Records, UAUH.
24. "University of Houston in Brazil."
25. Ibid.
26. For Atcon as Executive Secretary of CRUB, see, e.g., "Atcon cuida por sua conta da reforma universitária"; "Atcon pede algo mais do que crítica destrutiva," *Jornal do Brasil,* 2 June 1968; "Reitor da UFRJ é contra fundação." For the election of a new Executive Secretary, see "Conselho de Reitores tem novo Secretario Executivo," *Jornal do Brasil,* 27 June 1968. Not coincidentally, the selection of a new secretary came after a

month of large protests in Brazil, against the dictatorship and against the United States' role in the question of educational reform. Additionally, while news reports on Atcon had typically been front-section material, the announcement of his replacement was buried in the classifieds in what may have been a desire to remain out of the public eye.

27. "Materiais para Conferência Sôbre Renovação Administrativa Universitária," Series 29, Box 4, Faculty Senate Records, UAUH.
28. Ibid.
29. Individual interviews with Adriano Diogo, Cacá Diegues, and José Luis Guedes, PMME.
30. "Materiais para Conferência Sôbre Renovação Administrativa Universitária."
31. Ibid.
32. For educational data, see "Ensino Superior—Principais Resultados, por Unidades da Federação," 1968, Instituto Brasileiro Geográfica e Estatística (hereafter, IGBE); for population data, "População Estimada," *Anuário Estatístico do Brasil—1967*, IBGE.
33. "Materiais para Conferência Sôbre Renovação Administrativa Universitária."
34. Ibid.
35. Ibid.
36. Ibid.
37. Ibid.
38. JT pi tt Tiller, F.M., 1967.11.07, CPDOC.
39. JT pi tt Maclean, D.G. 1968.12.01, CPDOC.
40. See, e.g., "Plano de Metas da Educação Nacional," 1967, Caixa 299, Coleção Paulo de Assis Ribeiro, AN; *Diretrizes de Governo: Programa Estratégico de Desenvolvimento*, Caixa 283, Coleção Paulo de Assis Ribeiro, AN.
41. "Materiais para Conferência Sôbre Renovação Administrativa Universitária."
42. Ibid.

References

Almeida, Lúcio Flávio de. 2006. *A ilusão de Desenvolvimento: Nacionalismo e dominaão burguesa nos anos JK*. Florianópolis: Editora da UFSC.

Atcon, Rudolph P. 1957. "Reorganization of the Universidad de Concepción: Chile." UNESCO mission. https://unesdoc.unesco.org/ark:/48223/pf0000158866. Accessed 28 September 2017.

——. 1966a. *The Latin American University: A Key for an Integrated Approach to the Coordinated Social, Economic and Educational Development of Latin America*. Bogotá: ECO Revista de la Cultura de Occidente.

——. 1966b. *Rumo à reformulação estrutural da universidade brasileira*. Rio de Janeiro: Ministério da Educação e Cultura, Diretoria do Ensino Superior.

Boschetti, Vania Regina. 2007. "Plano Atcon e Comissão Meira Mattos: Construção do ideário da universidade do pós-64." *Revista HISTEDBR On-line* 27: 221–229.

Castelo Branco, Humberto de Alencar. 1966. *Discursos*. 3 vols. Brasília: Secretaria da Imprensa.

Cunha, Luís Antônio. 2007. *A universidade reformanda: O golpe de 1964 e a modernização do ensino superior*. São Paulo: Editora UNESP.

Dinius, Oliver J. 2010. *Brazil's Steel City: Developmentalism, Strategic Power, and Industrial Relations in Volta Redonda, 1941–1964*. Stanford: Stanford University Press.

Fávero, Maria de Lourdes de Albuquerque. 1991. *Da universidade modernizada a universidade disciplinada: Acton e Meira Mattos*. São Paulo: Editora Cortez.

Ginsberg, Benjamin. 2013. *The Fall of the Faculty: The Rise of the All-Administrative University and Why It Matters*. Oxford: Oxford University Press.

Iber, Patrick. 2017. "Social Science, Cultural Imperialism, and the Ford Foundation in Latin America in the 1960s." In *The Global 1960s: Convention, Contest, and Counterculture,* ed. Tamara Chaplin and Jadwiga E. Pieper Mooney, 96–114. New York: Routledge, 2017.

Ioris, Rafael R. 2014. *Transforming Brazil: A History of National Development in the Postwar Era*. New York: Routledge.

Kirkendall, Andrew J. 2010. *Paulo Freire and the Cold War Politics of Literacy*. Chapel Hill: University of North Carolina Press.

Langland, Victoria. 2013. *Speaking of Flowers: Student Movements and the Making and Remembering of 1968 in Military Brazil*. Durham, NC: Duke University Press.

Latham, Michael E. 2000. *Modernization as Ideology: American Social Science and "Nation Building" in the Kennedy Era*. Chapel Hill: University of North Carolina Press.

Lindo-Fuentes, Héctor, and Erik Ching. 2012. *Modernizing Minds in El Salvador: Education Reform and the Cold War, 1960–1980*. Albuquerque: University of New Mexico Press.

Long, Tom. 2015. *Latin America Confronts the United States: Asymmetry and Influence*. Cambridge: Cambridge University Press.

Moreira Alves, Márcio. 1968. *O Beabá dos MEC-USAID*. Rio de Janeiro: Edições Gernasa.

Newfield, Christopher. 2011. *Unmaking the Public University: The Forty-Year Assault on the Middle Class*. Cambridge, MA: Harvard University Press.

O'Brien, Thomas F. 2007. *Making the Americas: The United States and Latin America from the Age of Revolutions to the Era of Globalization*. Albuquerque: University of New Mexico.

Price, David H. 2016. *Cold War Anthropology: The CIA, the Pentagon, and the Growth of Dual Use Anthropology*. Durham, NC: Duke University Press.

Ribeiro, Maria das Graças M. 2002. "Educação Superior Brasileira: Reforma e Diversificação Institucional." Ph.D. dissertation. Universidade de São Francisco.
Rohde, Joy. 2013. *Armed with Expertise: The Militarization of American Social Research during the Cold War*. Ithaca, NY: Cornell University Press.
Rostow, Walt W. 1960. *The Stages of Economic Growth: A Non-Communist Manifesto*. Cambridge: Cambridge University Press.
Schrecker, Ellen. 2010. *The Lost Soul of Higher Education: Corporatization, the Assault on Academic Freedom, and the End of the American University*. New York: The New Press.
Simpson, Christopher, ed. 1998. *Universities and Empire: Money and Politics in the Social Sciences during the Cold War*. New York: The New Press.
Skidmore, Thomas E. 1988. *The Politics of Military Rule in Brazil: 1964–1985*. New York: Oxford University Press.
Soares, Walmer, 1968. "Os estudantes e a política educacional do governo." *Jornal do Brasil*, 9–10 June.
Snider, Colin M. 2016. "'An Incomplete Autonomy': Higher Education and State-Society Relations in Brazil, 1950s–1980s." *The Latin Americanist* 60 (1): 139–159.
Taffet, Jeffrey F. 2007. *Foreign Aid as Foreign Policy: The Alliance for Progress in Latin America*. New York: Routledge.
Vieira, Sofia Lerche. 1982. *O (Dis)curso da (Re)forma Universitária*. Fortaleza: Edições Universidade Federal do Ceará/PROED.
Vieira Pinto, Álvaro. 1994. *A questão da universidade*. São Paulo: Cortez Editora.

Chapter 9

Between the Eagle and the Condor

The Ford Foundation and the Modernization of the University of Chile (1965–1975)

Fernando Quesada

US philanthropic foundations are generally studied through the complex relationships they had with US foreign policy. Interpreting these Cold War relationships is quite complex because in some regions and countries, their interests were not completely congruent. On one hand, Frances Stonor Saunders (2001: 198) believes these US institutions were subordinate to American foreign policy and were its "conscious instruments." Gary Hess (2003: 323) maintains these institutions were an unofficial extension of US diplomacy. Volker Berghahn (1986) uses "Americanization" to encompass the process of spreading US practices and behaviors around the world by "Americanizers" who include philanthropic agencies. Some authors focus on the ideological similarities of US philanthropic institutions and the US government during the Cold War (Arnove 1980; Berman 1983; Fisher 1983).

Some researchers discuss the bureaucracy of these philanthropic institutions rather than their ideological foundations, which allows them to see institutions' greater autonomy from the US government (Bulmer 1984; Condliffe Lagemann 1999; Curti 1963). Ludovic Tournès (2010; Tournès and Scott-Smith 2018) articulates four dimensions to evaluate the actions of philanthropic institutions, which problematizes the binary of subordination–autonomy, and uses these dimensions to analyze the relationship between the two spheres. He defines philanthropic actions as a particular form of "transnational intellectual diplomacy," which has a dynamic that was sustained by intellectual networks that the institutions themselves built in four spheres: the realm of philanthropy, the United States as a nation, in international disputes and tension, and finally, in transnational dynamics.

With respect to Latin America, Gilbert Joseph, Catherine LeGrand, and Ricardo Salvatore (1998: 5) offer a more complex view of US cultural relationships in the region. These historians believe the "informal US Empire" had uneven impacts through different agents, in diverse realms and situations and through different transnational mechanisms. They call these "encounters," which "may represent attempts at hegemony, but are simultaneously sites of multivocality of negotiation, borrowing, and exchange; and of redeployment and reversal." Philanthropic institutions were one type of agent through which US power was deployed in the region. Along the same lines, Benedetta Calandra and Marina Franco (2012: 133) believe US philanthropic institutions were "wholesome bearers of the American dream: crucial actors in the exportation of the American way of life and at the same time main characters in the long Cold War."

This chapter's goal is to demonstrate that the binary categories used to interpret relationships between philanthropic institutions and the United States government are not always coherent with subordination or autonomy, especially for some countries and situations. Chile is a case study that shows some of the complexities of this phenomenon. The chapter presents an analysis of the Ford Foundation in Chile, particularly the agreement it orchestrated between the University of Chile and the University of California between 1965 and 1975. The foundation arrived in Chile at the end of the 1950s, motivated by the radicalization of conflicts throughout Latin America. In the early 1960s, the foundation articulated with the Alliance for Progress's geopolitics in the Americas and made Chile one of its preferred countries to allocate funds.

During the political events of 1970, which brought the Popular Unity coalition to power, led by Salvador Allende, the Ford Foundation was consistent in its democratic vision, maintained its modernization agreement between the University of Chile and the University of California, and even financed government projects. The reason behind this approach was based on the perception of the foundation's directors and officials of the "Chilean path to socialism," which they believed had emerged through the popular vote and not a revolution. In this sense, the Ford Foundation's position differed from that of the US Department of State's, which canceled all subsidies for Chile and continued funding only the army, the principal agent in the 1973 coup. With the fall of the democratic government in Chile, the Ford Foundation positioned itself against the new authoritarian regime, abruptly reduced many of its projects, including the agreement between the University of Chile and the University of California, closed its office in Chile, and started a human rights program with the goal of supporting scientists and students who were persecuted by the government. In this way, the Foundation distanced itself from the foreign policy of the United States, which openly supported the regime led by General Augusto Pinochet.

Between Fear and Hope

In 1950, the Ford Foundation began its international efforts with its Overseas Development Program, which provided assistance to regions it considered problematic. The first regions it began working in were Western Europe, Southeast Asia, and the Middle East. The chapter by Francisco Rodríguez-Jiménez (chapter 3) makes useful comparisons between different geopolitical appraisals the foundation had of two developing nations, Chile and Spain. The foundation was at first more interested in Spain, but toward the end of the 1950s, it became interested in Latin America and began to direct funds to the Western Hemisphere in 1959. To provide assistance to South America, the foundation sent a survey mission that included Alfred Wolf (Director of the foundation's Latin American program), Reynold Carlson (an economist from Vanderbilt University), Lincoln Gordon (a Harvard University professor), and Kalman Silvert. Silvert was a social scientist who had extensive knowledge of the region, had contacts with the most important academics in Latin America, and participated in the region's principal intellectual networks, which he supported during his work as a consultant for social sciences in the Latin American program of the Ford Foundation. He was one of the agents who led the institutionalization of the foundation in the hemisphere and possibly one of the most fervent supporters of Latin American social science (Quesada 2010).

The Ford Foundation officials shared US elites' anxiety about the Cold War, as described by Nils Gilman (2003). This anxiety came from a mixture of optimism in spreading the "American way of life" and modernization projects and fear in the face of advancing communism and a nonliberal view of development. In Chile, the foundation's directors expressed both sentiments upon arrival in 1959. They were optimistic because the country had a democratic political system and was relatively stable compared to its neighbors. They also believed the situation in Chile would be favorable to philanthropic influence because it had a university sphere that was rapidly modernizing. At the same time, they cautiously watched the growth of progressive and popular political movements.

In 1957, the main leftist political parties (the Popular Socialist Party, the Socialist Party of Chile, and the Communist Party of Chile) came together to form the Front for Popular Action and finished second in the 1958 presidential elections. The electoral victory went to Jorge Alessandri, a conservative candidate, but the observers at the Ford Foundation did not underestimate the rise in electoral power on the left. For this reason, they sent Robert J. Alexander to write a report on the political situation of the movements and organizations on the left. Alexander was a recognized historian from Rutgers University and an expert on communism in the region. In his 1957 book *Communism in Latin America*, he said the democratic left was the greatest danger to political systems in some countries. In his report to the Ford Foundation, he maintained, "Although the emergence of communism into legality once again does not pose an immediate threat to Chile's long-tested democracy, inflation is causing unrest and communism may be a long-range threat to the Republic."[1]

Later, after the Cuban Revolution and the activation of the Alliance for Progress (AfP), Chile became a notable country in US foreign policy in Latin America. In the first half of the 1960s, two significant events increased the symbolic, geopolitical, and strategic value of Chile for the AfP. First, the 1964 presidential elections again highlighted the progress of the leftist parties. The election results stoked the fear of US analysts in Chile. To the relief of the Americans, the Christian Democrat Eduardo Frei Montalva won the elections with the support of the Liberal Party and the Conservative Party with 56.08 percent of the vote.

Frei Montalva was a Catholic lawyer educated at the Catholic University of Chile. He founded the Christian Democratic Party in 1957. He was a charismatic leader who proposed a modern reform program called "revolution in freedom." This program brought together many of the AfP's proposals for progress—reforms in agriculture, education, and the tax system. This Chilean politician and John F. Kennedy met in early 1963 at a meeting organized by Ralph A. Dungan, the Special Assistant to the US President. The official US interest in building a relationship with Frei Montalva was based on the desire of the Kennedy administration to find support in the democratic and progressive groups in Latin America for its policies in the region, as a way to counteract the ideological influence of the Cuban Revolution (Henríquez and Klaveren 2016: 354).

Despite the 1964 victory of the moderates, the leftist coalition received 38.92 percent of the vote, which was 10 percent more than in the 1958 elections. For this reason, Chile became a principal benefactor of subsidies and loans from various international organizations and US federal agencies. Albert Michaels (1976: 77) estimates that during this period, Chile, with only 3.5 percent of the population in Latin America, received 13.4 percent of US economic aid. The only country that received more US funds was Vietnam. Jeffrey Taffet (2007: 7) lists the main beneficiaries of the Kennedy administration as Chile, Brazil, the Dominican Republic, and Colombia. These four countries accounted for about 60 percent of the funds distributed by the AfP. As part of this trend, the Ford Foundation established an office in Chile in 1963, which grew in importance until it became the regional headquarters in 1965. Chile rose to have a similar status as Brazil in the foundation's operations, and the two countries fought over extraordinary funds and institutional subsidies. From 1960 to 1969, the foundation sent $16.2 million to Chile and $15.2 million to Brazil, significantly more than the $11.1 million sent to Argentina.[2]

The other major event was the reaction to Project Camelot, which had repercussions throughout Latin America and rattled assistance agencies and philanthropic foundations. This social research project was contracted by the US Department of Defense and carried out by American universities. Its goals were to identify, diagnose, and contain social conflicts, political upheavals, and revolutions in Latin American societies. The project began in Chile but was meant to be used in several countries in the hemisphere. In 1965, when the project's intentions were finally known, it was condemned by scientists and created strong opposition in leftist politics, which labeled it as another form of US imperialism in the region (Navarro 2011). This may have been the crudest and most informal means of tying social science and politics together, of US intervention, and of causing science's loss of autonomy, which affected all Latin American science and led to a major rejection and criticism of funds from the United States, whether from government agencies or philanthropic foundations. This diplomatic scandal reverberated in the Chilean communist newspaper *El Siglo* and was continually used to denounce imperialism in Chile and the region (Navarro and Quesada 2010). In the end, the reaction against Project Camelot radicalized positions against US foreign investment and US interventions in Chile.

The Modernization of the University of Chile

Against this political background, the Ford Foundation actively participated in developing an agreement for university modernization, signed by the University of Chile and the University of California in 1965. This agreement was made in tandem with the Chile–California

Plan, financed by the US Agency for International Development (USAID), one of the principal organizations in the AfP. The Chile–California Plan was a 1963 agreement between the State of California and the government of Chile with the objective of developing the Maule River basin with hydroelectricity, agriculture, industry, education, and local communities. The project included a rural education program and a plan for developing human resources. It was part of US policies in the region and, as such, followed the view of the AfP, which considered the following elements essential to modernizing Latin American countries: industry, agriculture, urban and community development, education and human resource training, and communication (Quesada 2012).

The AfP made extensive use of such agreements between US states and Latin American governments, for example, Ecuador and Idaho, Costa Rica and Oregon, Bolivia and Utah, Peru and Texas, and Guatemala and Arizona. Generally speaking, these were aid programs based on economic, productive, climatic, and geological similarities. The goal was for the Latin American countries to reproduce the development model, to some extent, of the US state they worked with (Taffet 2007: 45). The agreement between the University of Chile and the University of California also arose under the auspices of the AfP. In 1961, a group of Chilean academics, mostly university administrators, as well as some in industry and business, made a long trip to the United States. The purpose of the trip was to create close ties between the two countries and develop ways of fostering cooperation between the two universities. The trip was financed by the International Cooperation Administration, which would soon become USAID, one of the principal US instruments of development in the Global South. The group included Juan Gómez Millas (Rector of the University of Chile) and rectors and deans of other Chilean universities. Gómez Millas's meeting with the president of the University of California, Clark Kerr, gave birth to the idea of an interuniversity agreement that the Ford Foundation later funded.

Gómez Millas was an intellectual humanist but also pragmatic; he was not a technocrat cut off from politics. Quite the contrary, he was an amphibian who performed very well in both academia and politics. He studied history at the Faculty of Philosophy and Education and graduated in 1922. In 1931, he was working as a professor of Universal History and directing the Institute of History and Geography when he was selected as the Secretary General of the University of Chile. This was the beginning of his road through the hierarchy of university administrative posts.

Throughout the 1930s, Gómez Millas filled an important post on the Chilean Commission of Intellectual Cooperation, whose goal was to create stronger ties between Chile and other countries in the League of Nations. Between 1943 and 1945, he was part of the Nationalist Union Party of Chile,[3] which brought together nationalism and fascism. In 1947, Gómez Millas was chosen as the Dean of the Faculty of Philosophy and Education, a position he held until 1952, when he was named Minister of Education by Carlos Ibáñez del Campo, a military officer and politician who became president of Chile for the first time in 1927. Even though Ibáñez del Campo reached the government through an electoral process, he wielded power like an authoritarian leader. After a first term from 1927 to 1931, he was re-elected in 1952. During his second administration (1952–1958), he tried to carry out right-wing nationalistic and populist policies. A few months after being named Minister of Education, Gómez Millas resigned after writing and passing Law 11,575, which allocated 0.5 percent of all direct and indirect taxes in the country to the Construction Fund and University Research, which principally benefitted the University of Chile. This law also established the Council of Rectors, whose main function was to coordinate university policies at a national level. In 1953, he became the Rector of the University of Chile, a position he held until 1963. When the Christian Democratic Party of Chile was created in 1957, Gómez Millas participated in its founding and strengthened ties with its leader, Frei Montalva.

Gómez Millas's term as rector was characterized by a large variety of educational reforms marked by their continuity. In the ten years he was rector (1953–1963), the University of Chile developed an innovative structure, institutional decentralization was consolidated, teaching was professionalized, the first graduate schools were created, and internationalization policies grew. The creation of the Valparaiso campus among the Regional Colleges arose from decentralization policies and because the university had to deal with growing university registration and demand outside of Santiago. The increase in full-time teaching positions contributed to the consolidation of research practices. The promotion of scholarships abroad, teacher exchanges, and protocol trips by university administrators grew out of the intention to internationalize the university's activities. During Gómez Millas's term, the creation of the Graduate School met the need for postgraduate education in most scientific disciplines and degree programs offered by the university. However, doctoral and master's degrees were not offered, which was one of the principal problems that administrators tried to address in the agreement with the University of California.[4]

Gómez Millas was in negotiations to acquire funds from the Ford Foundation starting with the first visit of Chilean delegates in 1959. Beginning then, he emphasized the development of a program of academic exchanges focused on basic sciences, social sciences, agricultural science, and technical assistance and materials for libraries, laboratories, and research institutes. Later, he was successful in having the foundation finance the creation of the Regional Colleges with an investment of $1.4 million. On his 1961 trip with the committee of rectors and deans to the United States, he was able to secure the foundation's promise for a long-term and comprehensive project of university modernization. The administrators of the Ford Foundation held Gómez Millas in high esteem and thought that under his leadership, the University of Chile would continue modernizing and contributing to the development of the country. In 1963, the foundation commissioned a mission to Chile that included Reuben Frodin and J. L. Morrill, with the goal of accelerating negotiations to put the agreement with the University of California into place. They suggested supporting and encouraging modernization reforms set into motion by Gómez Millas at the University of Chile:

> [Chile] has one of the highest literacy rates in all South America; there are probably more graduates of the University of Chile on the staffs of other Latin American universities than from any other single university on the continent; Santiago resembles Mexico City as a regional center for Latin America leadership in many aspects; the National University enrolls a sizeable plurality of all Chilean university students; and Don Juan Gómez Millas is the best known and perhaps the most widely respected rector in Latin America. For these reasons, together with the prospects of a turning point toward progressive reform and productive reorganization, it is our belief that earlier investments by the Foundation in the University have proved profitable in themselves and influential in stimulating the current impetus within the institution toward further reforms which may well merit continued assistance by the Foundation.[5]

However, Gómez Millas was not able to put into the agreement between the University of Chile and the University of California into effect because he lost the rector election in mid-1963 to Eugenio González Rojas. This new rector had deep political differences with Gómez Millas because of his political activism. Both had graduated from the same faculty and degree programs as humanists. However, González Rojas was a recognized member and founder of the Socialist

Party of Chile. During Ibáñez del Campo's first presidency, he was imprisoned for his socialist ideas and later appointed Minister of Education in 1932, in the period known as the Socialist Republic, an administration that lasted for only one year. Despite different politics and ideologies, Gómez Millas and González Rojas agreed on some aspects of university modernization. Both affirmed the need for profound changes to the institution, but they differed on the role of the university in the development of the country. Carlos Huneeus (1973: 77) believed the ideological differences over the role of the university lay in the fact that Gómez Millas focused on the scientific goals while González Rojas saw the university as an agent of revolutionary or social change. After losing the elections to the rector, in 1964, Gómez Millas was again named Minister of Education by the president, Frei Montalva.

The Agreement between the University of Chile and the University of California

The new rector continued the process of university modernization that Gómez Millas had started with slight differences. One of the projects González Rojas retained was the agreement between the University of Chile and the University of California. In 1964, the University of Chile created a special committee with representatives from all disciplines to specify the terms of the agreement. This committee was in charge of writing a document and seeking approval from the Superior Council before sending it to the University of California. Later, Ford Foundation Vice President Verne Atwater committed funds from the foundation. Planning and carrying out the basic points of the agreement was done through a series of 1964 meetings in Chile that included representatives of all three institutions. At these meetings, the philosophical foundation for the cooperation was agreed upon.

First, the "institutional nature of understanding" was emphasized, based on the institutional relationships between both universities and not between individuals. At the same time, "a principle of equality" was established for decision-making, in which the Ford Foundation would not intervene.[6] It only approved or rejected the payment of funds. In the creation of the principles that would define the relationship between the three parties, it was emphasized that the agreement was between universities and not individuals. This was meant to help avoid individual negotiations between academics, local representatives, and foundation administrators, which could endanger the fair academic development of all disciplines. This is an interesting part of the agreement because the philanthropic foundations that invested in Chile, especially the Ford and Rockefeller foundations, carried out projects focused on specific disciplines and sciences and devalued others. This asymmetric approach to university modernization had created tensions between institutions that had foreign support and those that did not. This problematic aspect of discretional use of philanthropic money is highlighted by Rodríguez Jiménez (chapter 3), particularly when he discusses how a group of academics from the University of Santiago de Compostela monopolized funds from the Ford Foundation.

Second, the project included all scientific disciplines, artistic and humanistic, which made it multidisciplinary and multi-institutional, and facilitated the participation of all faculties, institutes, schools, and research centers. Finally, the long-term development of shared activities was agreed on, and the length of the agreement was set to ten years with an optional extension. The Ford Foundation had been immersed in the process since the initial negotiations by Gómez Millas in the United States. It is necessary to understand the reasons the foundation decided to finance a project of such a scale in which it could not make decisions. Based on the documents that were reviewed for this chapter, diverse factors can be inferred that led to such a low-profile approach. First, there was an unfavorable climate for philanthropic US agencies due to the backlash to Project Camelot, so the Ford Foundation decided to pursue a minimally interventionist strategy that conserved the autonomy of both universities. It was neither involved in the decisions nor had influence over the agreement's activities.

The second motive was that it was an innovative approach to the relationship between the donor institution and universities that received funds. According to John Netheron, an official of the foundation, the educational agreement between the universities of Chile and California was unique "in the history of technical assistance" for its organization, duration, and design.[7] This meant the philanthropic agency was not ceding its administration to representatives of the universities, but instead, the administrative structure allowed all parties to be represented, but the foundation only had an advisory role. The educational agreement between the University of Chile and the University of California was signed in 1965 for a period of ten years. The Ford Foundation committed itself to fund it completely with $10 million and the possibility of a five-year extension with additional funds. The funds were granted directly to the University of California and its Los Angeles campus (UCLA) administered them. UCLA was responsible for all aspects of the management of the money for the agreement's many areas and programs.

The educational agreement focused on exchanges of academics between the two universities, on doctorates and Master of Science degrees undertaken by Chilean students and researchers, research collaborations on shared topics, and strengthening disciplines with graduate degree programs at the University of Chile. It should be noted that at the time it had only a few graduate courses and no graduate degree programs, while the University of California was one of the US universities with the largest offering of doctorates and Master of Science degrees in a range of specialties. Five scientific areas and disciplines participated in the agreement: agriculture and veterinary medicine, natural sciences and engineering, social sciences, arts and literature, and an area focused on updating and modernization libraries and training library staff.

Putting the project into place coincided with the first steps taken by Frei Montalva's pro-US government. For this reason, the project developed in a climate of suspicion in some—mainly Marxist and leftist-oriented—parts of the university and scientists, who distrusted money coming from US public and private institutions. Because of critiques of receiving foreign funding and the number of areas in the University of Chile that were opposed to these funds, the three participating institutions created an administrative structure that respected university autonomy. This guaranteed the autonomy of both universities with respect to the development of the program, management of funds, and the selection of grantees. At each university, a policy committee was in charge of determining the general principles of academic cooperation, funding priorities, and assessing program development. The committees from the two universities met annually to work as a joint policy committee. There were five subcommittees: (1) agriculture and veterinary medicine, (2) natural sciences and engineering, (3) social sciences, (4) arts and literature, and (5) library support. The subcommittees received and revised funding proposals, approved or rejected projects, recommended modifications, and administered and evaluated ongoing projects. The various areas and disciplines that the agreement covered were decided on during committee deliberations. Scientific disciplines were included in these five areas, excluding medicine and educational sciences, which both universities decided to exclude for different reasons. To administer the agreement, an administrative committee was created to handle the agreement's executive functions. In the institutional charter, the Ford

Foundation did not have any institutional representation, but some employees participated in advisory roles (Quesada 2015).

From its signing in 1965 to 1968, in the climate of university modernization and a reform government, the agreement was put into place heterogeneously based on the areas and disciplines. The institutional mechanisms that were put into effect allowed for an introductory phase, experimentation, and instrumentation of the many collaborative projects that were approved by the subcommittees. Some of these, in particular those in social science and arts and literature, were more successful in formulating specific objectives, policies, and procedures that were sensible to continue.[8] The central idea that underwrote the first stage had the goal of wide participation of academics at both universities and the development of collaborative research projects as well as planning graduate programs.

The first few years of the agreement were assessed positively by the Ford Foundation. The Faculty of Sciences was created at the University of Chile, and many Chilean graduates earned Master of Science and PhD degrees, many of which were done with studies at the University of California. The first doctoral programs were also created. In 1966, the doctoral degree program in Biology was started, and in 1968, doctoral degree programs in Chemistry and Math began to operate in the Faculty of Science, in addition to one in Geology at the Faculty of Physical Sciences and Mathematics. The largest problem the agreement had to face was turbulent university reform. The reform at the University of Chile, which started in 1968 and included a new rector in 1969, took place in a context of ideological conflicts between different groups. These ideological struggles were sustained for several more years and became radicalized with the ascent of Salvador Allende to the presidency. In the spasmodic process of university reform, several forces interacted: demands by the student senate for greater participation in the university government, demands for more pay and improvements to the workplace environment for university staff, and tensions between teachers and scientists, who were trying to maintain the autonomy of their institutions and obtain research funding. The university reforms were also a stage for ideological conflicts between student groups from different political parties (Huneeus 1988).

According to Tomás Vasconi and Inés Reca (1971), two groups formed at the University of Chile in the 1950s. First, the traditionalists wanted to maintain the status quo of the institution and not introduce innovations. Second, the modernizers were a heterogeneous group that aspired to transform the university. These authors argued that the 1968 university reform divided the modernizers into three major groups: (1) the democratizers, who sought institutional changes that would allow students and staff greater participation in the university government, (2) academics and scientists, who wanted improvements in teaching and research and to rationalize the university and update it with modern technology, and (3) the revolutionaries, who thought of the university as a strategic center for transforming wider economic and social structures. During the university reform that began in 1968, the academic authorities of the University of Chile brought about profound changes. The rector, Eugenio González Rojas, who supported a radical transformation of the university, could be called one of the revolutionaries. Many political parties had representatives in student movements. The Federation of Students was controlled by the Christian Democrats, and its critiques of the institution were focused on excessive professional education and scant student representation in the government. In terms of teaching and research, they proposed an organizational model of academic departments to break away from obsolete university structures. The Socialist Party of Chile also had student representatives, as did the Communist Party of Chile and the Leftist Revolutionary Movement.

The reform was started in 1968 in the Faculty of Philosophy and Education, when Dean Hernán Ramírez Necochea, an active communist, called elections that allowed a greater percentage of students to vote than university regulations allowed. This triggered the intervention and reorganization of the faculty and the resignation of González Rojas, who opposed this measure, and the student seizure of the university's main office. This began a long, tense period of more than two years. The period was accompanied by heightened sociopolitical conflict and mobilization, which led to constant assemblies, student strikes and seizures of buildings, and the resignation of deans and rectors, among other issues. After González Rojas's resignation, Ruy Barboza was made interim rector, and elections were held in all the faculties. This electoral process led to only two ratified deans. The new rector signed an Act of Agreement with the students, accepted student participation in the election of university officials, and began planning reforms to the university statutes. Despite taking these measures, the problems did not stop but instead became radicalized in tandem with an increase in ideological conflicts between student political parties, among which they were rivalries to take political advantage of the reform.

Before the 1968 university reform, Ford Foundation officials had adopted a neutral stance that followed its policy of not intervening in politics. But how did the university reform affect the foundation's higher education programs? On one hand, its main educational project in Chile (the project between the universities of Chile and California) was impacted by student occupations of faculties and schools. On the other hand, the foundation had a positive view of students' modernization proposals such as creating departments, articulating between teaching and research, professionalizing science degree programs, and improving connections between university and government activities—insofar as they matched its own objectives in the country.[9]

The university reform affected many activities of the University of Chile that had been included in the agreement. Scholarships that had been granted were halted, research was stopped, and some visits by teachers and scientists from the University of California were cancelled. However, generally speaking, the agreement and the Ford Foundation did not attract significant criticisms from the students on the left. In a letter to the president of the University of California, C. J. Hitch, the university's chancellor, Charles Young, said that "it is significant to note that during the reform, neither the University of California nor the Ford Foundation was attacked, although the Communist Party criticized the acceptance of US dollars and specifically named the Rockefeller Foundation and the US Air Force."[10] John Netherton corroborated this opinion in a report written in 1969:

> The sensitivities of the University of Chile called for a softening of the very idea of assistance. That of a strictly academic exchange, with the element of mutual benefit made very explicit, was much more palatable, and easier to explain to the larger constituency, where besides amour propre there is also widespread acceptance to the view of United States assistance as self-seeking intrusion, and a blurring of the difference between foundations and United States government agencies. It may be noted here that it was not until the third year of the project that the universities came to feel it advisable for a Foundation representative to be added to the Policy Committee. Yet a wide spectrum of ideologies is represented in the current Chilean committee membership, and the program has been almost completely free from political attack.[11]

What factors explain this more benevolent attitude of the student sector toward the agreement and the Ford Foundation? First, the autonomy of both the University of Chile and the University of California made the foundation less susceptible to student criticisms. Second, there was wide participation in the project by graduates, teachers, and researchers of different parties and ideologies. In fact, students and professors who received scholarships belonged to a range of political groups. For example, Ramírez Necochea was the dean of the Faculty of Philosophy and Education, a member of the Communist Party of Chile, and one of the people who started the university reform. This historian, who strongly criticized US financing in his writing and speeches, participated in the agreement as a member of the social science subcommittee. The reports reviewed here have no mention of him criticizing the agreement. On the contrary, the social science subcommittee became more active after the university reform. Two graduate programs were planned (master's degrees in Urban Planning and Demography), and the number of Chilean students with scholarships to study in California increased.[12]

Although the university reform did affect the project between the universities of Chile and California, it was not a significant problem for the Ford Foundation. However, the reform created a notable conflict in the administration of Frei Montalva and fragmented his political party, leading to the resignation of the Minister of Education Gómez Millas. He resigned in the face of the impossibility of placating the conflict and reaching an agreement between students and university authorities.

Close to Chile, Far from Nixon

As we have seen, Frei Montalva began his administration with a cordial bilateral relationship with the United States, but around 1965, disagreements began. They were over issues such as the refinancing of Chile's foreign debt, the increase in the price of copper proposed by the Chilean president—one of the country's best selling minerals that the United States needed for arms and communications in the Vietnam War, and Frei Montalva's critiques of US intervention in the Dominican Republic. Another factor to keep in mind was the cooling of relations between Washington and the Chilean administration caused by the AfP during the term of US President Lyndon B. Johnson. In the mid-1960s, Johnson abandoned the idealism and optimism that characterized the AfP during its first two years under the Kennedy administration (Taffet 2007: 60). This transformation toward a more pragmatic alliance was criticized by the Chilean president in an article in *Foreign Affairs* entitled "The Alliance That Lost Its Way" (Frei Montalva 1967).

Relations between Chile and the superpower did not return to the path of understanding or close cooperation during Johnson's presidency. On the contrary, the two became more distant when Frei

Montalva adopted some nationalistic policies that leaned toward nationalizing Chilean mining, which seriously affected the commercial interests of some US companies. In 1968, when Richard Nixon was elected president, relations between the two countries cooled even more (Henríquez and Klaveren 2016: 365–357). In addition, something happened in 1970 that the US government had tried to prevent through propaganda, diplomacy, and technical, economic, and educational assistance. Popular Unity, the coalition of the main leftist parties, won the elections. The victory of Salvador Allende "constituted the most significant revolutionary triumph in Latin American since the Cuban Revolution" (Tanya Harmer 2014: 198).

A socialist government in Latin America, under Cuban influence, was a serious geopolitical threat to the United States. In response, the Nixon administration followed a variety of strategies against Allende. First, through CIA agents and contacts in the armed forces, it attempted an army uprising to pressure Congress not to recognize the results of the election. This led to the assassination of General René Schneider for his loyalty to the constitution and opposition to the military uprising. Another tactic was boycotting the Chilean government and financing anti-communist propaganda to erode its popular support. Finally, it reduced loans while considerably increasing military aid, with the goal of winning the support of the Chilean Army (Gaudichaud 2016).

The socialist victory in Chile was not a surprise to the Ford Foundation, whose officials were aware of the possibility. One of them, Nagaraja Rao, visited the country to give a lecture on politics just before the elections and to assess the platform of the Popular Unity coalition. In his report, he was optimistic, saying, "It was exciting for me to be in Santiago at this juncture and witness the political processes that precede a new era in the national life of Chile."[13] Another official, Peter Hakim, witnessed the enthusiasm and affirmed, "It was a time of great optimism among most of the people at the Ford Foundation although some were very skeptical about Allende's economic proposals."[14]

Socialism's rise to power transformed Chile into one of the Cold War's geopolitical hotspots. The electoral victory of the left brought significant international attention, to the point that Ford Foundation President McGeorge Bundy and Vice President David E. Bell wanted to travel to Chile themselves to see the new socialist government. Bundy was a specialist in international relations. In 1961, he was the US National Security Advisor in the Kennedy administration and joined the Ford Foundation in 1966. Bell had served as the Administrative Executive to President Harry S. Truman, and while Kennedy was in the White House, he was named the USAID administrator in 1962. In

1966, he left public service to join the Ford Foundation. Both were part of the elite group of men that worked closely with Kennedy, whom David Halberstam (1969) called "the best and the brightest." Peter Bell, the foundation's representative in Chile, recommended against the trip for the following reasons:

> The Chileans were careful to emphasize that their advice, which coincides with our own, should not be interpreted as Government unfriendliness. To the contrary, their caution was based on their fear that Mac's visit might be used as a pretext by "others" to embarrass the Government and the Foundation. The pretext, of course, would not be Mac's position as president of the Foundation but his former role in the formulation of US foreign policy.[15]

In the end, Bundy and David Bell did not travel to Chile to avoid further clouding the local relationships that foundation officials had established in Chile. In the same report, Peter Bell did not perceive the situation as a problem for the foundation's activities:

> For the present my colleagues and I prefer to act on more "optimistic" assumptions, which point toward the building of a Socialist State through a democratic or pluralistic process. It seems to me that such action is justified, given 1—the lack of determinate indications for pessimism, 2—the low risk to the Foundation in being "wrong," and 3—the high gains for Chile, including our grantees, if we are right. If we were to take a more stand-offish tack, we would be abandoning both established relations and promising opportunities here and jeopardizing our future with what may be the "new wave" not only in Chile but much of Latin America. Within the current political framework, I believe that our prospects are largely of our own making.[16]

Unlike the US government and official agencies, which took a hostile position toward Allende, the Ford Foundation continued channeling funds to academic institutions in Chile and especially to the agreement between the University of Chile and the University of California. The foundation maintained its neutral stance on the political developments in Chile. Foundation officials believed the socialist government had taken power through elections and did not aspire to follow the Cuban Revolution. From this perspective, the "Chilean road to socialism" meant a series of social, cultural, and economic transformations to end the country's underdevelopment. Ford representatives also thought the socialist administration wanted to strengthen some socioeconomic measures that had been started by Frei Montalva's moderate and Christian Democrat government, specifically in the fields of education and agrarian reform, issues the Ford Foundation also supported with subsidies and projects. Hence, the socialist and transformative approach of Allende's government was not a danger to the Ford Foundation even though it was to Washington's interests. The Chilean government even received two subsidies from the Ford Foundation in 1972: one for $152,000 for agrarian reform (one of the foundation's major fields of action) and another for $170,600 for child nutrition.[17]

In this political context, the activities of the educational agreement between the universities of Santiago and California continued in a range of areas. The number of student scholarships that had dropped during the university reforms increased and graduate institutions were created. In the area of natural sciences and engineering, between 1970 and 1972, five doctorate programs were started: geophysics, chemical engineering, physics, seismology, and soil engineering and mechanics. In 1972, agriculture and veterinary medicine began offering master's degrees in animal health and pathology and animal nutrition. As mentioned above, two master's degrees were planned for the social sciences: Urban Planning and Demography.

Philanthropic Loyalty and Human Rights

In September 1973, a coup d'état led by General Augusto Pinochet overthrew Allende's constitutional government and proceeded to organize all state institutions under an authoritarian regime. At all universities, the military junta designated agents from the army as rectors with extensive powers. The strong ideological control that was imposed aimed to enact a major cleansing of academia. Professors and students were expelled. There were closures of departments, centers, and research institutes as well as unions and student and teacher associations. The new organization fractured the entire system of higher education. At the University of Chile, faculties, schools, centers, and research institutes were dismantled. Many academics were expelled from their institutions or jailed; some were assassinated or abducted and never heard from again (Póo 2016).

Peter Bell sent a report on the authoritarian regime to William Carmichael, the foundation's head of the Latin America and Caribbean Program. He described the coup as similar to many others in the region, though the Chilean coup was different for "the suddenness and virulence of change . . . [and] the brutality of repression." He added, "Over the next six months, I seriously doubt that we will want to make any new grants to Chilean government agencies or universities."[18] Even though Kalman Silvert thought the foundation should remain relatively neutral to the new government, he also believed he could not deny help to the academics and education experts they had relationships with: "The Foundation must not be subversive of regimes with which it operates. At the same time it must not ask of its officials that they suspend their most profoundly decent sentiments and refuse to assist fellow men who are lawlessly persecuted."[19]

The dictatorship's repression affected the gamut of economic, social, cultural, scientific, and educational transformations that had been ongoing, beginning with the Christian Democrat government and strengthened by the socialists. Once the dictatorship intervened in the universities and closed scientific and academic centers, the problem foundation officials faced was under what conditions they would maintain their investments and in some cases increase them. The other question was with whom to continue working, as many academics and researchers who had received scholarships from the Ford Foundation were fired, politically persecuted, jailed, or had gone underground to stay alive. It was not at all a positive situation. Faced with this situation, the Ford Foundation established a human rights agenda that, according to José Brunner and Alicia Barrios (1987: 230), has been used as a "behavioral model" by other institutions. The foundation had taken similar measures to relocate students with scholarships and academics from other Latin American countries whose governments had fallen to authoritarian regimes. In 1964, following the overthrow of Joao Goulart in Brazil, the foundation helped many scientists, mainly social scientists, flee the country, resettle abroad, and begin researching again. Chile was one of the countries they chose to resettle. This may be connected, as Fernanda Beigel (2010) suggests, to the appearance of dependency theory in Chile.

The foundation also helped many Argentine scientists resettle and reestablish research in other Latin American countries in 1966, when the dictatorship of General Juan Carlos Onganía intervened in the University of Buenos Aires. There was a strong repression of professors and students, and many instructors and researchers resigned en masse (Buchbinder 2005). In response, the Ford Foundation negotiated with Chilean Minister of Education Gómez Millas so that the two main state universities, the University of Chile and the State Technical University, hired a considerable number of Argentine scientists, fifty-two in total. The foundation provided these scientists with scholarships and gave them money to travel and resettle in Chile. The foundation also negotiated for a smaller group of researchers to move to Venezuela, Peru, Mexico, Costa Rica, and the United States (Braslavsky and Carnota 2018).

After the coup in Chile, the foundation took emergency measures to help academics who had been impacted and provided subsidies to help those who had been removed for political reasons. Since social science was one of the areas most persecuted by Pinochet's dictatorship, the foundation provided $242,000 to the Latin America Social Science Council with the goal of relocating these scientists. It also funded the Latin American Studies Association with $84,100.[20] In addition, the Ford Foundation subsidized the World University Service, a philanthropic nongovernmental organization, to help resettle exiled Chilean academics (Bayle 2008; Bayle and Navarro 2014).

Another measure taken by the Ford Foundation was to reduce the size of the Chilean office and reassign employees to Lima. This decision was a symbolical rejection of Pinochet's dictatorship and addressed the foundation's staff fear for their lives. The Chilean authorities considered Peter Bell "a suspicious person," and following a warning from the US Ambassador, he left the country. The educational project of the universities of Chile and California was significantly affected from the reorganization of faculties, departments, and institutes and the end of university autonomy, which had been a driving force in the agreement. Project activities were reduced considerably and in some areas stopped completely. The foundation froze funds earmarked for the agreement. There were no payments made in 1974 or 1975. Of the $10 million agreed upon at the beginning of the agreement, it paid out only $9,489,000 and canceled the possibility of extending funding for an additional five years, as had been mentioned in some meetings. The students with scholarships in 1974 and 1975 carried on with money paid out before the coup.

Natural sciences and engineering were also affected by the coup, given the number of scientists who had to flee in exile. Despite this, a master's degree in water science was started in 1974, which had been previously proposed. The disciplines on the subcommittee of agriculture and veterinary medicine were luckier than other institutional projects. In the first few years of the dictatorship, three new master's degrees were started: Animal Production (1974) and then Livestock, Forest Science and Fruit Cultivation (1975). However, the degree programs planned for the social sciences and master's degrees in Urban Planning and Demography did not start because some of the academics in these programs had been expelled.

According to a report by both universities in 1979, of the 279 Chilean students with scholarships from all areas, including library science, almost half (n=126) did not do any university activity in Chile. Of those, nine remained in the United States for graduate studies, research, or teaching as an extension of their participation in the agreement. A large number of these 126 grantees (n=19) had moved to the private sector. Another thirteen were categorized as having an unknown status; the report did not provide information on them in 1974 or 1978. For various political and work-related reasons, sixty-eight academics who had participated in the agreement were living abroad and were no longer part of the University of Chile. Some of the academics and students supported by the agreement had been expelled, tortured, or forced into exile.

In the face of the brutal intervention by the dictatorship in academia and science, the Ford Foundation began to finance independent academic centers and informal institutions that had no relationship to the universities. These centers, mainly in the social sciences, sheltered researchers who were expelled from their university jobs for diverse reasons but continued living in Chile. Through this strategy and from its Lima office, the foundation remained active in Chile and supported scientists during the transition to democracy. These scientists played an important role in criticizing authoritarianism and later, when democracy was restored in 1990, filled important political positions (Puryear 1994).

This chapter has shown the Ford Foundation in Chile was not always aligned with US foreign policy, though there were some affinities at certain junctures. At times, the foundation shared goals and interests with the regional strategy of the AfP, which was sponsored by the US government. For example, both organizations identified Chile's important role in geopolitics. However, the Ford Foundation's projects had strong continuity over time and did not always match the short-term interests of Washington's foreign policy and its fight against international communism. When foundation officials arrived in Chile during the 1960s, they were apprehensive about the growth of leftist coalition parties, but over time, they overcame distrust of the Popular Unity coalition because it was democratic, progressive, and transformative and not revolutionary or communist. Unlike the US Department of State, Ford Foundation officials in Chile were optimistic about Allende's victory. In this case, the foundation maintained its investments and even granted new financing to the socialist government.

Interpretive frameworks that reduce the actions of philanthropic foundations to either subordination to or independence from US foreign policy do not fit the historical evidence presented here. Hence, it is preferable to problematize these relationships and deduce the facts, historical processes, and empirical evidence, rather than adopting preconceptions bound to political or ideological interests. In this sense, Ludovic Tournès' (2010; Tournès and Scott-Smith 2018) perspective seems relevant and promising, because it incorporates new dimensions of analysis and relational aspects that fit the situation in Chile. This is especially true for the Ford Foundation's continuing focus on maintaining academic and scientific networks even in unfavorable situations such as the dictatorship under the rule of Pinochet. As Jeffery Puryear (1994) has shown, the networks that were saved and relocated played an important role in Chile's transition to democracy.

Fernando Quesada is Associate Researcher in Argentina's National Council of Scientific and Technological Research (CONICET) and Professor at the National University of Cuyo, Mendoza. He obtained his doctorate at the National University of Córdoba. He is author of *La Universidad Desconocida: El Convenio entre la Universidad de Chile–Universidad de California y la Fundación Ford* (2015). He researches relations between philanthropic foundations and science in Latin America. His research topics include scholarships programs, transnationals flux of scholars and researchers, and financial support of science. He is currently researching the Rockefeller Foundation's funding of agricultural science in Chile and Chile's importance in the international Green Revolution.

Notes

1. Robert Alexander, "Notes on Chile," Reports 000062/1959, Catalogued reports, Reports 1-3254, 1936–2005, Ford Foundation Archives (FFA), Rockefeller Archive Center (RAC).
2. Data from the Annual Reports of the Ford Foundation, 1960–1969, FFA, RAC.
3. The Nationalist Union Party of Chile was created in 1943 and after the Wold War II it was dissolved.
4. Consejo de Rectores, 1965. Guía informativa de las universidades chilenas (Estudios que ofrecen, requisitos y títulos). Santiago de Chile: Centro Nacional de Información y Documentación.
5. *Comprehensive Report, 1965–1978: A Cooperative Education and Research Program between the University of Chile and the University of California*, Narrative Report, vol. 1, July 1979, 14, FFA, RAC.
6. Ibid.,18.

7. John Netherton. "The Case of the Chile-California Program," Reports 002695-015/1969, Catalogued reports, Reports 1-3254, 1936–2005, FFA, RAC.
8. Informe comprensivo de las actividades del Convenio Universidad de Chile-Universidad de California entre 1965–1972 (1972), Universidad de Chile.
9. Netherton, "The Case of the Chile-California Program."
10. *Comprehensive Report: 1965–1978*, 53–54.
11. Netherton. "The Case of the Chile-California Program," 5–6.
12. "Programa de largo plazo de las actividades del Convenio, 1970–1975" (1970), Un programa cooperativo en educación e investigación entre la Universidad de Chile y la Universidad de California.
13. Rao K. Nagaraja. "A Report on My Recent Visit to Chile, 1970," Reports 008505/1970, Catalogued reports, Reports 6262-9286, 1936–2005, FFA, RAC.
14. Interview with Peter Hakim, 29 May 2008.
15. Peter Bell, "On a Visit to Chile by McGeorge Bundy and David Bell," Inter-Office Memorandum to William D. Carmichel and John Nagel, 21 January 1971 (Confidential), 6, Reports 011634/1971, Catalogued reports, Reports 9287-11774, 1936–2005, FFA, RAC.
16. Ibid., 5.
17. 1972 Annual Report of the Ford Foundation.
18. Peter Bell, "The Aftermath of the Military Coup in Chile," 22 November 1973, Reports 010668/1973, Latin America and the Caribbean Program Files on the 1973 Coup d´Etat in Chile, 1971–1978, FFA, RAC.
19. Kalman Silvert, "Chile," 1 April 1974, Reports 008959/1974, Latin America and the Caribbean Program Files on the 1973 Coup d´Etat in Chile, 1971–1978, FFA, RAC.
20. Anita Isaacs (Program Officer), "Support for Employment Clearinghouse, Relocation Costs, and Fellowships for Latin American Scholars Displaced by Political Events," Grant no. 07400187/1973–1976, reel no. 3179 5202 5283; and James R. Himes (Program Officer), "Support for the Operations of an Emergency Committee to Bid Latin American Scholars," Latin America and the Caribbean Program Files on the 1973 Coup d'Etat in Chile, 1971–1978 (FA721), FFA, RAC.

References

Alexander, Robert J. 1957. *Communism in Latin America*. New Brunswick, NJ: Rutgers University Press.

Arnove, Robert, ed. 1980. *Philanthropy and Cultural Imperialism: The Foundations at Home and Abroad*. Boston: G.K. Hall& Co.

Bayle, Paola. 2008. "Emergencia académica en el Cono Sur."*Ícono: Revista de Ciencias Sociales* 30: 51–63.

Bayle, Paola, and Juan José Navarro. 2014. "Le World University Service et l´Amérique Latine."*Monde(s)* 6: 89–110.

Beigel, Fernanda. 2010. "La teoría de la dependencia en su laboratorio." In *Autonomía y dependencia académica: Universidad e investigación científica en un circuito periférico: Chile y Argentina (1950–1980)*, ed. Fernanda Beigel, 129–144. Buenos Aires: Biblos.

Berghahn, Volker R. 1986. *The Americanization of West German Industry, 1945–1973*. New York: Cambridge University Press.

Berman, Edward H. 1983. *The Influence of the Carnegie, Ford, and Rockefeller Foundations on American Foreign Policy: The Ideology of Philanthropy*. Albany: State University of New York Press.

Braslavsky, Silvia, and Raúl Carnota. 2018. "Operativo Rescate: La Fundación Ford y la emigración posterior a la Noche de los Bastones Largos." In *Filantropía, ciencia y universidad: nuevos aportes y análisis sociohistóricos sobre la diplomacia académica en América Latina*, ed. Juan Jesús Morales, 67–111. Santiago: Ediciones UCSH.

Brunner, José Joaquín, and Alicia Barrios. 1987. *Inquisición, mercado y filantropía: Ciencias Sociales y autoritarismo en Argentina, Brasil, Chile y Uruguay*. Santiago de Chile: FLACSO.

Buchbinder, Pablo. 2005. *Historia de las Universidades Argentinas*. Buenos Aires: Sudamericana.

Bulmer, Martin. 1984. *The Chicago School of Sociology: Institutionalization, Diversity, and the Rise of Sociological Research*. Chicago: University of Chicago Press.

Benedetta, Calandra, and Marina Franco. 2012. *La guerra fría cultural en América Latina: Desafíos y límites para una nueva mirada de las relaciones interamericanas*. Buenos Aires: Biblos.

Condliffe Lagemann, Ellen, ed. 1999. *Philanthropic Foundations: New Scholarship, New Possibilities*. Bloomington: Indiana University Press.

Curti, Merle. 1963. *American Philanthropy Abroad: A History*. New Brunswick, NJ: Rutgers University Press.

Fisher, Donald. 1983. "The Role of Philanthropic Foundations in the Reproduction and Production of Hegemony: Rockefeller Foundations and the Social Sciences."*Sociology* 17 (2): 206–233.

Frei Montalva, Eduardo. 1967. "The Alliance That Lost Its Way."*Foreign Affairs* 45(3): 437–448.

Gaudichaud, Franck. 2016. *Chile 1970–1973: Mil días que estremecieron al mundo*. Santiago: LOM.

Gilman, Nils. 2003. *Mandarins of the Future: Modernization Theory in Cold War America*. Baltimore: Johns Hopkins University Press.

Halberstam, David. 1969. *The Best and the Brightest*. New York: Ballantine Books.

Harmer, Tanya. 2014. "Chile y la Guerra Fría Interamericana, 1970–1973." In *Chile y la Guerra Fría Global*, ed. Tanya Harmer and Alfredo Riquelme Segovia, 193–223. Santiago: Ril Editores.

Henríquez, María José, and Alberto van Klaveren. 2016. "Reformismo y pragmatismo: La política exterior de Eduardo Frei Montalva, 1964–1970." In *Eduardo Frei Montalva: Un gobierno reformista: A 50 años de la "Revolución en Libertad,"* ed. Carlos Huneeus and Javier Couso, 343–369. Santiago: Editorial Universitaria.

Hess, Gary R. 2003. "Waging the Cold War in The Third World: The Foundations and the Challenges of Development." In *Charity, Philanthropy, and Civility in American History*, ed. Lawrence J. Friedman and Mark D. McGarvie, 319–339. Cambridge: Cambridge University Press.

Huneeus, Carlos. 1973. *La Reforma Universitaria en la Univesidad de Chile*. Santiago: CPU.

——. 1988. *La Reforma Universitaria veinte años después*. Santiago: CPU.

Joseph, Gilbert, Catherine C. LeGrand, and Ricardo D. Salvatore. 1998. *Close Encounters of Empire:Writing the Cultural History of U.S.-Latin American Relations*. Durham, NC: Duke University Press.

Michaels, Albert L. 1976. "The Alliance for Progress and Chile´s "Revolution in Liberty" (1964–1970)."*Journal of Interamerican Studies and World Affairs* 18(1): 74–99.

Navarro, Juan José. 2011. "Cold War in Latin America: The Camelot Project (1964–1965) and the Political and Academic Reactions of the Chilean Left." *Comparative Sociology* 10 (5): 807–825.

Navarro, Juan José, and Fernando Quesada. 2010. "El impacto del proyecto Camelot en el período de consolidación de las Ciencias Sociales Latinoamericanas." In *El desarrollo de las ciencias sociales: Tradiciones, actores e instituciones en Argentina, Chile, México y Centroamérica*, ed. Diego Pereyra, 51–75. San José de Costa Rica: FLACSO.

Póo, Ximena, ed. 2016. *La dictadura de los sumarios (1974–1985): Universidad de Chile intervenida*. Santiago: Editorial Universitaria.

Puryear, Jeffrey M. 1994. *Thinking Politics: Intellectuals and Democracy in Chile, 1973–1998*. Baltimore: Johns Hopkins University Press.

Quesada, Fernando. 2010. "Sobrevolando la tormenta: la sede chilena de la Fundación Ford." *Cuadernos Americanos* 3(133): 89–101.

——. 2012. "Un modelo para el desarrollo: la cooperación entre Chile y California y el papel del financiamiento público y privado norteamericano."*Estudios Avanzados* 18: 11–34.

——. 2015. *La Universidad Desconocida: El Convenio Universidad de Chile-Universidad de California y la Fundación Ford*. Mendoza: EDIFYL.

Saunders, Frances Stonor. 2001. *La CIA y la guerra fría cultural*. Madrid: Debate.

Taffet, Jeffrey F. 2007. *Foreign Aid as Foreign Policy: The Alliance for Progress in Latin America*. New York: Routledge.

Tournès, Ludovic, ed. 2010. *L'argent de l'influence: Les fondations américaines et leurs reseaux européens*. Paris: Autrement.

Tournès, Ludovic, and Giles Scott-Smith. 2018. *Global Exchanges: Scholarships and Transnational Circulations in the Modern World*. New York: Berghahn Books.

Vasconi, Tomás A., and Inés C. Reca. 1971. *Modernización y crisis en la universidad latinoamericana*. Santiago: CESO.

Chapter 10

Between Modernization and University Reform (1957–1973)

Technical Assistance from UNESCO to the University of Concepción

Anabella Abarzúa Cutroni

From 1945 to 1984, the technical assistance from the United Nations Educational, Scientific and Cultural Organization (UNESCO) to developing countries materialized in many initiatives, which we can include in the concept of sponsorship. The sending of experts with an assigned mission was the central activity around which other activities of technical assistance were organized. These activities comprised the organization of meetings, preparing publications, financing libraries and scientific infrastructure, teacher training, and the start-up of academic centers, among others. All these initiatives were developed through complex institutional mechanisms that mediated between the national and international spheres and between the political and academic fields of member states and UNESCO itself. The officials of this organization were very careful not to sponsor initiatives that did not enjoy significant support from the local academic authorities. This was because they knew the commitment of local academics gave a higher degree of feasibility and durability to the activities undertaken. This was perceived as a benefit for the prestige of UNESCO.

I have carried out my research work over the past few years from the point of view of academic dependency (Beigel 2013). UNESCO constitutes a privileged space from which to observe empirically the complex interdependence that was historically established between academic centers and peripheries. "Dependence" is a historical condition that is not a unilateral imposition by the centers on the periphery but is a dynamic relationship between different poles. These poles have different degrees of centrality—both at the world and regional levels—and, in turn, specific conditions that make them peripheral. My research work has been devoted to explaining how, by means of the technical assistance of UNESCO, concrete cases of dependency or academic autonomy were originated. In the case of UNESCO, observing situations of academic dependency empirically involved making a cross section through the local, regional, and international ambits, as well as articulating political and academic plans in the analysis.

A small number of the experts that UNESCO sent around the world were specifically devoted to advising on higher education and scientific policy. In Latin America from 1945 to 1974, the technical assistance by UNESCO was principally oriented toward the area of education. However, very few experts gave specific advice regarding higher education. The process of modernization of the University of Concepción, started in 1957, was considered by the UNESCO officials and bureaucrats as a special case in which a "pilot project" of university modernization could be carried out which would be an example for the universities of Latin America.

The technical assistance given by UNESCO to the University of Concepción was based mainly on the recommendations of two "international consultants on higher education," Rudolph P. Atcon and Joseph Lauwerys. Both experts made stays at the university that lasted two to three months. Atcon was the first to come to the University of Concepción. He carried out an institutional diagnosis and planned a first stage of "modernization" during his two visits in 1957. Then, the implementation of his recommendations began during a visit in 1958.[1] Years later, in 1963, Lauwerys evaluated the implementation of the reforms planned by Atcon and made some new recommendations. In 1965, he participated actively in the implementation of a second stage of "modernization" at the University of Concepción, based on the recommendations he had made earlier.

Rudolph P. Atcon (1921–1995) was born in Greece and became a US citizen. In the United States, he studied Civil Engineering at Union College (Schenectady, New York) in 1943 and Liberal Arts at Amherst College (Massachusetts). In 1951, he obtained a postgraduate degree in Philosophy of Science and Symbolic Logic from Harvard University. Once he had finished his postgraduate studies in the United States, Atcon settled in Brazil as an international adviser on education. In 1952, Anísio S. Teixeira hired him as an assistant for the restructuring of the Campanha de Aperfeiçoamento de Pessoal de Nível Superior (Campaign for the Upgrading of Higher Level Personnel) in the field of education. Then, he was hired by the Ministry of Education and Culture and the Council of Vice Chancellors of Brazilian Universities, and he carried out sporadic consultancies for various Brazilian universities. From his settling in Brazil onward, he worked as a consultant in various countries in the region—Venezuela, Chile, Colombia, the Dominican Republic, Honduras, Mexico, and Argentina—under contracts with international organizations such as the Organization of American States (OAS) and UNESCO (Bernardet Bittencourt 2011; Inhan De Souza 2015).

Joseph Lauwerys was born in Belgium and taught Comparative Education at the Institute of Education at the University of London from 1947 onward. Between 1939 and 1951, he had been a visiting lecturer at Columbia University. In 1945, he had formed part of the Conference of the Allied Ministers of Education as Director of the Research Commission. From 1946 to 1948, he was the consultant of the preparatory commission and UNESCO's Department of Education. After his work at the University of Concepción, he continued working as a UNESCO expert in Brazil.[2]

Brief Characterization of Higher Education in Chile

From 1842 to 1956, eight universities were created in Chile, which are currently the oldest and most prestigious in the country. They made up an institutional nucleus powerfully led by the University of Chile, which laid the foundations for the higher education system. The budget for these universities was largely financed by the state, including in the case of private universities, which also had other sources of finance. Despite this special feature, the governmental authorities recognized these institutions as autonomous. This original nucleus was made up of two public universities—the University of Chile (1842) and the Technical State University (1947)—two private universities with a confessional origin—the Catholic University of Chile (1888) and the Catholic University of Valparaíso (1928)—and four private universities of lay origin—the University of Concepción (1919), the Federico Santa María Technical University (1925), Austral University (1954), and the Catholic University of the North (1956) (Brunner 2009; Garretón and Martínez 1985a).

From the late nineteenth century onward, Chilean universities acquired a professionalizing character, in the sense that they were assigned the task of training the professionals that "national development" required. Toward the mid-1950s, both the academic and governmental authorities proposed to modernize the universities. This implied above all the teaching of basic sciences (both exact and natural versions and social sciences) and the development of research (Brunner 2009; Garretón and Martínez 1985b: 64).

The University of Concepción was set up in 1919 on the initiative of local freemasonry and under the leadership of the philosopher Enrique Molina,[3] who would be the Vice Chancellor of this institution from the date it was founded until 1956. It is a private university, financed at the moment of its creation by the local elite through the Pro-University Committee and the Concepción Clinical Hospital and subsequently by a system of donations by prize draw and by fiscal contributions. From the beginning, the University of Concepción stood out from other Chilean universities, as it defined itself as lay, liberal, and modernizing. Another particular characteristic of this university was the high degree of radicalization that its students achieved during the 1960s with the boosting of the Movimiento de Izquierda Revolucionaria (Left-Wing Revolutionary Movement—MIR), which achieved the presidency of the Federación de Estudiantes de Concepción (Concepción Student Federation—FEC) in 1967 (Garretón and Martínez 1985a, 1985b; Huneeus 1988).

The Modernization Plan of the University of Concepción

In 1954, Chile had completed the necessary requirements for its full incorporation as a member state of UNESCO. From that moment on, Chilean authorities began to ask for technical assistance. Chile, together with Brazil, functioned as a kind of "laboratory" for the initiatives of the organization in Latin America. A good example is the emblematic sponsorship of UNESCO for the Latin American Faculty of Social Sciences. In parallel, UNESCO also contributed to sustaining the process of modernization, which took place in the University of Concepción between 1956 and 1967. The documentary sources consulted on this mission indicate to us that the modernization of the University of Concepción was from the beginning an initiative of the local university authorities. They had sufficient governmental support, which made possible the request for international technical assistance both from UNESCO and other agencies. In 1956, Vice Chancellor Molina had to stand down because of the conflict triggered by the FEC. The students were demanding the creation of a commission made up of academics, students, and authorities that would start up a process of "university reform." In view of the intransigence of the Vice Chancellor, they called a strike. As a result of this protest, the university authorities decided to expel the students responsible and suspend classes for thirty days (Huneeus 1988). Despite these disciplinary measures, the Vice Chancellor felt obliged to resign.

That same year, instead of Molina, the lawyer David Stitchkin Branover was elected Vice Chancellor and immediately called on academics and students to modernize the University of Concepción.[4] As part of this policy, the technical assistance of UNESCO was called for. But Vice Chancellor Stitchkin Branover already had a clear diagnosis of the university's situation before receiving the recommendations of this international organization. In a letter addressed to the specialists of the UN Technical Assistance Board, the Vice Chancellor claimed the University of Concepción was following the model of Spanish universities; that is to say, it was organized in faculties that were independent of each other, which set down a rigid curriculum for a professional qualification. The objective of the restructuring that was proposed was to adopt a system of credits similar to that implemented by US universities, above all for the "new specializations," that is to say, for the creation of nontraditional degrees. Toward the end of 1956, the UNESCO specialists initiated the process of recruiting the experts requested by Chile to advise on the reform of the University of Concepción. As a result, Atcon was selected as an adviser, together with other candidates, by the Chilean government itself. The funding of the first two stays this US expert made in Chile was provided by UNESCO, while the cost of the third was covered by the Contingency Fund of the UN Expanded Programme of Technical Assistance.

Over the past few years, I have tried to reconstruct Atcon's route and the itinerary of this international expert in Latin America. Up to the present, I have a mosaic of activities and institutional relationships that do not entirely reveal the identity and interests of this controversial expert. In the documents consulted about his stays at Concepción, I find indications that Atcon was acting with a certain degree of autonomy with regard to UNESCO. This may be explained by the fact that he had the support not only of the Chilean governmental and academic authorities[5] but also other international agencies that were also giving technical assistance in the region, such as the Rockefeller Foundation and the International Cooperation Agency, known as the ICA Point Four Program.[6] As is recorded in the correspondence dealing with the hiring by UNESCO, his stay in Chile had to be authorized by the US government. That is to say, even though Atcon was acting as a UNESCO expert, with the diplomatic privileges and immunities this implied, and he was practically settled in Brazil, his designation to work in Chile had to go through the processes of control and supervision of the US government.

During this period, Atcon established contacts and networks with prestigious academics in the region. For example, in Brazil, he had been hired by Anísio Teixeira, and before arriving in Chile, he had met Bernardo Houssay in Buenos Aires.[7] It might be said Atcon's agenda of meetings is a clear example of how the technical assistance missions required the deployment of what I call perpendicular diplomacy. This concept refers to a relationship with three vertices, which combines the scientific links between colleagues, the official sponsorship of the member states, and the capacity for recruitment and prestige supplied by the international employees of UNESCO. This diplomacy was deployed with the aim of carrying out the international cooperation initiatives at the national level (Abarzúa Cutroni 2017).

The consensus for carrying out an ambitious modernization plan was general. From the start, the relationship between Stitchkin Branover and Atcon was cordial and had no significant disagreements about the kind of reorganization they wished to implement at the University of Concepción. Toward the end of 1957, the reform plan was wholly approved by the faculties and the University Council. This approval implied, at least in formal terms, that the University of Concepción Institutes of Basic Sciences (Physics, Chemistry Biology, and Mathematics) should be created immediately. The UNESCO employees were also in agreement with the content and orientation of the reform plan created by Atcon. This blossoming process was considered a "pilot project" that, if successful, could be established as a model for modernization for universities all over Latin America. In 1959, UNESCO published the report Atcon had prepared in 1957 for the authorities at the University of Concepción: "Estudio Preliminar de una Proyecto de Reorganización de la Enseñanza y la Investigación de la Ciencias Básicas en la Universidad de Concepción" (Preliminary study of a reorganization project of teaching and research in basic science at the University of Concepción). As I will show later, both the employees of the UN Technical Assistance Board and the UNESCO General Secretariat made great efforts to give continuity to Atcon's prescriptions, that is, to turn this project into a long-term initiative (of four or five years) that would develop, as Atcon recommended, deep roots at the University of Concepción.

The report published in 1959 was a brief document, carefully drawn up in a diplomatic style. In the introduction, Atcon made a positive diagnosis of the state of the University of Concepción and emphasized the virtues of its authorities. The content of the report dealt with formal reforms of the university structure. It recommended the faculties restructure their internal subunits into departments with the aim to have greater administrative flexibility, which would promote collaborative research and might fund their own research, without the mediation of the faculties. In general, each recommendation aimed to centralize the academic management in the Vice Chancellor's Office to the detriment of the autonomy of the faculties. In his recommendations, Atcon gave special importance to the creation of the Institutes of Basic Sciences. These institutes, centralized in the orbit of the Vice Chancellor's Office, would give undergraduate and postgraduate courses to more than one faculty and, furthermore, would foment pure and applied research for the university as a whole. These institutes would be organized by detaching subunits from the faculties that housed these disciplines. The staff of these subunits would be absorbed by each new institute, although it would be possible to keep the status of a teacher in the original faculty. The main lack that Atcon identified at the University of Concepción was the absence of social sciences in its academic options.[8]

Nevertheless, Atcon's recommendations exceeded those concerned with an academic and administrative reform of the structure of the University of Concepción. Before the report I just mentioned, the US expert explained to Vice Chancellor Stitchkin Branover his project in a series of internal memoranda. One of these documents attracted attention to its political connotations: "Policy of the University about Politics and other Student Activities." In the document, Atcon proposed a series of measures aimed to have the university authorities adopt a neutral attitude vis-à-vis political activities that were taking place in the university and discourage specifically the politicization of the students. These measures were as follows: (1) diminishing the importance of the student representation in the university structure; (2) condemning all political activity on the part of the students that was linked with national political groups; (3) encouraging students to concentrate on academic activities; (4) promoting extracurricular activities in "nonpolitical" areas of interest; and (5) establishing of institutions in which the students could learn democratic parliamentary procedures without any specific political orientation.[9]

As noted earlier, the FEC had a great capacity of organization and mobilization. In fact, when he had become Vice Chancellor, Stitchkin Branover had recognized this as an integral part of the process of modernization. From that moment on, the students would also be the leading actors in the process of radicalization of the university, which would reach its high point with the election of the MIR for the management of the FEC in 1967. With the result that, if they had become known to public opinion, these suggestions by Atcon to the Vice Chancellor would have aroused the indignation of the students. Indeed, the perfectly foreseeable student protest against these recommendations made their application practically impossible. Toward the end of November 1957, the Chilean university authorities, this time also those belonging to the University of Chile and not only the University of Concepción, began to manage a third stay of Atcon in Chile with UNESCO and the Technical Assistance Board of the UN for 1958. During this third stay, the objective of the mission would be to coordinate the creation of the Institutes of Basic Sciences.

Despite the full support Atcon had achieved at the local level, some UNESCO employees did not agree with this US adviser taking on a third mission hired as a UNESCO expert. This was because Atcon did not entirely follow the instructions given to him by UNESCO and made explicitly political recommendations to the academic authorities of the University of Concepción. This was a clear transgression of his status as an international consultant. For this reason, the UNESCO employees feared the reputation of the organization would be damaged if it persisted with the association of UNESCO with the controversial figure of Atcon. This group of employees tried, without success, to impose another candidate for the mission in Chile. In view of the fact that Atcon was explicitly requested by the Chilean authorities, the employees regretfully had to accept that, despite the protests made, this expert still had influential contacts at UNESCO who backed his behavior.

In November 1958, the tenth UNESCO General Conference was held. At that conference, the permanent delegate from Chile to the organization in Paris, Carlos Morla Lynch, presented UNESCO Director-General Vittorino Veronese with a draft resolution that referred to the "pilot experience" of the University of Concepción as an example for the region and model of technical assistance in higher education for UNESCO.[10] This resolution was preapproved at one of the working groups of the Programme Commission of the UNESCO General Conference, but the same commission understood it could not be approved as it involved an imputation of costs to the UN Special Fund, which was a question that was technically outside the competence of UNESCO.[11] I believe this technical excuse hid the political intention, on the part of the UNESCO officials, of preserving, publicly at least, the prestige of the organization vis-à-vis Atcon. After 1959, Atcon was no longer hired as a UNESCO expert. Nevertheless, this did not mean his contacts were severed with the organization or that the Technical Assistance from UNESCO ceased at the University of Concepción, as the organization recruited and hired several specialists to collaborate on the start-up of the Institutes of Basic Sciences.

The Creation of the Institutes of Basic and Social Sciences

From 1950 onward, the promotion of the basic sciences at the regional level was a programmatic priority for UNESCO.[12] In Latin America, this UNESCO resolution did not have any impact until 1958, when the tenth General Conference created the Latin American Centre of Mathematics—informally known as the Regional Math Centre of Buenos Aires—through an initiative of the Argentine government.[13] Other similar initiatives took place in Brazil with the establishment of the Latin American Physics Centre in 1960, in Mexico with the Latin American Chemistry Centre in 1962, and in Venezuela with the Latin American Biology Centre in 1964. At the University of Concepción, the start-up of Institutes of Basic Sciences would take four years, from 1959 to 1963. At its sessions in June 1958, the University Council approved the regulations of the central institutes prepared by Atcon and authorized by the Vice Chancellor to hire the heads of the institutes. In 1959, UNESCO began supplying experts in basic science. I have found two UNESCO experts specializing in biology (G. F. Asprey, Dutch) and chemistry (Enrique Costa, Spanish), who collaborated on the start-up of the respective institutes. As is shown by Asprey's extensive mission report, the UNESCO experts were not the only ones to work on the creation of the Institutes of Basic Sciences. What is more, the experts hired by this organization executed a plan prepared by a group of advisers from the United States.[14]

According to Asprey, the biology section of the US report had been prepared by A. R. Davis,[15] who had established the principles that should be borne in mind for the preparation of the curriculum for the Institute of Biology. He mentioned, among other requirements, simultaneous dedication to teaching and research. Regarding the content of the courses, they should cover three great thematic areas (general biology, botany, and zoology) and include the disciplinary foundations of mathematics, chemistry, and physics; the teaching of Spanish and English; and, notably, some social sciences. Asprey maintained that preparing the study plan from the "Davis Report" was simple but that the true difficulty was rooted in the practical application of these imported plans to a totally new setting. Bearing this difficulty in mind and adding his own principles, the Dutch biologist created the curriculum of the Institute of Biology, which would be put into practice in March 1960. On Costa's mission, I do not have many details. Before his arrival in Chile, the authorities from the University of Concepción established which tasks would be assigned to this chemistry expert. His mission would be (a) assistance for the development of the inorganic chemistry section of the Central Institute of Chemistry, and (b) assistance for the development of technical chemistry at the Technological Research Institute. Likewise, among his tasks was establishing the frontiers of activities between this institute and the Central Institute of Chemistry. Unfortunately, I do not have the mission report by this expert, which prevents us from knowing exactly which tasks he carried out.

In 1962, a new University of Concepción Vice Chancellor was selected, the doctor Ignacio González Ginouvés.[16] By then, the four Central Institutes of Basic Sciences had already been started, the result being that the new university authorities decided the first stage of modernization was at an end. However, the integral modernization of the university that Atcon proposed was far from consolidated. According to Carlos Huneeus (1988), the new Vice Chancellor again emphasized the faculties to the detriment of the process begun in 1957. However, in 1963, the University of Concepción authorities again began the steps to obtain technical assistance from UNESCO. They asked for an expert in University Planning to collaborate on the second stage of academic reorganization consisting of the creation of Institutes of Social Sciences. Unlike the previous occasions, the Vice Chancellor formally suggested a candidate for the position, Joseph Lauwerys, with whom he had made contact in London. Together with the request for technical assistance, the Vice Chancellor included a preliminary plan for the second stage of reorganization of the University of Concepción. As is recorded in the document, the plan had the support of the deans of all the faculties at the university and cost more than one million dollars.

In the aforementioned document, the Vice Chancellor identified three main problems: (1) the University of Concepción still had a professionalizing profile, which made the establishment of scientific research difficult; (2) the students who joined the university had not achieved a sufficient academic level to study there, which caused people to give up and led them to opt for traditional degrees; and (3) the university did not have any courses devoted to social sciences and humanities. The plan grouped the international technical assistance into three axes: financing of infrastructure, cooperation of experts on educational and scientific matters, and the award of grants for training in foreign countries of members of the institute. This assistance needed to be articulated to carry out this second stage to create the Institutes of Social Sciences and Humanities.

The result of Lauwerys's first visit to the University of Concepción was a diagnosis of the general situation of higher education in South

America. In a confidential report dated 4 November 1964, Lauwerys—as Atcon had done years earlier—gave his vision of the university in Latin America to the UNESCO officials.[17] He identified problems, proposed solutions and even a strategy for their success. According to Lauwerys, the main problems of South American universities in general and of the University of Concepción in particular were, among others, the high cost of the university if the investment was calculated in relation with the number of degrees achieved, the high rate of drop-outs, the fragmentation of the universities into independent professional schools (faculties), the training in a utilitarian spirit as opposed to the cultivation of science as an autonomous discipline, the habits of teaching and learning that replaced understanding by memorizing, and, again, the politicization of the students.

In view of these problems, Lauwerys suggested a series of significant reforms: the creation of an admissions office in the university and of an organization for student welfare (with responsibility for residences, loans, medical and dental services, and sports and extracurricular activities); the establishment of a new system of teaching (by means of tutorials and seminars) and a new general basic year (propaedeutic), in which the students would learn subjects without any kind of professional specialization; the adoption of a system of credits that would replace the end-of-year examinations; the promotion of a spirit of research and enquiry; and the elimination of the catechistic approach. It is interesting to note this UNESCO expert recommended a series of strategies to generate consensus about the measures he had proposed. For instance, Lauwerys suggested not attacking the faculties directly, as they were very powerful and establishing autonomous institutes for the basic disciplines (exact sciences and natural sciences / social sciences and humanities). He also pointed out that the admission to the institutes or faculties should have a relationship with the economic and social needs, adopting a quarterly system for the courses. In the planning of the reform, he considered convenient to consult all the interested parties (local politicians, teachers, head teachers of secondary schools, and even student organizations) and ensure nobody believed he would lose his job.

The general basic year (propaedeutic) was one of the measures that attempted to correct, according to Lauwerys, a main defect of the universities in Latin America: the tendency toward training of a professional type.[18] This common basic year was implemented from March 1965, and student admission was run by an office established at the level of the university. The students had to fill out a form about which degree they preferred to study, giving first, second, and third choices.

That year, according to Lauwerys, there were 2,500 applicants, of whom 800 had put down Medicine as their first choice. This expert said only 80 to 100 students could be admitted to that degree given the installed capacity (laboratory, number of teachers) of that faculty. About one year later, this restriction would cause student protests as a result of the difficulties in access to the desired faculties.

The second visit by Lauwerys took place from March to May 1965. During this time, he worked, in a close relationship, together with the Vice Chancellor, with the aim of starting up the aforementioned proposals. To be exact, the basic general course was organized, about one hundred tutors were selected and trained for the faculties, and a good number of social science teachers were hired full-time. According to the resident representative of the UN Technical Assistance Office in Chile, the university's full-time teaching staff increased by 40 percent. With the collaboration of Lauwerys, the Central Institutes of Social Sciences and the Humanities were created in 1964 from the restructuring of the Faculty of Education.[19] The non-pedagogical subjects that were taught at this faculty were grouped in four new institutes—Social Sciences, Language, Philosophy and Logic, and History and Geography—while the faculty would, from then on, devote itself only to pedagogical subjects or to subjects related with the sciences of education. It was established that the title of "State Teacher" would be gained after four, instead of five, years. The first year would be the propaedeutic one, the second and third years would be set by the institutes in relation to specific subjects, and the Faculty of Education would give the professional specialization in the fourth year.

Finally, Lauwerys in his mission report evaluated the impact of the reform undertaken in 1957. He indicated that achieving consensus on the reform plan had not been an easy task and that it had involved active protests and, on occasions, tough discussions in the university community. Atcon's proposals and recommendations had built up resistance among students and the teaching staff who wanted to preserve the autonomy of the faculties. In the end, the creation of the Central Institutes of Basic Sciences had not dissolved or weakened the faculties. In fact, students were admitted by the faculties and took only some of their courses at the central institutes. As a result of the persistent mobilization of the Chilean students, Lauwerys, unlike Atcon, recommended incorporating students into the reform process through the consultation of the FEC. This proposal was achieved with the incorporation of a student representative on each of the four commissions that advised the coordinator of the propaedeutic year. Almost at the end of his period in office, Vice Chancellor González Ginouvés created a tripartite commission (authorities, academics, and students) to study the demands in favor of the educational reforms (Huneeus 1988). But the demands of the students were much more radical than those contemplated in the plans for academic modernization that had been implemented at the University of Concepción over the previous ten years.

University Reform at the University of Concepción

The University Reform in Chile (1967–1973) was a complex process that had as its epicenter the Catholic University of Chile first and later the University of Chile. This process of transformation of Chilean universities had, according to Manuel Garretón and Javier Martínez (1985a), four stages: (1) the process of gestation, in which the universities went through a process of modernization; (2) unleashing and rupture, the moment when student protests led to a breakdown in communication with the university authorities via the takeover of the premises of the universities; (3) development of transformation measures; and (4) a moment that is distinguished by the identification of the political actors in the university with the social and political scene in the country.

At the University of Concepción, the academic authorities wanted to develop an integral process of modernization, which had certain limits. On the one hand, the faculties kept their autonomy vis-à-vis the central institutes. On the other was the radicalization of the demands from the student movement. In 1967, the MIR achieved the leadership of the FEC. The leftist student organizations maintained that true reform of universities would be possible only if there was a global social transformation (Garretón and Martinez 1985a). MIR General Secretary Miguel Enríquez Espinosa[20] declared, after suffering repression by the police after a series of protests carried out by the students at the University of Concepción, the aim of the students was a university revolution, by means of which the structure of power at the university would be transformed and put at the service of the interests of laborers and peasants. For this purpose, it was fundamental to install student co-government as a form of democratization of the university, the defense of their autonomy and the struggle against US penetration.[21]

In 1968, Stitchkin Branover was again elected to the role of Vice Chancellor. As a first management measure, he democratized the government of the University of Concepción because he considered it fundamental that there should be participation by the entire university community (teachers, nonteaching staff, and students) on the decision-making organs.[22] A Reform Commission was then created with a representation of 40 percent of the members reserved for students. On the Superior Council, the students achieved a representation of 25 percent, and the FEC president was included on it. Meanwhile, deliberative organs were also established in the faculties with 25 percent student representation (Huneeus 1988).

In December 1968, new authorities had to be chosen, as the Reform of the University Status in that year established direct elections. At the University of Concepción, it was necessary to have an absolute majority of the weighted vote to reach the position of Vice Chancellor and his deputy. The weighting by faculties was divided into three: academics 72 percent, students 25 percent, and nonacademic staff 3 percent. Finally, Edgardo Enríquez Fröden, the father of Miguel Enríquez, was elected Vice Chancellor.[23] This last election consolidated the principle of university co-government. Since 1970, with the triumph of the Popular Unity and the election of Salvador Allende as President, the University of Concepción was driven through with the political polarization that this political stage involved. However, the academic management was plural and democratic (Huneeus 1988).

The coup d'état of 11 September 1973 affected the universities, replaced the democratically elected authorities, and imposed state-sponsored terrorism by means of purges based on the political and ideological criteria of teachers, non-teachers, and students. The student federations were closed down. Between 1973 and 1979, the measures taken during university reform were dismantled, the academic study plans again became rigid, and training again adopted its professionalizing character and its orientation toward traditional degrees (Garretón and Martínez 1985a). In 1981, the military regime imposed a new university regime characterized by privatization and the decentralization of higher education (Brunner 2009).

Conclusions

The process of modernization that was carried out at the University of Concepción shows how the local demands, from academics and students who were trying to transform the university of which they were a part, were articulated in a complex manner with the interests of UNESCO. This international organization was trying to generate a pilot project that would make it possible to prepare a model of modernization that would be viable for all Latin American universities. The peculiarities of higher education in Chile and the power of the political processes that took place in the country in the 1960s and the early 1970s meant this pilot project took on a life of its own and was then abruptly dismantled with the coup d'état in 1973.

In this process of modernization, the university authorities stood out as indispensable mediators, as they mediated between the experts and the international officials, and the teachers and the students. In this regard, both Atcon and Lauwerys were able to translate their international diagnoses, schematic and generalized, into recommendations likely to be implemented at the University of Concepción. These recommendations resulted in the introduction of research and teaching of science at university and professionalization of the teaching body. However, this did not imply the weakening of the faculties or the end of the structure of professorships.

Anabella Abarzúa Cutroni is Associate Professor at the National University of Cuyo and Postdoctoral Fellow of the National Council for Scientific and Technical Research in Argentina. She is also a research member of the "Research Program on Academic Dependency in Latina America" at the National University of Cuyo. She holds a PhD in Social Sciences from the University of Buenos Aires and has a degree in Political Science and Public Administration from the National University of Cuyo. Her main publications include "El poder simbólico de la UNESCO en América Latina: Sobre el vínculo FLACSO—UNESCO" (*História da Educação*, 2018) and "Partículas universales: Las misiones científicas de la UNESCO en Argentina (1954—1966)" (*Revista Iberoamericana de Ciencia, Tecnología y Sociedad*, 2017).

Notes

As sources for this work, I consulted the correspondence folders corresponding to technical assistance to the universities in Chile and the reports of the experts sent to the University Concepción. These documentary sources are hosted at the UNESCO Archive (UA) in Paris.

1. There are indications that Atcon continued to work as an adviser to the University of Concepción in 1959 and even 1960. Nevertheless, I do not know whether he did so continuously and was present or whether he was only consulted by correspondence. However, I was able to confirm that from 1959 onward, he was no longer hired by UNESCO.
2. "Index of Field Missions Reports 1947–1968," p. 161, 53, Brief biographical details of J. A. Lauwerys, Memorandum of Welling to Bentancur

Mejía (Assistant of the Director General in Education), 8 June 1964, DC/JL Papers of Joseph Albert Lauwerys, Biographical history, Institute of Education, University of London.

3. "Graduate of the first year of the Teacher Training Institute of the University of Chile, Vice-chancellor of the Liceo de Talca, he soon became a progressive figure on the national stage" (Garretón and Martínez 1985b: 24).
4. David Stitchkin Branover (1912–1997) was a lawyer from the University of Chile (1937) and Professor of Civil Law at the same institution.
5. On his first visit to Chile, in Santiago he met representatives of the Ministry of Foreign Affairs who led the Technical Assistance Committee, with the head of the Superintendencia de Educación and University of Chile Vice Chancellor Juan Gómez Millas.
6. He specifically made contact with the specialists at the University of California who were working on an ICA Point Four Program for the School of Agriculture of the University of Concepción.
7. Anísio Teixeira (1900–1971) was an outstanding Brazilian teacher and founder of the Escola Nova. In the 1940s, he was an adviser to UNESCO on higher education. In 1951, he agreed to manage the Campanha de Aperfeiçoamento de Pessoal de Nível Superior. Bernardo Houssay (1887–1971) was an outstanding Argentinean scientist. He won the Nobel Prize in Medicine and Physiology in 1947. Houssay was the holder of the Physiology Professorship of the Faculty of Medicine at the University of Buenos Aires. He was also President of the National Council of Scientific and Technical Research from its creation in 1958 until his death.
8. "Estudio preliminar de una proyecto de reorganización de la enseñanza y la investigación de la ciencias básica en la Universidad de Concepción" (Preliminary study of a project for the reorganization of teaching and research in basic sciences at the University of Concepción), Co-Ord. Unit-ED. Chile, Reports from field experts, Mr. R. ATCON, University Organization. CHILED 3, UA.
9. Memorandum no. 3 from Atcon to Stitchkin, Vice Chancellor's Office at the University of Concepción, 24 November 1957, Co-Ord. Unit-ED. Chile, Reports from field experts, Mr. R. ATCON, University Organization. CHILED 3, UA.
10. Proyecto de Resolución 10 C/DR/28, Paris, 6 November 1958.
11. 10° Conferencia General, Resoluciones, C. Anexos, 1, Información de la Comisión de Programas, 108.
12. 5° Conferencia General, Res. 2.21, 1950.
13. 10° Conferencia General, Res. 2.33, 1958.
14. "Mission Report by G. F. Asprey," November 1959, UA.
15. There is no record of institutional or professional references to this.
16. González Ginouvés was a doctor and surgeon from the University of Chile (1928). He was Dean of the Faculty of Medicine of the University of Concepción from 1948 to 1955.

17. "Brief Informal Report and Suggestions from Professor Lauwerys." 4 November 1964, UA.
18. "Reform of the University of Concepción: Mission Report by J. Lauwerys," 1965. UA.
19. In parallel with Lauwerys's mission, I recorded a six-month mission (November 1964 to March 1965) by the economist of the Latin American and Caribbean Institute for Economic and Social Planning, Pedro Paz. This expert acted as an adviser of the Department of Economic Science at the University of Concepción. Part of this expert's work was to collaborate in the implementation of the new curriculum for the School of Economics. Paz describes the main reforms carried out at the Faculty of Economics, where he says that from 1964 onward, the system of professorships was eliminated—the classes were given on a six-monthly basis in accordance with the new plan—a system of credits was decided on and research was aimed at local problems. "Informe de Misión de P. Paz," 1965, UA.
20. Miguel Enríquez Espinosa (1944–1974) was a doctor and leftist militant. He completed his secondary studies at the Liceo de Concepción. He began studying Medicine at the University of Concepción in 1961. In 1962, he began to be active in the Federación Juvenil Socialista (Socialist Youth Federation). When he broke with the Socialist Party, he founded the MIR in 1965. After the military coup, on 5 October 1974, Miguel was murdered in Santiago by agents of the National Intelligence Directorate (DINA).
21. "Balance de una lucha," *Revista Punto Final* 40, October 1967, 37.
22. David Stitchkin Branover, *Annals of the University of Chile*, April–June 1969.
23. Edgardo Enríquez Fröden (1912–1996) was a doctor and surgeon from the University of Concepción (1937). He was Professor of the Faculty of Medicine and Head of the Hospital de Talcahuano (1953–1969). Enríquez Fröden became Minister of Education of Salvador Allende from June 1973 until the coup. He was arrested by the military regime and sent to the concentration camp at Isla Dawson. Subsequently, he sought exile in England and Mexico.

References

Abarzúa Cutroni, Anabella. 2017. "Partículas universales: Las misiones científicas de la UNESCO en Argentina (1954–1966)." *Revista Iberoamericana de Ciencia, Tecnología y Sociedad* 12 (36): 33–60.

Beigel, Fernanda. 2013. *The Politics of Academic Autonomy in Latin America*. London: Ashgate.

Bernardet Bittencourt, Agueda. 2011. "Cooperação científica internacional e a criação da CAPES." *Revista Colombiana de Educación* 61: 117–140.

Brunner, José Joaquín. 2009. *Educación Superior en Chile: instituciones, mercados y políticas gubernamentales (1967—2007)*. Santiago de Chile: Universidad Diego Portales.

Garretón, Manuel Antonio and Javier Martínez. 1985a. *Universidades chilenas: Historia, reforma e intervención*. Vol. 1 Santiago de Chile: Ed. Sur.

——. 1985b. *Antecedentes estructurales de las Universidades Chilenas*. Vol. 5. Santiago: Ediciones del Sur.

Huneeus, Carlos. 1988. *La Reforma Universitaria veinte años después*. Santiago: CPU.

Inhan De Souza, Gabriella. 2015. "Rudolph Atcon, entre o educacional e o urbanístico na definição de diretrizes para Campi universitários no Brasil." MA thesis, Universidade Federal de Juiz de Fora.

Index

Lightning Source UK Ltd.
Milton Keynes UK
UKHW021142181219
355558UK00003B/203/P

9 781789 205459